REFORMERS IN THE WINGS

REFORMERS IN THE WINGS

From Geiler von Kaysersberg to Theodore Beza

Second Edition

David C. Steinmetz

OXFORD
UNIVERSITY PRESS

2001

OXFORD
UNIVERSITY PRESS

Oxford   New York
Athens   Auckland   Bangkok   Bogotá   Buenos Aires   Calcutta
Cape Town   Chennai   Dar es Salaam   Delhi   Florence   Hong Kong   Istanbul
Karachi   Kuala Lumpur   Madrid   Melbourne   Mexico City   Mumbai   Nairobi
Paris   Saõ Paulo   Shanghai   Singapore   Taipei   Tokyo   Toronto

and associated companies in
Berlin   Ibadan

Copyright © 2001 by David C. Steinmetz

Published by Oxford University Press, Inc.
198 Madison Avenue, New York, New York 10016

Oxford is a registered trademark of Oxford University Press

Library of Congress Cataloging-in-Publication Data
Steinmetz, David Curtis.
Reformers in the wings : from Geiler von Kaysersberg to
Theodore Beza / David C. Steinmetz.—2nd ed.
p.   cm.
Includes bibliographical references and index.
ISBN 0-19-513047-2; ISBN 0-19-513048-0 (pbk.)
1. Reformation—Biography.   I. Title.
BR315.S83   2000
270.6'092'2—dc21   99-048788
[B]

1 3 5 7 9 8 6 4 2

Printed in the United States of America
on acid-free paper

TO VIRGINIA

PREFACE

Reformers in the Wings was first published in 1971 and enjoyed a fairly long life in print, first as a hardbound book with Fortress Press and then in a paper edition by Baker. Both editions have been out of print for more than a decade but have not been replaced by any other work that tried to do what they did; namely, illustrate the wide diversity of theological reforms attempted in Reformation Europe by offering biographical studies of a carefully selected group of lesser-known reformers.

It occurred to me that the book, if thoroughly revised, might have a renewed life capable of engaging a new generation of readers. Cynthia Read at Oxford University Press agreed with me and encouraged me to rework the material. Revising a book without losing the freshness of the original proved more of a challenge and took a good deal longer than I had anticipated. However, I was helped in this task by a number of people who deserve to be thanked. Elaine Cooper typed the original book into the computer so I could have the manuscript in a form that could be revised over and over again. Paul Leslie, my research assistant at the time, prepared a new and expanded bibliography for me on all twenty figures in the book, a bibliography later revised and updated by my current research assistant, Sujin Pak, who also checked and corrected a penultimate draft of the revision. My new research assistant, Deborah Marcuse, subjected the introduction to the book to a searching criticism that led to its recasting. The index was prepared by J. Samuel Hammond. Most of the rewriting took place in 1998 at the Herzog August Bibliothek in Wolfenbüttel, Germany. I am grateful to the director, Professor Helwig Schmidt-Glintzer, who invited me to come to the library, and to Dr. Gillian Bepler, his associate, who provided me with a large and quiet study, an unproblematic e-mail connection, and numerous kindnesses, both personal and professional. I should add, as is customary in academic prefaces, that the mistakes that remain in the book are all mine and should never be attributed to my friends and colleagues. But everyone knows that authors alone are to blame for whatever howlers and inaccuracies remain in their text. I think we can therefore take that traditional disclaimer as already read.

CONTENTS

Contents

REFORMERS IN THE WINGS

INTRODUCTION

THIS BOOK IS INTENDED not only to introduce to the general reader some of the lesser known figures of the Reformation but also to provide within the context of the stories of their lives an introduction to some of the most fiercely debated theological issues in the sixteenth century. Every chapter introduces a problem as well as a figure. Readers are therefore presented with more than a collection of biographical studies; they are offered what amounts to a primer of Reformation theology.

The reformers discussed in these pages are divided into four confessional families: Catholic, Lutheran, Reformed, and Radical. The late medieval Catholic reformers died in communion with the church of Rome. Even though they were critical of the theology and practice of the late medieval church and may not be judged fully Catholic on some point or another by the standards of later Roman Catholic orthodoxy, still they expressed a willingness to submit to the teaching authority of the magisterium of the Catholic church or, at the very least, a hesitancy to be caught up in open schism.

The fact that these reformers wished to remain within the framework of medieval Catholic thought does not mean that their ideas were homogeneous or that they exercised no influence on the theology of Protestant reformers, who were willing, however reluctantly, to bear the scandal of schism. There is a great gulf fixed between the celebration of the human coming-of-age in the theology of Johannes Geiler von Kaysersberg and the exaltation of the all-sufficiency of divine grace in the theology of Johannes von Staupitz—yet both men made a profound impression on the generation of Protestant theologians who followed them. Luther's indebtedness to Staupitz is well known and widely discussed. Less well known, perhaps, is the veneration of the young Melanchthon for Geiler.

The Lutheran reformers shared a common confessional loyalty to the teaching of Martin Luther. Luther's understanding of justification, of the relation of law and gospel, and of the ubiquity of the body of Christ were theological starting points for these reformers. Even when, as in the case of Melanchthon, they deviated from Luther's teaching, they did so by modifying rather than rejecting it outright. Indeed, the fiercest struggles within Lutheranism were often between men like Andreas Osiander and Nikolaus von Amsdorf, who held diametrically opposite views on an issue and who claimed, both with some justification, to be faithful to motifs in Luther's thought that had been obscured by other Lutherans.

The Reformed, including early Anglicans like John Hooper, regarded themselves to some extent as heirs of Luther, though not of Luther alone. They shared with Luther a common conviction about such issues as the bondage of the will, justification by faith, and predestination as a comfort for believers. They differed from him, however, in their understanding of the nature of the presence of Christ in the Eucharist and in their stress on the importance of discipline for the life of faith. These differences arose in part because the Reformed were more open than Luther to the voice of the humanists, with their accent on moral reform and their interest in ethics. But in part these differences grew out of disagreements over the teaching of Scripture and the early Christian Fathers, in which philosophy had very little to do with the shape of the conflicting arguments.

The Radical reformers learned lessons from both Luther and Zwingli. They were marked, however, less by their indebtedness to the Lutheran and Reformed traditions than by their rejection of them. Whereas Luther and Calvin stressed the bondage of the human will in sin, the Radicals emphasized human freedom. Whereas Martin Bucer and Zwingli defended infant baptism and the Christian society of the later Middle Ages, the Radicals argued for adult baptism and the formation of an alternative and voluntary Christian society composed of visible saints in covenant with God and with each other.

But the Radicals were no more homogeneous than any other group in the sixteenth century and were divided sharply on issues of a fundamental nature. The debate between Caspar Schwenckfeld, who regarded the structure of the visible church as a matter of total indifference, and Pilgram Marpeck, who showed all the passion of a medieval canon lawyer in arguing for the salvific significance of visible structures, illustrates as well as anything the broad spectrum of opinion one can find among the Protestant Radicals.

The Reformation was never monochromatic. Luther's condemnation of Aristotle finally fell on Melanchthon's deaf ears, and his predilection for Occamist philosophy never swayed Bucer or Peter Martyr, who preferred the views of Thomas Aquinas. It is the polychromatic character of the Reformation that this book attempts to stress and which, I think, may be its primary contribution.

Why sixteenth-century Europe should have produced such an extraordinarily large number of interesting theologians is not easy to explain, any more than it is easy to explain why, after the relatively barren reign of the first four

Tudors, English letters flowered under Elizabeth. There is about the givenness of history a mysterious quality that eludes easy explanation. Still one cannot read the stories of these twenty reformers without being struck by the variety and richness of theological discussion in the sixteenth century. Balthasar Hubmaier and Johannes Brenz are less well known than Luther and Calvin, but they provide the context in which the real achievements of such better known reformers can be assessed. Hubmaier and Brenz (indeed, all the figures whose stories are told here) were reformers in the wings, supporting members of the cast, who by their often unnoticed activity furthered the course of the Reformation to its final curtain.

I

Catholic Reform

I

JOHANNES GEILER VON KAYSERSBERG
(1445–1510)

Pastoral Care and Human Responsibility

IT IS NOT THE CASE, as Protestants have often thought, that the Protestant reformers were the first to recover the importance of the sermon and of the act
of preaching for the life of the church. In the later Middle Ages there was a
resurgence of interest in good preaching. The town councils in the larger cities
of Europe wanted to hear a good sermon on Sunday instead of a dry adden-
dum to the Eucharist and were willing to pay a fine salary to install a talented
preacher in the pulpit of the local cathedral. Zwingli first rose to prominence
as one of these popular preachers. But the prince of the pulpit in the late
fifteenth and early sixteenth centuries was the people's priest in the imperial
city of Strasbourg,[1] Johannes Geiler von Kaysersberg.[2]

Geiler was born on March 16, 1445, in Schaffhausen in Switzerland. His family moved within a year of his birth to Ammerschweier in Upper Alsace. After
Geiler's father, who was the city clerk of Ammerschweier, was killed in a hunt-
ing accident, Geiler was raised by his grandfather in the nearby town of
Kaysersberg. He was sent at the age of fifteen to the University of Freiburg in
Breisgau, where he distinguished himself as a student of philosophy. From 1465
to 1470 he taught philosophy and grammar at Freiburg; he was even chosen as
dean of the philosophical faculty. He left Freiburg in 1470 to study theology at
Basel. In 1475, after earning his doctorate in theology, he returned to Freiburg
(by popular demand of the students!) to teach theology. The following year he
was elected rector.

His academic career was successfully launched. He was popular with the students and esteemed by his colleagues. Nevertheless, he was restless and
dissatisfied with life in the university community. There lurked at the back of
his mind the thought, which gradually grew into a conviction, that his real vocation was to the pulpit rather than to the lectern. Unable to shake the feeling
of a missed vocation, he finally yielded to it. When the city of Würzburg in-

vited him to preach a trial sermon, he readily accepted. The people of Würzburg were delighted with his sermon and invited him to stay. He was willing to do so, and even set out for Basel to collect his books. On his way to Switzerland, however, he stopped in the city of Strasbourg. The casual visit proved to be a fateful one. The Ammeister of Strasbourg, Peter Schott, persuaded Geiler to decline the invitation to Würzburg and to accept the post of preacher at the Strasbourg cathedral instead.

Geiler never regretted his decision to become the people's priest in Strasbourg. For thirty-two years he preached at the appointed times in the municipal cathedral. His sermons were a ringing cry for the improvement of the moral level of clergy and laity alike and a stirring denunciation of the abuses of Christian discipline within the church. He remained at his post until his death on March 10, 1510, when he was buried under the carved pulpit built in his honor by Peter Schott.

In spite of his friendship with Jacob Wimpfeling and Sebastian Brant, Geiler was no humanist.[3] He could read neither Greek nor Hebrew and showed little interest in philosophy. According to tradition, he was familiar with the writings of Pico della Mirandola and Marsilio Ficino, though there is no record that he ever cited them in his sermons. What Geiler shared with the humanists was an interest in education and a desire for moral reform.

Geiler's relationship to late medieval scholastic theology is clearer and somewhat easier to establish. His favorite theologian was Jean Gerson, the former chancellor of the University of Paris, whose writings he frequently cited and some of which he translated into German. Though Geiler knew Thomas Aquinas and Duns Scotus, he was drawn not to them but to the central nominalist position in theology, represented by such figures as Gabriel Biel, professor of theology at the University of Tübingen and Geiler's personal friend. Geiler was, as E. J. Dempsey Douglass has convincingly demonstrated, the persuasive advocate of a pastorally oriented nominalism, which urged men and women to be mature and to accept full responsibility for the state of their relationship to the living God.[4]

The key to nominalist thought may be found in the nominalist doctrine of God.[5] The nominalists drew a sharp distinction between the absolute power of God (his unlimited ability to do whatever he pleases) and his ordained power (the choices and commitments God has made that limit his otherwise unlimited freedom of action). The mystery of God's sovereign freedom as Creator and Lord can only be understood by giving careful attention to the interplay of these two powers.

The nominalists wished to stress the fact that God is not under any natural obligation to his creation. There are no innate laws written into the very structure of things that God is bound to observe. God is not obligated, to take an easy example, to create a world in which water runs downhill or in which the sun rises in the east. He could have, had he chosen to do so, created a world quite different from the one we know, a world more like the one Alice discovered when she stepped through the looking glass and less like the one scientists presently observe and measure. Grass is not green by necessity; it is green by choice. The wonder and mystery of the divine choice that made grass green is that God could have, had he chosen to do so, made it indigo or magenta instead. The world that surrounds us is a product of the ordained power of God. But it can only be appreciated for what it is when it is seen against the background of the absolute power of God, against the background of the infinite choices that were possibilities for divine action but that God in his wisdom and freedom rejected.

That does not mean that there is anything uncertain about the ordained power of God or that the laws of nature are in immediate danger of sudden and arbitrary suspension. The nominalists did not expect to rise from bed one morning to find to their dismay that the law of gravity had been repealed by divine fiat. They simply wanted to stress their belief that the world in which we live is the contingent product of divine choices. They did not want to imply that it is an unreliable mechanism subject to the arbitrary whims of sovereign caprice. God has entered into a covenant with the world he has made—to preserve it as he made it. God remains faithful to the decisions he has made. But his fidelity is not grudging or coerced. It is a commitment freely and gladly assumed. In the last analysis the structures of creation and redemption rest on no other basis than a free and uncoerced decision of the sovereign will of God. There is no guarantee for creation and redemption outside that will, but only in it. The God of the nominalists is the faithful God of the covenant.

The covenant God has made with the church is two-sided. It assumes responsibilities and obligations for both parties in the contract. God has promised to give his grace to people who will assume full responsibility for their status in the presence of God and who will exercise their own natural powers to the utmost in turning from sin and toward God. The nominalists believed that the fall into sin had done such little damage to human beings that it was still possible for sinners to love God above everything else and their neighbors as themselves without any divine assistance whatever, apart from the natural virtues and capacities God gave to men and women when he made them. God will give his grace to those who do their very best. And the best sinners can do is very good indeed! Sin makes it more difficult to love God supremely, but it does not make it impossible. The nominalists shared with humanists like Erasmus an optimistic view of human freedom and capacities.

On the face of it, it sounds very much as if the nominalists taught that human beings could earn their salvation by trying a little harder to keep the moral law and that grace had almost no place in the scheme of salvation. But that would be too simple a judgment. It would attribute to the nominalists a more naive view of salvation than they actually taught. The nominalists tried to preserve a place for the grace and mercy of God at several points in their under-standing of the drama of redemption.

In the first place, it was an act of divine mercy that established a scheme of redemption in which people could earn grace by their works. God was under no obligation to establish such a system. He could simply have allowed sinners to perish in their sins. That he made any way of salvation at all is clear evidence of his merciful intention toward sinners.

Furthermore, the good works human beings do are not really full merits but only a kind of half-merits. Human good works have no natural claim on the mercy of God. The best works sinners can do under optimum conditions are always flawed, and in any case they are finite. God promises to give an infinite reward for finite works. The very incommensurability between the inherent value of the works sinners do and the inherent value of the reward God gives is further evidence of divine mercy. The flawed works of men and women are only able to earn eternal life because God in his mercy accepts them. God's act of acceptation attributes more worth to human works than they inherently have.

Finally, one should also note that the natural capacities that sinners are able to exercise in order to dispose themselves for grace are themselves God's gra-cious gift to sinners. There is a sense in which creation itself is a divine bene-fit, a gift from the gracious hands of a merciful God. It may be true that sin-ners do not need some inner divine power to assist their fallen natures to turn to God. But the fact that human beings can assume full responsibility before God without the aid of such assistance was ample proof to the nominalists of how great a gracious benefit is creation itself. Like Augustine, though with a quite different meaning, the nominalists could say, "What do you have that you have not received?"

After all this, it still must be admitted that the nominalists stressed the jus-tice of God rather than his mercy, that they emphasized human responsibility rather than divine grace, and that they extolled the act of creation and mini-mized the negative results of the fall. Even predestination was reinterpreted by the nominalists in keeping with their emphasis on human responsibility. For the nominalists, predestination was equated with foreknowledge. God knows in advance which sinners will assume responsibility for their status in the pres-ence of God and which will not. God elects the responsible group to eternal life and reprobates the recalcitrant. There is nothing mysterious about God's choice. God's act of election is a response to human initiative or lack of it. It is fully explicable in terms of divine justice.

The gospel Geiler preached in the cathedral at Strasbourg was shaped by these convictions about the relationship of God and erring humanity. In times of moral decay and of the collapse of ethical norms, it may be necessary to stress once again human responsibility before God and the innate possibility sinners have, even at the worst of times, to fulfill the rigorous demands of

God's law. Though mercy belongs to the gospel as well as justice, the preacher is obligated to stress divine justice in a time of moral crisis and to warn people against presuming on God's mercy. God will give his grace to those who do their very best. First draw near to God and then God will draw near to you. That is the gospel one should preach in a time of moral disintegration.

The preacher has a high and holy office to discharge, fully as important as the role of the priest at the altar.[6] The medieval understanding of preaching, which Geiler shared, regarded the sermon as an instrument for preparing sinners for the reception of grace through the sacraments. The sermon calls men and women to the sacraments. The medieval image is the image of a priest, standing on the steps of a cathedral, calling his listeners to come into the cathedral to the confessional chair, the baptismal font, or the altar, where saving grace is dispensed. God does not give saving grace through the sermon. At best God gives a kind of preparatory grace, since the action of God in forgiving sins takes place in and through the sacraments. But since the preacher calls men and women to the sacraments, above all to the sacrament of penance, his office shares, by a kind of reflected glory, in the dignity of the sacrament to which he calls. Since penance remits mortal sin, the task of the preacher is fully as important as the work of the priest presiding at the Eucharist, whose sacrifice is only able to remit the lesser or venial sins of the church.

Geiler followed an established routine in his preaching. On entering the pulpit he first removed his hat and then knelt to pray. On rising he made the sign of the cross and read the Latin text of his sermon. After repeating that text in German, he knelt to recite the Ave Maria. He then stood up in the pulpit, put his hat back on his head, and proceeded to explain the Gospel lesson for the day. When he finished the Gospel lesson, he would take up the topic on which he had been preaching during that season of the church year. He kept one eye cocked at the hourglass, and when the sands ran out, he brought his sermon to a punctual conclusion.

His sermons were direct and pointed. Though they were written out in advance in Latin, they were preached in a homely and often pungent German. Geiler believed that the preacher, unlike the lecturer at the university, dared not run the risk of being obscure. It is the business of the preacher of the gospel to be plain, to be understandable—if necessary, to be crude—in order to carry home to the hearts of his listeners in a direct and unforgettable way the simple truth that lies at the center of all Christian proclamation. The preacher cannot be an instrument of reform if he restricts himself to the delivery of learned and—from the standpoint of the common people at least—generally incomprehensible essays in Latin. If the use of secular literature will assist the preacher in the performance of his task, then secular literature should be gratefully received and gladly used. But above all the sermon must be simple.[7]

Geiler's reform efforts received their first official encouragement from Bishop Albert of Bavaria, who had been elected to the see in Strasbourg the same year that Geiler had been called to the cathedral. On April 18, 1482, the bishop summoned a diocesan synod to Strasbourg in order to consider reform measures, and he appointed Geiler the official preacher to the assembled clergy. Geiler preached an optimistic sermon, anticipating the beginning of a great reform movement within the diocese. The results of the synod, however, fell far below expectations. Aside from a few prescriptions concerning moral discipline and the establishment of an inspection tour within the diocese, the lasting effects of the council were negligible. But at least a start had been made, however feeble and faltering.

When Bishop Albert died on August 20, 1506, he was replaced by Wilhelm von Honstein, a man even more devoted to the cause of moral reform espoused by the humanists. The new bishop lost no time in aligning himself with the forces of reform in the diocese. Like the humanist reformers before him, he was convinced that the fundamental reforms to be undertaken were in the area of moral and ecclesiastical discipline, not in the area of doctrine. When the Reformation finally broke out in the city of Strasbourg, Bishop Wilhelm unequivocally identified himself with the conservative forces of the Catholic counterrevolutionaries. The reforms he envisioned were matters of the church's life, not of her thought.

The new bishop took Wimpfeling, Brant, and Geiler into his confidence and made them his advisers. The ideal of a bishop, which Geiler had preached about from the pulpit of the cathedral, Bishop Wilhelm conscientiously struggled to incarnate in his own person. Even after Geiler's death in 1510, Wilhelm remained true to the original ideas of the reform and on July 6, 1515, issued a mandate concerning moral conduct in his diocese. But since human nature proved more resistant to reform than the bishop had anticipated, he found it necessary to repeat the injunction on February 19 and August 12, 1524.

The Catholic reform movement bore surprisingly little fruit. This was due in part to the strength of the forces opposing reform, including a large number of the canons of the cathedral. It may also have been partly due to the nonpolemical and peace-loving nature of the bishop, who was reluctant to provoke discord and could be convinced on occasion that inconvenient reforms could be postponed to a more convenient season. After all, there were many other concerns that bore heavily on the mind of the bishop, including his political activities as an adviser and ambassador for the emperor and the archbishop of Mainz. But perhaps the modest results were chiefly due to the tidal wave of Protestant reform that followed close upon the less ambitious efforts of the Strasbourg humanists and engulfed their results in its own.

2

JOHANNES VON STAUPITZ
(1460 / 9–1524)

Theology of the Praise of God

JOHANNES VON STAUPITZ was Luther's superior in the Augustinian order, his predecessor in the chair of Bible at the University of Wittenberg, and his adviser in an especially critical period of his theological development. While Luther seems at times to have overestimated the degree to which Staupitz influenced him, it can nevertheless be demonstrated with reasonable certainty that Staupitz did aid Luther in developing a positive attitude toward temptation and in reshaping his theological views on the questions of predestination and penance.[1] And yet Luther, though he was by far the most important, was by no means the sole figure in the sixteenth century to acknowledge his indebtedness to Staupitz. Johannes Altenstaig, the author of the *Vocabularius Theologie*, a highly influential dictionary of late medieval theological terminology, dedicated the *Vocabularius* to Staupitz in a letter dated October 4, 1517. Similarly, Andreas Bodenstein von Carlstadt, who had been forced by Luther to a re-study of the theology of Augustine, dedicated his commentary on Augustine to Staupitz. Even Caspar Schwenckfeld, who was not personally acquainted with Staupitz, thought so much of Staupitz's little book on the love of God that he reissued an edition of it after Staupitz's death.

Staupitz was born in the town of Motterwitz sometime between 1460 and 1469. Unlike Luther, whose father was in the copper mining industry, Staupitz belonged to the Saxon nobility and numbered among his childhood friends Frederick the Wise, the future elector of Saxony. Staupitz studied the liberal arts at Leipzig and Cologne, beginning at Cologne in 1483. Apparently he took his vows as a member of the Order of the Hermits of Saint Augustine in the cloister at Munich. In 1497 the order sent him to Tübingen to complete his theological education and to serve as the prior of the Augustinian house in Tübingen. Staupitz's career at Tübingen was brief but successful. Within three years he was able to complete all the requirements for the doctor's degree in theology. He also preached a series of learned sermons on Job, which have survived and are the oldest writings from his hand.

Older scholarship on Staupitz stressed the fact that he had studied at Leipzig and Cologne, where the thought of Thomas Aquinas seems to have exercised an important influence on the intellectual life of the university community. Staupitz certainly held Thomas in great esteem and quoted him copiously in his sermons on Job. At Tübingen, however, Staupitz was exposed to Scotist and nominalist theology and to many of the themes and ideas preached at Strasbourg by Geiler von Kaysersberg. Gabriel Biel, the most important nominalist theologian to teach at Tübingen, was already dead when Staupitz arrived at the university. But his thought was represented by his disciple, Wendelin Steinbach. Though Staupitz was never converted to Biel's view of grace and free will, he did nevertheless adopt a number of important nominalist themes, which he used in the service of a far more radically Augustinian theology.[2]

In 1500 Staupitz left Tübingen for Munich, where he became the prior of the Augustinian cloister for two years. His quiet life in Munich was interrupted by a call from Frederick the Wise to become professor of Bible at the newly founded University of Wittenberg and to serve as the first dean of the theological faculty. He had hardly settled into the routine of his new responsibility as a theological professor when he was summoned to assume an additional responsibility as the vicar-general of the Reformed Congregation of the Hermits of Saint Augustine.

The Augustinian order in Germany, like many other mendicant orders, was divided into two different and often hostile groups, the Observants, known as the Reformed Congregation, and the Conventuals. The Observants insisted on a strict adherence to the rule of the order; the Conventuals took a rather more relaxed and liberal view of the rule. In the fifteenth century Andreas Proles had succeeded in uniting the Observants in a semi-independent confederation known as the Reformed Congregation, which could elect its own chief administrative officer, the vicar-general, and which was in certain respects directly responsible to the pope and not to the general of the order. The Observants did not secede from the order, but they did gain a high degree of independence within it.

In cooperation with Giles of Viterbo, the general of the Augustinian order, Staupitz attempted to reform the Augustinian order in Germany by merging the Reformed Congregation with the Conventuals of the Saxon province.[3] The Saxon province favored the merger, but the Reformed Congregation was divided in its attitude toward it. The German legate, Cardinal Carvajal, issued a bull authorizing the merger of the two groups, which were to meet jointly to elect a common superior. Staupitz did not follow the letter of this authorization, though he tried to preserve its spirit by being elected to a new term as vicar-general of the Observants and a first term as provincial of the Saxon province. Since the stipulations of the bull had not been met, the Saxon province and the Reformed Congregation were not in fact merged by meeting separately and electing Staupitz vicar-general and provincial. They simply shared a common superior.

Even as an interim strategy this move failed to assuage the elements in the Reformed Congregation that were opposed to the proposed merger. Seven of the twenty-nine monasteries of the Reformed Congregation disapproved of the merger outlined in the papal bull when the terms of the merger were published in 1510. The Observants in Saxony were afraid that Staupitz would some day be replaced by a Conventual superior. The Observants, who were part of the Reformed Congregation but who lived in one of the other provinces in Germany, resented coming under the control of the Saxon provincial. And in any case the Observants were worried that a merger with the Conventuals would force them to surrender their hard-won independence from the control of the general of the order and to compromise their rigorous loyalty to a strict interpretation of the rule. Their opposition to the merger was so uncompromising and so effective that Staupitz finally gave in to them and announced at the meeting of the chapter of the Reformed Congregation in Cologne in 1512 that he had abandoned all hope of bringing the merger off.

Since Staupitz was busy in his administrative activities as vicar-general and provincial, he had very little time to spend as professor at the University of Wittenberg. Because he felt that his work as an administrator was more important than his work as an educator, he decided to prepare a younger man to take over his post at the university. Martin Luther had already been appointed to the University of Wittenberg to teach ethics on the faculty of arts. In 1511 Staupitz encouraged Luther to earn a doctor's degree in theology and to assume the chair, which Staupitz felt he could no longer fill. As Luther later recounted the story, he opposed the suggestion that he become a theologian with a long list of excuses, only to have them all wittily countered by Staupitz, who was not to be thwarted in this matter.[4] In 1512 Luther was inaugurated as professor of Bible at the University of Wittenberg, a position he kept until his death in 1546.

During the early years at Wittenberg, while Staupitz was still a professor on the theological faculty, Luther had sought Staupitz out as his confessor and spiritual adviser. Staupitz, whose theology was firmly rooted in the thought of Augustine and whose disposition was marked by an unbounded confidence in the mercy of God, found it difficult to understand the complexity and depth of the spiritual torment through which Luther was passing. Nevertheless, as Luther himself later acknowledged, Staupitz was able to help him to see the positive purpose of God in the temptations and trials that assailed him and to understand and embrace a more Augustinian view of grace and predestination.

Like Geiler von Kaysersberg, Luther had been raised in the school of Gabriel Biel to understand the relationship between God and human beings as a two-sided covenant in which God promises to give his grace to those who do their very best and who assume full responsibility for their status before God. Even the most hardened sinners, if they will only try, can love God supremely and their neighbors as themselves. The moment sinners fulfill this condition of the covenant, God will justify them. Although the nominalists tried to protect the mercy of God in this understanding of justification and to guard against a naive view of the relationship between God and fallen humanity that affirmed without qualification that sinners earn their salvation by their own works, it is nevertheless clear that for them one's destiny was principally one's own responsibility, that divine assistance for the human will was superfluous and not to be expected, and that the demands of the gospel were, if anything, more rigorous than the demands of the law.

Staupitz agreed with the nominalists that the relationship between God and sinners should be understood in terms of a covenant, but he understood the character of that covenant in a radically different fashion.[5] Whereas the nominalists thought of a two-sided covenant in which there are mutual obligations binding on both parties and in which human responsibility is stressed, Staupitz thought of a one-sided covenant in which God not only sets the terms of the agreement but also fulfills them himself in Christ and offers everything to the elect unconditionally.

God created human beings to praise him.[6] However, though men and women are under obligation to praise God by virtue of their creation by him, they no longer do so because of their fall into sin. Unlike the nominalists, Staupitz was convinced that the consequences of the fall were nothing short of cataclysmic. The problem is not that sinners have lost sight of the demand of God that is laid on them or are slothful and unwilling to make use of their ability to obey the will of God. If that were so, then moral education and exhortation could awaken sinners to their predicament and enable them to assume their responsibilities towards God and the neighbor. The problem is, rather, that the human will is the prisoner of its own self-love and cannot release itself from that bondage. This misdirected love has worked havoc in the human soul. There is no inner citadel of the soul that has fought the enemy to a standstill and escaped the effects of the fall. On the contrary, sinners are not only unable to earn merits, they are even, as Augustine had rightly argued, unable to act virtuously. When the nominalists urged sinners to do their very best and assured them that God would reward their very best with his grace, they were reading a sentence of death over the human race. Fallen men and women cannot love God supremely even if they try—and there is no reason to be sanguine about the possibility that they will try.

The key to the human predicament is found in the doctrine of election. For nominalists like Biel election was nothing more than the response of God to foreseen human behavior. Because election was identified with foreknowledge and viewed as a secondary response to human initiative, it was easy for the nominalists to rationalize the doctrine of predestination in terms of God's justice. For Staupitz, however, predestination was a gracious and mysterious act of God, which was not motivated by God's prior knowledge of human activity and which could not, no matter how assiduously one attempted to do it, be reduced to simple rational intelligibility. Human salvation begins with and rests at every point on the act of divine election. The gospel is a proclamation not of a divine demand and of the human capacities to fulfill that demand but, rather, of a divine initiative that seeks sinners out and comes to their aid when they despair of their own ability to liberate themselves.

Staupitz's stress on the initiative of God in predestination led him to redefine the doctrine of justification. The entire scholastic tradition, and not simply the nominalists, defined justifying grace as the grace that makes sinners pleasing to God. This definition seemed to Staupitz to mirror inadequately the nature of God's act. It is not justification but predestination that makes sinners pleasing to God. The function of the grace given in justification is to make God pleasing to sinners. Justification is simply the fruition in time of a sovereign decree of election made before time. When God chose the elect, God placed Jesus Christ under obligation to give justification to them through his work as mediator.[7] The function of the mediatorial work of Jesus Christ is, therefore, not to make men and women dear to God,[8] but rather to make God dear to them.[9] The elect are the beneficiaries of a covenant initiated and fulfilled by God in Jesus Christ.

Justification can also be defined as the restoration of the ability to praise God.[10] There was no doubt in Staupitz's mind that the elect would be justified. His conviction in this matter did not rest on any illusions about the merit of the elect or the stability of their faith[11] but was based rather on his conviction that God will be faithful to his decree of election.[12] The calling of the elect, their justification, their restoration to conformity to Christ, and their final glorification are all covenanted mercies of God given unconditionally to the elect. Like the nominalists Staupitz had no other guarantee for human salvation than the fidelity of God.

When Staupitz pointed Luther to the love of God for humankind made evident in the crucified Redeemer in order to bolster his faith[13] and when he assured Luther that the temptations that beset him from every side were themselves signs of God's election,[14] he was doing nothing more than applying a traditional remedy for the spiritually disturbed that might have been used in that situation by any other confessor. The evidences were traditional, and they were recommended by Biel as well. Yet Luther found help in these remedies when they were applied by Staupitz as he had not found help in them before.

Perhaps the reason for this is to be sought not in the evidences themselves but rather in the theological context in which they occur. Biel divided the work of Jesus Christ into what he called the work of hope and the work of justice.[15] The work of hope refers to God's redeeming act in the death and resurrection of Jesus Christ, on which ultimately all hope of salvation rests. The work of justice refers to Christ's work as judge, which began with the ascension and will continue until the last judgment. Biel tried to balance these two works in order to keep the Christian in the middle of the road that leads to the heavenly Jerusalem, oscillating between hope and fear. But since the work of hope lay largely in the past for Biel, the work of justice tended to overbalance it and to hold the center of the stage.

Staupitz, on the other hand, had very little to say about the work of Christ as judge. The work of hope was expanded for him from the past into the present. He did not think simply in terms of the first advent of Christ in the flesh (which for Biel was the basis of the work of hope) or the final advent of Christ in glory (which for Biel was the culmination of the work of justice). Rather, he laid heavy emphasis in his theology on the advent of Christ in grace. Grace is not an impersonal power or habit of love, though in his early thought he could speak of it in these terms. Grace should be defined instead as the personal presence of the risen Christ and justification as an intimate marriage between Christ and the Christian. Life in the present is lived out of the boundless resources of the indwelling Christ, who provides at every moment all the Christian needs in order to persevere. Because in his union with Christ the Christian has access to all the unlimited resources of grace, Staupitz could not be anxious about the impending judgment of God. His certitude was grounded in the love of God, a reality that is not subject to change and fluctuation.

After Staupitz was relieved of his responsibility as professor of Bible at Wittenberg, he was able to devote his time to the duties of visitation that his high position in the order imposed on him. He found special satisfaction in visiting Nuremberg, where his preaching was favorably received and where he became the leader of a sodality composed of many of the leading citizens of Nuremberg. Some of the sermons Staupitz preached at Nuremberg and elsewhere were reworked for publication. The most important of the treatises written in this way was his little book on predestination, which was an adaptation of his Advent sermons preached at Nuremberg in 1516. The Latin edition of this work was translated into German by his good friend Christoph Scheurl.

When the indulgences controversy broke out in Germany in the fall of 1517, Staupitz at first stood by Luther, though he urged him to consider the possibility of recantation. Even when Luther was summoned to appear before Cardinal Cajetan, Staupitz joined him in Augsburg and attempted to mediate the dispute. As soon as it became clear to Staupitz that the dispute could not be mediated and that Luther was in danger of arrest, he released Luther from his vows to the order so that Luther could act with greater freedom.

After Augsburg, Luther and Staupitz corresponded and even saw each other again in Saxony. But Staupitz was frightened by the turn of events and even fearful for his own safety. When the general of the Augustinian order sent

Staupitz a letter, admonishing him to aid in bringing the struggle with Luther to an end, Staupitz resolved to take himself out of the conflict between Luther and Rome and to seek a quiet sanctuary where he could spend his last years in peace. And so in 1520, after seventeen years as vicar-general of the Reformed Congregation, Staupitz resigned his position at a meeting of the Augustinians in Eisleben.

Staupitz accepted the invitation of Cardinal Lang to become a preacher and adviser at his court in Salzburg, and in 1521 he received permission from Rome to leave the Augustinian order and to join St. Peter's Benedictine monastery in Salzburg, where he was consecrated as abbot. From 1520 to 1522 there was no contact between Luther and Staupitz. When Luther attempted in 1522 to reestablish contact, he received no answer to his letter from Salzburg.[16] Undaunted by the failure of his first attempt to reopen lines of communication, Luther wrote again in 1523.[17] This time Luther chided Staupitz for accepting his post as abbot. Although he acknowledged his great debt to Staupitz, he urged him to forsake his service to Cardinal Lang and his loyalty to the pope for the sake of Christ.

Staupitz did reply to Luther's second letter.[18] He reaffirmed his faith in Christ and in the gospel and compared his love for Luther to the love David had for Jonathan. However, he also made it clear that he was not in complete sympathy with the direction the Reformation had taken. It seemed to him that the adherents of the new movement had made issues of conscience out of matters that were theologically neutral and had abused the freedom of the gospel by their conduct. Shortly after composing his reply to Luther, Staupitz died on December 28, 1524. His body was buried in the Benedictine monastery in Salzburg. Though Staupitz had not broken communion with the Roman Catholic church and had even attempted to put some distance between the Protestant Reformation and himself, his works were nevertheless placed on the Index by Pope Paul IV in 1559.

The theology of Johannes von Staupitz is important, not simply for the intellectual stimulus it provided for Martin Luther but as evidence of one late medieval attempt at theological reform. Gabriel Biel and Geiler von Kaysersberg, in their endeavor to shape a pastoral theology relevant to the situation in which the church found itself in the late fifteenth century, had diluted in what seemed to Staupitz a dangerous fashion the church's message of the grace of God. Staupitz attempted to reform the proclamation of the church by making the praise and glory of God, rather than the pastoral needs of his listeners, the central motif of this thought. One ought, if one's act of self-renunciation would render praise to God, to be willing to be damned for the glory of God. In order to make the motif of the praise of God central in his theology, Staupitz was willing to break with elements of the medieval tradition at certain crucial points, though far less radically than Luther, and to redefine theological concepts. Staupitz was one of a long line of theologians in the late Middle Ages who protested in the name of Augustine the direction the church was taking in its interpretation of the gospel. The Reformation led by Luther, Zwingli, and Calvin is a continuation of that protest, even though the form their protest took was somewhat different and although the content of their answers was often radically new.

3

GASPARO CONTARINI
(1483–1542)

The Search for a Consensus

THE YEARS IMMEDIATELY preceding the convocation of the colloquy at Regensburg in 1541 were years filled with increased activity aimed at the final reconciliation of Protestant and Roman Catholic Christians. The initiator of this policy was in large measure Emperor Charles V. The threat of an impending conflict with France made it desirable for the emperor to have a united empire behind him. The religious controversy that divided Germany only served to weaken the position of Charles and to strengthen that of his opponent, Francis I, the king of France.[1]

The Catholic electors also favored the reunion of the empire, but for a different set of reasons. They were convinced that if Charles succeeded in crushing the power of the Protestant League of Schmalkalden, the resulting victory would upset the delicate balance in Germany between imperial and electoral power. Any weakening of the Protestant princes would mean a weakening of the Catholic princes as well. The emperor would be the only real victor in such circumstances. The Catholic electors therefore supported Charles in his attempts to reach an understanding with the Protestant princes, in the hope that a reconciliation would curtail the extension of imperial power.[2]

In 1539 Charles sent Johann von Weeze, the expelled archbishop of Lund, to negotiate an agreement with the Schmalkaldic League. The immediate result of these negotiations was the Recess of Frankfurt of April 19, 1539. According to the terms of the agreement reached at Frankfurt, the league promised to provide money for war against the Turks in return for a fifteen-month suspension of suits against its members. This agreement was, of course, not a final solution of the German problem but only a preliminary arrangement intended as a first step toward ultimate reconciliation. The second step toward this goal was to be a conference at Nuremberg to which the pope was not invited.[3]

Needless to say, the agreement von Weeze had negotiated was not greeted with enthusiasm by the papacy. On August 18, 1539, Giovanni Ricci was sent to the court of the emperor in Spain. He had been instructed to prevent the ratification of the Recess and, if possible, to put an end to the diplomatic career of von Weeze. Ricci was able to persuade the emperor to dismiss the Frankfurt negotiations, but he was not able to bring down von Weeze, who remained a confidant of the emperor.[4]

In November 1539, Cardinal Farnese visited the court of Charles V as a peace legate, hoping thereby to dissuade the emperor from pursuing his policy of reunion. The emperor, however, had made up his mind in this matter and was not to be dissuaded by the cardinal's arguments. Farnese was able, nevertheless, to get the emperor to agree that the pope would be represented at any future religious conference held in Germany.[5]

Meanwhile the political situation in Europe had deteriorated. In April 1540, negotiations with Francis I had reached an impasse. At the same time intelligence reports from the East indicated that the Turks had begun a buildup in their military preparations. Faced with the prospect of war on two fronts, the emperor was forced to act swiftly and decisively. On April 18, 1540, he summoned the estates of the empire to a conference in Speyer.[6]

With the sudden outbreak of an epidemic disease, Speyer proved an unsuitable location for this conference. Moreover, to add to the difficulties Charles faced, the two principal states of the Protestant League, Hesse and Saxony, declined the imperial invitation and refused to send representatives. When the conference finally met in Hagenau in June 1540, only a fraction of the delegates originally invited were present. With so few in attendance the delegates were unable to discuss common religious problems fruitfully and so disbanded without tackling the issues they had been convened to discuss. They did manage, however, to fix October 28, 1540, as the date for a new religious conference at Worms.[7]

Pope Paul III hesitated to send a representative to Worms, and only after he had received assurances from the emperor that no decision would be taken at Worms without the express approval of the papacy did he decide to send the bishop of Feltre, Tommaso Campeggio, as his delegate. Campeggio, a renowned canon lawyer, was empowered only to serve as an observer. He was not empowered to give papal approval to any of the doctrinal formulations made at the conference.[8]

The first weeks of the colloquy continued the procedural discussion that had begun before the opening of the conference. Each particular item of procedure—the matter of voting, the number and order of speakers—was discussed in great detail and decided on with painstaking care. It was January 14, 1541, before the theological negotiations could begin in earnest. Johann Eck and Melanchthon opened the debate with a discussion of the articles of the Augsburg Confession. Within four days the two parties had agreed on a common definition of the doctrine of original sin.[9]

Catholic Reform

Meanwhile behind the scenes at Worms another series of negotiations was in progress. Johann Gropper and Martin Bucer were engaged in composing a series of articles of their own to be used in debate by the other delegates. Gropper, a Catholic theologian from Cologne, had written in 1538 a book, the *Enchiridion*, which was intended to be a systematic exposition of the fundamental tenets of the Roman Catholic position. The book discussed the Apostles' Creed, the seven sacraments, the Lord's Prayer, and the Ten Commandments.[10]

The real significance of Gropper's work, however, lay in his discussion of the doctrine of justification. One can describe medieval thought on justification by drawing a distinction between the justice of Christ and the justice of God.[11] The justice of Christ is the grace given to the Christian in baptism and renewed in penance. It is understood both as pardon and as the power of divine love that transforms sinners and makes them pleasing to God. Christians cooperate with this justice in order to earn merits and to prepare themselves for the last judgment. The justice of God, on the other hand, is the standard by which God judges the Christian's appropriation and use of the justice of Christ. The justice of God is not given at the same time as the justice of Christ. It stands at the end of the Christian's pilgrimage as the justice of Christ stands at the beginning. The Catholic pilgrim, aided by the justice of Christ given in justification, sets out on the narrow path leading to the last judgment, which will be governed and regulated by the justice of God. Catholic men and women must prepare themselves through their cooperation with grace to meet the requirements of that justice. In order for them to withstand the final judgment the justice of Christ must be supplemented with their own inherent righteousness. This will take place in one or more ways: through ontological elevation, which makes men and women fit to have fellowship with God on God's level and, possibly, through the acceptation of works, which bestows on human works a meritorious dignity they do not have inherently.

In his study of Romans 1:17 Luther discovered that the justice of Christ and the justice of God are not separated in time but coincide and are granted simultaneously. In other words, the justice of God was identified for Luther with God's grace in Jesus Christ. Jesus Christ has by his obedience fulfilled the requirements laid on human beings by the justice of God. God imputes this justice of Christ to the sinner, who possesses it in faith.

Luther tried to make clear what this means in terms of a distinction from canon law between property and possession. In marriage two people who have their own property enter into possession of the property of their partner in marriage. The same holds true in justification. The sinner's property is his or her sin; Christ's property is his righteousness. When the sinner is united with Christ by faith, then the righteousness of Christ becomes the sinner's possession, even while remaining the property of Christ. At the same time the sinner's property, his or her sin, becomes Christ's possession.

This reunification of the justice of Christ and the justice of God meant that Christians are justified before God at the beginning of their pilgrimage to the heavenly Jerusalem and not at the end of a long process of sanctification. Christians no longer look fearfully ahead to a last judgment, whose outcome is uncertain. The judgment of God has already taken place in Christ. God's gracious word of acceptance and acquittal has already been spoken in the crucified Lord.

The fact that the justice of God was understood by Luther as the justice of Christ means, furthermore, that Christians are no longer called to supplement the justice of Christ with their own works of cooperation. Luther's teaching resulted in a radical secularization of good works. Christians do good works as a good tree bears good fruit. But they do not offer these works to God or try to supplement the merits of Christ with their own merits. Since Christians are totally accepted by God, even in their continuing imperfection, they are liberated from concern for themselves and their own ultimate destiny and free to offer works of love to their neighbors, who may now be loved as ends in themselves and not as stepping-stones for the gaining of merit. As God in his overflowing bounty has perfectly justified and accepted sinners because of Christ, so Christians in gratitude for all they have received from God do acts of love for their neighbors. Christians live in two spheres that must not be confused. In their relationship to God Christians bring nothing but open hands to receive whatever God has to give them. The relationship to God is the proper sphere for faith. But in the relationship to the neighbor it is not faith but works that are demanded of the Christian. In the relationship between God and humankind, men and women are the recipients, never the givers; while, in the relationship between one human being and another, Christians give gladly to their neighbors what they have received from God. All doctrines of human merit are excluded from this framework of thought. Charles Wesley described the heart of Luther's thought when he wrote the lines, "What shall I render to my God for all his mercies' store? I'll take the gifts he hath bestowed and humbly ask for more!"

Gropper was familiar with both the medieval understanding of justification and Luther's new and radical reinterpretation of it. Gropper was, generally speaking, a Thomist in his theology. But his study of Augustine had led him to revise his understanding of the very Augustinian Saint Thomas in an even more radically Augustinian direction. Unlike the nominalists, Gropper was impressed with the damage that had been suffered by human nature as a result of the fall. Even in Christians, concupiscence, the dreadful power of perverted self-love, is actively at work. While Gropper was committed to the medieval understanding of justification, he was reluctantly forced to admit that concupiscence prevents Christians from ever attaining a state of inherent righteousness adequate to withstand the scrutiny of the divine Judge. Christians can only stand in the presence of God if their inherent righteousness is supplemented by an imputation of the righteousness of Christ.[12] Apart from such a supplementary imputation, certitude of salvation is impossible.

Gropper's proposal seemed to mark out a middle way between the two extremes of the central medieval tradition and the new teaching of Luther. This doctrine is generally called the doctrine of double justice, though it would probably be more accurate to call it the doctrine of triple justice, since there are three terms to be distinguished: (1) the justice of Christ, which in agreement with the medieval tradition Gropper identifies with the grace given in baptism and penance; (2) the inherent justice of the Christian, who cooperates with the justice of Christ and earns merits; and (3) the imputed justice of Christ, which is granted at the last judgment. When Christians stand before the justice of God at the last judgment, the combination of the justice of Christ, seen as the power of love released in them, and their own inherent justice, understood as the product of their own cooperation with grace, falls short of the justice of God because of the continuing power of concupiscence. Merits of Christ are then imputed to Christians, not to replace their own merits but only to supplement them in sufficient quantity to meet the demanding standard of the justice of God.

Using the *Enchiridion* and its sharply Augustinian doctrines of sin and grace as a foundation, Gropper attempted to compose a series of brief chapters that could be used as a formula of reconciliation between Protestants and Roman Catholics. He was assisted by Bucer, who modified the articles slightly with material taken from his own commentary on Romans. By and large, however, Bucer accepted the work of Gropper without modification. From December 15, 1540, onward, the two men worked side by side in the home of the chancellor. When they were finished, they presented the articles to Granvella, who was extremely pleased with the results of their work. These articles came to be known in the following days as the *Regensburg* or *Ratisbon Book*.[13]

The debates between Eck and Melanchthon had yielded some fruit, when they were suddenly cut off; the colloquy was suspended by the emperor until it could be resumed at Regensburg, where the diet was soon to convene. In order to smooth the road toward agreement, the emperor himself promised to be present. The pope, on the other hand, was to be represented by the popular and moderate Italian cardinal Gasparo Contarini.[14] The appointment of Contarini as papal legate was hailed by both sides as a propitious omen for the success of the colloquy. Contarini was born in 1483 into a noble Venetian family. Following his student days at Padua, he lived a strict religious life with his two friends Tommaso Giustiniani and Vincenzo Quirini. In 1511 Contarini had a spiritual experience that convinced him of the insufficiency of human merits to achieve justification and of the necessity for the action of divine grace. While Contarini's two friends entered a religious order, Contarini resolved to live a Christian life in the world. He entered the diplomatic service of the Republic of Venice and in 1521 attended the Diet of Worms as a Venetian envoy.[15]

In his capacity as a professional diplomat, Contarini familiarized himself with the main tenets of Lutheran theology. Partly as a result of his own religious experience and partly as a result of his own appreciation for the theology of Augustine, Contarini was sympathetic to the appeal of Luther, though he could not agree with it. In 1530 at the request of a friend, he wrote a short treatise that expounded the principal teachings of the Lutherans and offered a short critique of them. In this treatise Contarini took his stand generally with Thomas Aquinas.[16]

On May 20, 1535, Pope Paul III elevated Contarini, who was still a layman, to the College of Cardinals. A number of other cardinals were created at the same time: Reginald Pole, John Fisher, Gian Pietro Carafa, Gaetano dā Thiene, and Jacopo Sadoleto. Even Erasmus was considered for this honor. Pope Paul had a clear perception of the desperate situation of the papacy and saw that heroic measures must be taken. He asked the new cardinals to investigate the state of the church.

The cardinals met in 1536 for the first time and offered their report, the *Consilium de Emendanda Ecclesiae*, in 1538. They urged the pope to use his power with restraint, though they did not exalt the power of a general council of the church over that of the pope. They complained about the appointment of unworthy candidates to positions in the church and condemned the way philosophy was taught, especially at Padua. They even objected to the use of the *Colloquies* of Erasmus as a text for schoolboys. They were profoundly split, however, in their attitude toward the crisis in the church. Contarini and Sadoleto felt that it was not too late for compromise and reunion. Carafa felt that the time for compromise was past. The appointment of Contarini, therefore, as papal legate to Regensburg was an indication that Pope Paul III entertained serious hopes for significant progress toward reunion and intended to keep men like Eck and Johann Cochlaeus in check.[17]

Contarini entered Regensburg on March 12, 1541. His arrival was greeted with enthusiasm, especially by the Protestant delegates to the conference. The atmosphere, which had been heavy with suspicion and distrust, seemed to lighten perceptibly. In fact Granvella and the emperor took such pains to satisfy the Protestant representatives who were present that they slighted the Catholic members of their own party. Everything, it appeared, had changed. And yet it could be said with equal justification that nothing had changed. The divisions between Protestants and Roman Catholics remained unaltered by the presence of Contarini. Only the atmosphere had improved.

On April 21, 1541, the theological discussions between the German Protestant and Catholic theologians resumed. Granvella and Frederick, the count Palatine, presided over the colloquy. Six representatives of the estates were chosen to act as auditors. The foundation for the ensuing debate was the *Regensburg Book*, the twenty-three articles composed by Bucer and Gropper at Worms on the basis of the *Enchiridion* and the so-called Leipzig Draft. Melanchthon and Eck, who thought that the basis of the debate was to be the Augsburg Confession, at first opposed the substitute articles, though at last they were persuaded to agree to their use.[18] The Catholic theologians were required to report twice a day to Cardinal Contarini, once in the morning and once in the evening. This enabled the legate to keep his fingers on the pulse of the debate.

The discussion proceeded quite smoothly. Within a very few days the theologians of both parties had reached an agreement on the first four articles of the *Regensburg Book*, the articles dealing with the original state of humankind, free will, the cause of sin, and the nature of original sin. On May 2 the representatives reached an agreement on article 5, the chapter dealing with justification. This article spoke of a double justice.[19] Though the article owed much to the *Enchiridion* of Johann Gropper, it had been written in its final form by Cardinal Contarini himself.

Contarini felt the acceptance of article 5 to be an event of great significance, and he sent copies of it to his friends. The reception accorded the formula was almost universally chilly. Only two cardinals, the evangelical Pole and the hopelessly untheological Pietro Bembo, were willing to defend it.[20] Cardinal Gonzaga commissioned his theological adviser to write a critique of article 5 and send it to Contarini. On May 25, 1541, Contarini replied to this criticism in his famous *Epistola de Iustificatione*, an eloquent essay in defense of the doctrine of double justice.[21]

According to this doctrine, Christians cannot rely on their own righteousness for justification. The grace given to Christians in penance transforms them, but this transformation is always imperfect in this life. The inherent righteousness that is a product of human cooperation with the justice of Christ falls short of the demanding standard of the justice of God. It is necessary to supplement human inherent righteousness with the imputed merits of Christ. Christians stand before God with both their inherent justice and the imputed merits of Jesus Christ, which supplement the deficiencies in their own inherent justice. Both are needed to withstand the judgment of the justice of God.[22]

Contarini's defense of the doctrine of double justice failed to convince the members of the curia, who perceived—rightly, as it happens—that this formulation deviated from the central medieval tradition at several important points. Nevertheless, they did not interrupt the course of the discussions at Regensburg.

Although the Protestant and Roman Catholic theologians were able to agree on article 5, they found themselves at odds on several of the other chapters. Articles 6 and 9, dealing with the church and its teaching authority, proved a troublesome source of disagreement. The Protestant theologians were convinced that a council of the church could err; the Catholic theologians were just as firmly convinced that it could not. Contarini, sensing a storm in the offing, had the discussion of these articles postponed to the end of the colloquy.[23]

This maneuver delayed the final breakdown of negotiations but did not prevent it. As soon as the theologians reached article 14, the chapter dealing with the doctrine of the Eucharist, it became painfully obvious to all that the disagreements between the two parties were of a fundamental nature. The Catholic theologians were determined to defend to the last man the doctrine of transubstantiation as it had been authoritatively articulated by the Fourth Lateran Council in 1215. The Protestant theologians were just as thoroughly determined to oppose it as a distortion of the truly Christian understanding of the real presence of Christ in the sacrament.[24]

Contarini, who up to this point had been sensitive to the feelings of the Protestant divines, stood his ground against them. As far as he was concerned, the doctrine of transubstantiation was not a negotiable matter. When someone suggested that the colloquium agree to an inoffensive declaration that Jesus Christ was truly present in the sacrament without specifying the manner of that presence, Contarini vetoed the idea. The doctrine of transubstantiation was a matter on which a council of the church had already spoken. It was not a matter that required further definition. To act as if it were in need of such definition was to obscure the truth in the interests of a hollow formula of concord. Contarini had no intention of being a party to an empty agreement.[25]

On May 14, 1541, the Protestants administered the *coup de grâce* to the negotiations by insisting that the confession of grave sins was useful but not essential. The discussions had reached an impasse. Either the emperor could force an agreement by commanding the Protestants to submit to the teaching authority of the Roman Catholic church, or he could dismiss the dreams of a reconciliation. All other avenues seemed to have led to a dead end.[26]

The emperor, however, was reluctant to take action before it was absolutely necessary. He did agree to Contarini's request to exhort Hesse, Saxony, and Brandenburg to renounce their allegiance to the Protestant cause, though he entertained no illusions about the effectiveness of such a pious exhortation. As long as the colloquy was in session, Charles was determined to support it. Gropper and Julius von Pflug, Melanchthon and Bucer were able, by much blowing on the dying embers of the conference, to keep it going until May 22, 1541. But their finest efforts merely forestalled the inevitable. It was an ironic afternote when on June 8, 1541, a communiqué arrived from Rome rejecting the disputed article on justification. The conference was already dead.[27]

The colloquy at Regensburg thus spluttered to an inconclusive and disappointing finish. The emperor failed to reunite Germany, though he did gain a momentary alliance against the Turks. Gropper and Bucer failed to bridge the theological gap between the Protestant and Roman Catholic camps, though they inadvertently succeeded in uncovering the depth of the disagreement between the two parties. Contarini failed to effect a rapprochement between Rome and Wittenberg, though he did manage to convince many of the members of the curia that he was a crypto-Lutheran. In short, the colloquy at

Regensburg succeeded only in a negative way. It showed perceptive men and women of all persuasions that the dream of any easy settlement between Protestant and Roman Catholic Christians was no more than a dream. When Contarini died in 1542, the Roman church had already begun the process of turning its face away from the hope of reconciliation and toward the implacable and uncompromising policies of Carafa.

4

FABER STAPULENSIS
(1455–1536)
The Letter and the Spirit

THE PROBLEM OF LETTER and spirit was not a problem created by theologians in the sixteenth century (although they devoted considerable attention to it) but was inherited from the patristic age.[1] The Christian exegete, when striving to expound the meaning of the biblical text, was confronted by the fact that certain passages of Scripture, if taken literally, either created insoluble theological and textual difficulties or, at the very least, contributed nothing to the edification of the Christian community.[2] How were these troublesome passages to be understood? The problem was especially acute in the case of the Old Testament, though it was by no means limited to it.

The usual answer of the medieval expositor was the one suggested by Origen and repeated in different ways with varying modifications until the time of the Protestant Reformation.[3] Behind the letter of Scripture there is a spiritual sense, more or less deeply hidden but nonetheless accessible to the eyes of faith. To understand Scripture rightly one must press beyond the mere letter to the spirit that underlies and animates it. The method used to uncover this spiritual meaning of Scripture was, generally speaking, the allegorical method.

That is not to say that the Fathers approved of an arbitrary and undisciplined interpretation of Scripture that gave free rein to the allegorical imagination of the exegete. Augustine argued, for example, that the more obscure parts of Scripture should be interpreted in the light of its less difficult sections. The interpreter of Scripture ought not to put forward an allegorical exegesis of a troublesome passage that was not supported by the manifest testimonies of other less ambiguous portions of the Bible.[4]

This meant, of course, that an easy equation of the literal sense with the "letter that kills" (2 Cor. 3:6) and the allegorical interpretation with the "Spirit that makes alive" was never wholly accurate. The letter of Scripture was not simply to be rejected as deadly in itself. There are historical accounts in Scripture that can and should be taken at face value and that are of spiritual significance in their mere historical facticity. The passion narratives would be for medieval interpreters a case in point. The literal sense is never without some value, even in the more barren stretches of Leviticus and Numbers. Indeed, it is the foundation of all Christian teaching in theology and ethics. Sometimes, however, it is of lesser worth in comparison with the spiritual sense.

Medieval theologians inherited the distinction between letter and spirit, but they did not inherit a clear criterion for distinguishing them in practice. The suggestion of Augustine that one should understand literally only what can be referred to faith or love was too subjective to provide a clear line of demarcation.[5] It was generally agreed that the literal sense should be distinguished from the spiritual sense, but there was little unanimity on the best way for doing this.

Thomas Aquinas elaborated a solution to the problem that stressed the primacy of the letter without condemning Christian exegetes to abandon all hope of a spiritual interpretation. Aquinas returned to a distinction found in Augustine between "things" and "signs," though he substituted for the Augustinian terminology (i.e., things-signs) the language of Aristotle (i.e., things-words). Words are the signs of things. But, under certain circumstances, things designated by words can themselves become the signs of still other things.[6] In all branches of human knowledge, words alone have a sign-character. But in Holy Scripture, the things designated by words can themselves have the character of a sign. The literal meaning of Scripture has to do with the sign-character of words; the spiritual meaning of Scripture has to do with the sign-character of things.

The effect of such a distinction was clear. It meant that the spiritual sense of Scripture is always based on the literal sense and is, in fact, derived from it. No argument can be advanced on the basis of the spiritual meaning of Scripture alone, not because the spiritual interpretation of the Bible lacks all authority in matters of faith but because a thing might have a multiplicity of figurative meanings. The lion, to take only one example, is a figure in the Bible, not only of Christ but also of Satan.[7] While the spiritual sense, therefore, assists the Christian in right conduct and in right belief, there is nothing faith needs that is not found somewhere in Scripture in the clear, literal meaning of the text.[8]

Nicholas of Lyra, following in the footsteps of Thomas, applied the Thomistic hermeneutic to the practical task of interpreting the text of Holy Scripture. Like Thomas, Lyra was inclined to take the literal meaning of Scripture with more than customary seriousness and to minimize the spiritual interpretation. Nevertheless, he did not wish to neglect the spiritual meaning of the text entirely. Building on the Thomistic principle that the literal sense is the meaning of the text "which the author intends" (the Author in this case being God), Lyra suggested that it was possible to speak of a double-literal sense.

While it had been the general contention of the previous tradition of medieval scholarship that the literal sense is limited to a referent within the immediate historical environment of the human author of the text, Lyra offered a new perspective, based on elements in the view of Thomas Aquinas. If the literal meaning of Scripture is to be sought in the intention of the author, is it then possible to believe that the intention of the author (presupposing, of course, that the principal Author of Scripture is God) might embrace a distant, rather than a near object? Could it be that a prophet in the Old Testament, acting under the inspiration of the Holy Spirit, might refer directly to Jesus Christ? Lyra believed not only that it was possible but that it had in fact occurred.[9]

The letter of Scripture could thus in certain instances have a double referent, both parts of which were understood to fall within the literal meaning of the text. This theory of a double-literal meaning of Scripture, built on a Thomistic basis (though going beyond Thomas), was adopted by other medieval theologians as a useful tool for the interpretation of the Old Testament. But perhaps the most famous early-sixteenth-century humanist to make use of this theory, at least as a starting point and framework for his own approach to Scripture, was the French biblical scholar Jacques Lefèvre d'Etaples, commonly known by his Latin name, Faber Stapulensis.[10]

Faber was born in 1455 at Etaples in Picardy in the north of France.[11] Though he entered holy orders, he was not in the strict sense of the term a theologian but was, rather, one of the company of humanist scholars who devoted their lives to the editing of ancient texts and to general philological study. Faber first gained a reputation in France for his work in recovering a better text of Aristotle than had been available for centuries. His interest in Aristotle had been stimulated by a trip to Italy. When he returned to France he lectured at the Sorbonne on the philosophy of Aristotle, which he found clearly preferable to the philosophy of Plato, and published corrected texts of Aristotle's works.

Gradually, however, Faber's interest in Aristotle gave way to an interest in the recovery of the Christian past. Hours that had been devoted to the careful and painstaking editing of classical texts were now given over to the study of the Fathers and the medieval mystics. Among the Fathers, his favorite works were the writings of Ignatius and Polycarp; among the mystics, the writings of the Victorines, Ruysbroeck, Mechthild, and Hildegard.

Faber's study of the ancient Christian past and of the mystical theology of the Middle Ages whetted his appetite for the study of Scripture itself, the common source of inspiration for both the Fathers and the mystics. In 1508 Faber, though not himself a monk, was given the privilege of residence in Saint-Germain-des-Près, a monastery with rich manuscript collections. In the quiet of his new surroundings and with the help of its resources, Faber edited the Psalms in 1509 and the letters of Paul in 1512.

Faber's edition of the Psalms was called the *Quincuplex Psalterium* because of its unique structure. The Psalter consisted of five versions of the Latin text of the Psalms: the three Latin versions of Jerome, the Old Latin Version used in the church before the Vulgate was prepared, and the *Conciliatum*, the critical version prepared by Faber himself. The idea of a critical edition of Scripture, utilizing parallel texts, was not original with Faber. Origen's *Hexapla* is perhaps the earliest attempt to provide the church with a better text through a comparative study of various extant versions. The method, if old, was nevertheless sound, and Faber's edition of the Psalms was eagerly devoured by the scholarly world.

Even more important than the text-critical work of Faber was the commentary on the Psalms, appended to the purified text. The church in general and monastic communities in particular were committed to the devotional use of the Psalms. The use of the hymns of Israel in the liturgical life of the church, however, created certain important theological problems, which could not be skirted. How could the church, which had been commanded to love its enemies, pray the warlike and vengeful sentiments of certain of the more martial and unforgiving Psalms? What sense did it make for a French monk who had never wandered farther east than Rouen to repeat the ancient nostalgic cries of the Israelites in exile who longed for a glimpse of Jerusalem? What significance could a Catholic Christian, who celebrated the Feast of Corpus Christi, find in a hymn composed for the celebration of Passover?

Faber agreed with the prevailing sentiment in many quarters that the Psalter could only be used by the church if it was shown to be in some sense a book that witnessed to the gospel. Where Faber differed from the mainstream of biblical interpretation was in his rejection of the contention of Christian exegetes that the significance of the Psalter as a book serviceable to the church could only be regained by retreating from the literal or primary meaning of the text to a spiritual or secondary meaning. He could not even accept the solution of Lyra, which distinguished the literal-historical meaning of the psalm, known to the prophet who composed it, from the literal-prophetic meaning, known only to God, the principal Author of Scripture, who later revealed it to the church. For Faber that was a theological ruse, a subtler way of reintroducing a fundamentally unpalatable distinction.

The literal sense of Scripture is the meaning that the Holy Spirit intends it to have.[12] If Psalm 22 is a witness to the crucifixion of Jesus Christ, then that is the only meaning Psalm 22 has ever had. What Lyra called the literal-historical sense is abruptly dismissed as unacceptable by Faber. David spoke consciously and directly of Jesus Christ. The church does not find a meaning in the Old Testament that was alien to the writers of the Old Testament themselves. If this reduces the human authors of the Bible to the level of passive instruments, it nevertheless establishes the Christian meaning of the Old Testament as the primary meaning. Isaiah 53 witnesses directly to Jesus Christ. Any attempt to equate the Suffering Servant with Israel in exile rests on a basic misunderstanding of the intention of the text. An historical-literal sense that deflects the reader away from Jesus Christ is a mere product of human fancy. For Faber the spiritual meaning of the Old Testament *is* the literal meaning. God's witness is not divided against itself. Therefore Faber did not hesitate to identify the historical-literal sense with the letter that kills.

It is one thing, however, to identify the literal with the spiritual sense of Scripture and another thing to show how the spiritual meaning of Scripture is discerned. Surprisingly enough, for all his interest in the philological study of the Bible and the preparation of better texts, Faber did not feel that grammar provided the key for unlocking the meaning of Holy Scripture. Spiritual things are discerned by the Spirit. Insight into the meaning of Holy Scripture is not a human work, not a product of human erudition. Scripture can only be understood as a result of illumination by the Holy Spirit, who makes intelligible the mysteries of divine revelation. Since the Holy Spirit grants illumination only to those men and women whom he indwells, the problem of the right exegesis of Scripture becomes, in the last analysis, the problem of the justification of the human interpreters of Scripture.[13]

Scripture is "the letter that kills" to sinners who are carnal, who have not been justified by the grace of God. The same Scripture is "the spirit that makes alive" to those men and women who, having been justified by divine grace, are indwelt by the Holy Spirit. The crucial difference is found not in the Scripture that is to be interpreted but in the character of the interpreters themselves. The contrast of letter and spirit is a contrast in human beings rather than in the text. The real hermeneutical problem is the human interpreter.

Faber's philological and exegetical work attracted the interest of a circle of highly talented men, who became his theological disciples.[14] They were inspired by Faber's ideal of the reform of the church according to the model of faith found in the primitive church.[15] Like many other humanists, Faber hoped for a restitution of primitive Christianity through the study of the Bible and the Fathers and the reintroduction into the church of high ethical standards.

In 1516 Faber and his disciples were presented with an opportunity to implement their vision of reform in concrete action. William Briçonnet, the abbot of Saint-Germain-des-Près, was appointed bishop of Meaux. The new bishop briskly set about to reform his diocese. He grouped the parishes into districts, in order to administer them more effectively and to encourage better pastoral care of the congregations. He banned dances and games, which he felt had often provided opportunities for moral abuses of various kinds, not to say debauchery. Priests who had neglected their pastoral functions were brought up short. And the mendicant orders found themselves, much to their discomfort, under a measure of episcopal control. In all these reforms Faber served as adviser and as a constant source of inspiration.

Faber's teaching, however, did not remain unopposed. Noel Beda, the principal of the College of Montaigu in Paris,[16] was outraged when Faber contended, against the commonly accepted tradition, that Mary Magdalene, Mary the sister of Martha, and the woman who washed the feet of Jesus with her tears were three different women. Beda quickly became the leader of the fac-

Catholic Reform

tion at the Sorbonne opposed to the teaching of Faber and the reforms instituted by the circle of Meaux. Matters came to a head in 1525 when Faber was denounced by the Franciscans. He had already been condemned by the Sorbonne in 1521. But new factors had entered the picture. Men professing to be his disciples had been arrested and executed. In this dangerous and volatile situation Faber decided that it was the better part of wisdom to flee for safety to Strasbourg. He returned to France only when the king, at the specific intervention of his sister, ordered an end to the persecution.

The flight to Strasbourg marked the demise of the circle of Meaux and the noble experiment of Bishop Briçonnet. Pope Clement VII put a stop to the reformatory work in the diocese of Meaux. There was nothing for the bishop to do but submit. The circle that had gathered with such high hopes in 1516 broke up. Josse Clichtove, Gerard Roussel, and Michel d'Arande remained within the Catholic fold. William Farel and François Vatable became Protestants. Caroli, who had become a Protestant for a brief time, at the end joined the majority by reconverting to Catholicism.

Faber himself retired to the court of Marguerite d'Angoulême in Nérac, where he was safely out of the grasp of his enemies. Though Faber's influence on Luther and Farel is clear and can be documented,[17] Faber was not, in the customary sense of the word, a Protestant.[18] The attempts of older scholarship to classify Faber with the Protestant reformers have proved largely abortive. Faber followed his own path to reform,[19] the path of a gentle Christian intellectual. But Faber's vision, though it inspired other intellectuals, did not capture the popular imagination. The times were harsh and called for heroic measures. The work of Faber in France, like the work of John Colet in England and Geiler in Strasbourg, was superseded by more fundamental and thoroughgoing movements of reform. When Faber died at eighty-two, his reforms had largely been absorbed by the work of other men. He had served as the herald for an age that he had not fully anticipated and that he could not guide.[20]

5

REGINALD POLE
(1500–1558)

The Loss of Eden

NO FIGURE IN THE English reformation lost more and was less deserving of the losses he suffered than Reginald Pole. Though a cousin of the king, he was forced to spend most of his adult life in exile because of Henry's ill will toward him—always fearful, while Henry lived, of the long arm of the king's vengeance. While the Catholic church showered on him the honors that his native country had denied him, he saw the theological positions he defended rejected at Trent, his hope for election to the papacy thwarted by one vote, and his orthodoxy questioned by Pope Paul IV. Even when shortly before his death he returned to aid Queen Mary in her attempt to reclaim England for the Catholic faith, he watched his valiant efforts for reform come at last to nothing, defeated by a Spanish marriage and the fires of Smithfield.

Pole was born on March 3, 1500, in Stourton Castle, Staffordshire, to Margaret of Salisbury, the niece of King Edward IV, and Sir Richard Pole, a cousin of Henry VII.[1] With Tudor and Plantagenet ancestry, Reginald Pole was related to the royal houses of both Lancaster and York. Indeed, Catherine of Aragon, the first wife of Henry VIII, always cherished the hope that her daughter, Mary, and Pole might someday be united in marriage in order to strengthen the Tudor claim to the throne.

Pole was tutored in Greek by William Latimer and then sent away to school, first at the Carthusian monastery of Sheen and later at Magdalen College, Oxford. Through Latimer, Pole was introduced to Christian humanism, a movement of reform that attempted to link the Christian present with the humane values of classical and Christian antiquity. The voice of Christian humanism, however, tended to be drowned out by the controversies that dominated England in the sixteenth century. The controversy over royal supremacy and then over the issues of doctrinal and liturgical change, and not the more moderate reform of morals and of education envisioned by the humanists, stirred the passions of Pole's contemporaries and claimed their loyalties.

From 1519 to 1527 Pole, with the financial support of Henry VIII, continued his education on the continent, studying at Rome, Padua, and Venice. The years spent at Padua were decisive for Pole. There he met and became fast friends with Bembo, Contarini, and Sadoleto, men known not only for the breadth of their learning but also for the genuineness of their concern for reform.

In 1527 Pole was recalled to England by Henry, who was quietly trying to find a way out of his marriage to Catherine of Aragon. Catherine had been married to Arthur, Henry's brother, but Arthur had died before the union could be consummated. Marriage with a brother's widow was forbidden by canon law, since the two were regarded by the church as brother and sister. But Ferdinand of Spain, whose dynastic plans had been spoiled by the death of Arthur, had convinced the pope to legalize a marriage between Henry and Catherine. Though Catherine bore Henry several children, only one survived, a baby girl. England needed a prince, but Henry and Catherine could not seem to produce a living male heir to the throne.

Henry, who had not been faithful to Catherine, became infatuated with Anne Boleyn, a lady-in-waiting of his wife and a sister of his former mistress. Anne, however, had learned from the mistake of her sister and refused to confer any favors on Henry without marriage. Accordingly, Henry, moved both by his attraction to Anne Boleyn and his desire for a living male heir, professed to have qualms of conscience about the validity of his marriage with Catherine.

Pole wanted no part of the divorce proceedings against Catherine and retired to the monastery at Sheen on the pretext of taking up again the studies that had been interrupted by his recall to England. He left England for Paris, with Henry's permission, to study theology and to disengage himself from the "King's Great Matter." He was followed, however, by Henry's appointment of him as ambassador to the court of Francis I and by Henry's command that he take part in a special mission to the University of Paris. Henry wanted Pole to convince the faculty at Paris to support Henry in his contention that his marriage to Catherine was invalid. Pole protested that he lacked the skill and experience for such a commission. Paris did finally support Henry, but only, as Pole had rightly feared, by the slimmest of margins.

When Henry summoned Pole to return to England in 1530, there was every reason to believe that the king intended to confer new honors on his younger cousin. Cardinal Wolsey had fallen and left empty the sees of Winchester and of York. The king needed an ally to offset the influence of Bishop John Fisher, whose persistent opposition to the divorce threatened its success. Pole could have either Winchester or York, if he would only swallow his principles and throw his wholehearted support to Henry. But Henry had misjudged his man. In a stormy interview in the king's private drawing room Pole refused the tempting bribe which Henry dangled before him. By defying Henry, Pole lost the favor of the king and very nearly lost his life as well.

In 1532 Pole received the grudging permission of the king to leave England and return to Italy. Two years later Parliament passed the First Succession Act, which validated Henry's secret marriage to Anne Boleyn, and the Act of Supremacy, which acknowledged Henry to be the supreme head of the church in England. Once again Henry needed an ally to support his cause in the face of the opposition his radical policy had evoked. And once again he turned to Pole.

In 1535 Thomas Starkey, who had served as Pole's chaplain on an earlier visit to Italy and who was now the chaplain to the king, relayed to Pole by letter the king's plea for his support. Pole did not immediately reply to Henry. Indeed, it was not until Pole heard of the execution of Bishop Fisher and Sir Thomas More that he felt impelled to enter the public lists against Henry. From September 4, 1535, to March 30, 1536, he was absorbed in writing his reply to the king. His treatise, *De Unitate*, was a classic defense of the doctrine of papal supremacy and an impassioned attack on Henry's schismatic policy.[2]

Henry was outraged by what he regarded as Pole's stubborn opposition to his wishes and vented his anger on Pole's family in England. He ordered the immediate execution of Pole's brother and the imprisonment of his mother, Margaret of Salisbury, who later—also by Henry's order—was beheaded in the Tower of London. The break between Henry and Pole was final. Had Pole dared to face down the king's wrath and return to England Henry would have seized and executed him on the spot. As it was, he lived in constant fear of Henry's hired assassins.[3]

While Pole's defense of the papacy had earned the undying hatred of the king of England, it had also merited the admiration of the Vatican. Pole was called to Rome, where he was made a cardinal by Pope Paul III and employed by the Roman curia. His duties were various. He was immediately appointed to the commission, on which Contarini and Carafa also served, that recommended certain measures for the reform of the church in an important white paper entitled the *Consilium de Emendanda Ecclesiae*. When twenty thousand men in Lincolnshire rebelled against Henry in 1536 in the so-called Pilgrimage of Grace, Pole was named papal legate to England. The rebels wanted an end to religious innovation and a restoration of the ecclesiastical status quo ante. The pope believed that Pole, with his extensive family connections in England, was the proper man to take maximum advantage of Henry's temporary embarrassment. By the time Pole reached Paris, however, the rebellion had already been crushed. Pole's later attempt in 1537 to unite Francis I and Charles V in an alliance dedicated to the invasion of England and the reduction of Henry to obedience to the Roman church also ended in failure. Pole had been associated from the very first with the reform party in Rome, which supported the Colloquy at Regensburg between Protestants and Catholics.[4] By the summer of 1541 it had become clear that the discussions at Regensburg had failed to produce the hoped-for reunion with the dissident Protestants. Indeed, the discussions had had precisely the reverse effect. They had shown to moderates of both sides how wide the chasm between Rome and Wittenberg had grown.

Furthermore, the cause of Protestantism was prospering. The evangelical movement had crossed the Alps into Italy and was daily growing in strength in the duchy of Milan. Evangelical groups had even been uncovered at Modena and Lucca. The penetration of Protestantism into the Latin nations of Christendom had begun.

The failure of Regensburg and the growing strength of Protestantism fortified the determination of Pope Paul III to propose a general council to the German estates. However, the convocation of a general council was no easy matter. The political situation in the Catholic world was inflammable. War seemed imminent between Emperor Charles V and Francis I of France.

Cardinal Giovanni Morone was dispatched to Germany to encourage church reform and to sound out the attitude of the Catholic estates toward the location of the coming council. On March 23, 1542, Morone presented himself before the German estates at Speyer with a list of five cities recommended for the site of the proposed council—a list from which the estates could choose. After some debate among themselves and in spite of a last-minute and clumsy diplomatic move on the part of Pope Paul III, the Germans agreed on the city of Trent as an acceptable location. Morone returned to Rome with the written decision of the estates tucked securely in his pouch.

On May 22, 1542, the bull of convocation, *Initio Nostri Huius Pontificatus*, was issued. Nuncios were commissioned to carry the bull to the bishops of the Catholic church. But while these preparations were still being made, Francis I undermined the likelihood of their success by declaring war on the emperor. French forces pressed to the attack in Spain and in the Netherlands.

Faced with war between the great powers, the pope adopted an attitude of neutrality. The emperor resented the neutrality of the papacy, since in his eyes this attitude made no distinction between aggressor (namely, Francis) and victim (namely, Charles). Consequently, in a letter of August 25, 1542, Charles urged the pope to abandon his impartial stance and pled with him to side with the empire in the conflict with Francis. As long as Francis remained unpunished, it would be impossible for Charles to send delegates to a council at Trent. The implication of the letter was clear: no alliance, no council—at least for the time being. But the pope was not to be shaken from his neutrality, especially since he feared the possibility of a French schism.

The invitation to the council met a similarly stony response in France. As early as May 17, 1542, Francis had flatly rejected the idea of a council in Trent. In fact, the king was so opposed to a council at Trent that Cardinal Sadoleto, who had been sent as a peace delegate to Montpellier, felt it the better part of wisdom not to broach the subject in his audience with the French monarch.

In spite of the disheartening response from Charles and Francis, the pope proceeded with his plans for the council. On September 18, 1542, the bishops of Verona and La Cava were dispatched to Trent as commissaries of the council. Orlando Ricci, the inspector of the fortresses of the Papal States, joined them as billeting officer. On October 16, 1542, nearly a month later, three legates were appointed for the council: Cardinal Pierpaolo Parisio, formerly a professor of civil law at Padua; Cardinal Morone, who had obtained the agreement of the German estates to the city of Trent as the site of the new council; and Cardinal Pole, who had served since August 1541 as the governor of Viterbo and the Papal States. The legates were given instructions that had been drafted by the canonists Giovanni Del Monte, Bartolomeo Guidiccioni, and Tommaso Campeggio.

When Pole and his fellow legates arrived in Trent on November 21, 1542, they found only two bishops awaiting them: Tommaso Sanfelice, one of the two papal commissaries, and Christopher Madruzzo, the bishop of Trent. The French bishops, for the most part, hid behind the refusal of Francis to take part in the council. The Spanish cardinals were kept at home by Charles. The bishops of Germany had refused to take the long journey to Trent before the Italian bishops, who lived much nearer, began to stir. In Switzerland, the announcement of a council had not even been taken seriously.

The months dragged by. On May 10, 1543, the first German delegates arrived at Trent, swelling the total episcopal congregation to ten. Though some interest in the council had been generated at the Diet of Nuremberg, it was not sufficient to save the rapidly expiring council at Trent. On May 5, 1543, the pope recalled Cardinal Pole from Trent to give a personal report to the papal court in Bologna. On May 13, Cardinal Parisio was similarly recalled. Morone alone was left in charge at Trent.

Pope Paul was faced with three courses of action. He could suspend the council until the war ended. He could transfer the council to a city within a papal state. Or he could do nothing and on July 6, 1543, after consultation with the cardinals and with the emperor himself, the pope took the anticipated step and suspended the council. The first attempt of Paul III to hold a general council had ended in failure.

The situation changed, however, with the defeat of Francis by Charles. According to a secret clause in the peace treaty, Francis agreed to a council at Trent, Cambrai, or Metz at a date to be determined by the emperor. He furthermore agreed to send his own bishops and theologians to the council. Assured of his own military power and eager to deal with the Protestant menace in the empire, Charles urged the pope to re-call the council he had suspended. The pope was willing, indeed eager, to do so, provided that the emperor agreed to keep the religious question off the agenda of the coming diet at Speyer.

The new bull of convocation, *Laetare Jerusalem*, was read on November 19 and 22, 1544. It fixed the date for the opening of the council as March 15, 1545. The bull was published on November 30 and dispatched to the emperor on December 3. It was February 22, 1545, however, before the papal legates—Del Monte, Marcello Cervini, and Pole—were appointed and given the legatine cross. By the time Del Monte and Cervini had arrived in Trent, it was already March 13, only two days before the day appointed for the opening of the council. Two days passed. Laetare Sunday came and went. No one stirred to open the convocation. The Council of Trent had entered its second period of incubation.

As anticipated, morale at Trent sagged. By September 12, 1545, more than a dozen prelates had abandoned Trent without permission. Other bishops, who had not yet started for Trent, were disposed to remain at home and adopt a policy of wait and see. Finally, on October 30, 1545, the pope felt that he could delay no longer, regardless of the emperor's plans, and announced his intention of opening the council before Christmas. On December 11, 1545, the formal order for the opening of the Council of Trent was delivered to Pole and the other legates by a courier from Rome. The long-awaited opening was at hand.

The announcement arrived on December 11. The council was due to be inaugurated two days later. At nine-thirty in the morning on December 13, 1545, the procession formed in the Church of the Most Holy Trinity. The hymn *Veni, Creator Spiritus* was chanted, and the procession began. Approximately four hundred bishops filed into the cathedral and took their places. Cardinal Cornelio Masso preached; the Mass of the Holy Ghost was celebrated; the papal bull, *Laetare Jerusalem*, was read. By two o'clock in the afternoon the service was over. The Council of Trent had been officially inaugurated.

The second session of the council was held on January 7, 1546. The opening address, though it was delivered by Angelus Mascarelli, had in fact been written by Cardinal Pole. The address was a stirring summons to the Catholic church to repent and reform itself. Rather than allowing the council to choose the easy path of recrimination against the Protestants, Pole urged it to examine its own life and to acknowledge the guilt of its own sins:

> We exhort you! . . . We are all in the same boat! . . . In the midst of tempests and dangers we must arouse ourselves and be vigilant lest we crash on the rocks. . . . Strong in faith and hope, let us direct our voyage, so we may arrive at the port of salvation for the glory of God. . . . Before the tribunal of God, we ourselves are guilty. . . . Truly we the shepherds are the cause of the evils now oppressing the Church. If anyone thinks this is an exaggeration . . . facts themselves which cannot lie, bear witness to the truth of these words. . . . How will the Holy Spirit guide us if we do not admit that our shameful faults merit the just judgment of God? . . . With our prayers and a humble voice and contrite heart let us invoke the Holy Spirit to illumine our hearts. . . . We exhort you, with love in the Lord, with one heart and spirit to glorify God the Father in Christ Jesus, Who is God the Blessed, for ever, Amen![5]

Some historians have argued that of all the delegates to Trent, Pole was clearly the delegate most open to the theological influence of the Protestants.[6] Only a short time before, he had served as the spiritual director of a group that numbered in its membership the Italian poets Marcantonio Flaminio and Vittoria Colonna.[7] Flaminio in particular was enamored of Luther's teaching concerning justification. Nevertheless, he was persuaded by Pole, who was himself not unmoved by Luther's profound interpretation of Paul, to adhere to a more traditional understanding of justification and to remain in communion with Rome.

At Trent, Pole's sensitivity to the Protestant critique of Pelagianizing tendencies in Catholic theology and his openness to the recovery of a more biblical theology made him a natural ally of the general of the Augustinian order, Girolamo Seripando. Seripando had taken up the cause of the doctrine of double justification where Contarini had left it at his death, and argued—unsuccessfully, as it proved—for its adoption by the Fathers at Trent. Seripando also fought, again with the support of Pole, against the formula, later adopted by the council, that the written Scriptures and the unwritten traditions of the church should be treated with equal reverence and affection. Seripando believed the formula should read "similar" rather than "equal." In 1548 at the end of the tenth session, Pole withdrew as papal legate to Trent. By that time the council had rejected not only Luther's understanding of justification, which was to be expected, but also the more moderate doctrine of double justification defended by Seripando. Though the motives for Pole's withdrawal from Trent are still in dispute—he pled ill health at the time—there is good reason to believe that he left in part because of his dissatisfaction with the conciliar decree on justification. Not that Pole was a heretic! On the contrary, he submitted to the teaching of the Catholic church and resisted any temptation to break with it.

Pope Paul died on November 10, 1549. Pole, along with his rival Carafa, was a leading contender for the papal crown and came within one vote of election. A delegation of imperial cardinals approached Pole and offered to give him the chair of Peter by acclamation. Pole refused their offer and insisted that he would only accept the papacy if he were elected to it by proper canonical procedure. The next day, however, he fell five votes short of the number needed for his election. Finally, with the help of the French cardinals who arrived at the conclave after the earlier balloting had been completed, Del Monte was chosen as a compromise candidate and crowned as Julius III. Pole himself wryly noted: "When two Cardinals came to offer homage, I thought of the two disciples whom our Lord sent to fetch the ass on which He was to ride into the Holy City. . . . I prayed them to wait and leave the issue to be proved by daylight, and as the event proved the Lord did not require this particular ass."[8]

In 1553 Mary Tudor fell heir to the throne of England.[9] Unlike her half brother Edward VI, Mary was a Catholic, who proposed to restore the Roman Catholic system and papal supremacy set aside by her father. Pole was ap-

Catholic Reform

pointed in 1554 to serve as Mary's adviser and papal legate to England. Though delayed a while by Charles, who wanted to see Mary safely married to Philip of Spain and who was suspicious of Pole's intentions, the cardinal arrived at last in England and absolved it from its schism. The church in England was once again in communion with the church of Rome. When Cranmer was executed by Mary for his part in the divorce proceedings against her mother, Pole succeeded him as the archbishop of Canterbury and the primate of all England. Immediately he set about to enforce in the English realm the reform measures taken by the Council of Trent. He recommended the establishment of seminaries—a word he coined—for the proper training of priests.

In the last analysis it was Pole's allies and not his enemies who undercut his work. Mary launched, against Pole's advice, a policy of severe repression against the Protestants. The privy council and Parliament went along with the queen because they had only expected a few heretics to be burned. They were taken aback when over two hundred and fifty perished in the flames. In spite of Pole's attempt to reform the Catholic church in England and not simply reinstate it, Mary's persecutions and her unpopular Spanish marriage undid much of his work before it could take root. The Roman Catholic church became identified in the minds of many English people with bigotry, blood, and Spain.

If anyone was slow to link the Catholic church with bigotry and blood, the lesson was hammered home by John Foxe's *Acts and Monuments*, written after Pole's death. This account of the Marian persecutions became an effective tool of Protestant propaganda. Foxe knew the power of an individual case study to kindle the imagination of his reader. The pages of his book are filled not with statistics about the incidence of persecution or with analyses of the causes— political, sociological, and theological—that created the environment favorable to persecution but with living portraits of the men and women in the England of Cardinal Pole who suffered persecution and who chose to give up their lives rather than yield their faith.

Portrait follows portrait; vignette follows vignette. With a deft touch and a sure sense for concrete and vivid detail, Foxe recreates what was individual and warmly human about each of his subjects. Here is Lady Jane Grey, blindfolded and groping for the block; Bishop Hooper, forced to walk silently to his execution; Rowland Taylor, careful to bequeath a prized Latin book to his son; Rawlins White, the simple fisherman, weeping at the sight of his wife and children but undeterred in his purpose; Matthew Plaise, the weaver, matching wits with the bishop of Dover; Joyce Lewis, abandoned by her husband; Roger Holland, the gambling tailor, converted by the servant of his master; short Mrs. Prest, thickset and stubborn; Thomas Benbridge, throwing his velvet cap away before mounting to the stake.

Yet while Foxe is concerned with the individual, it is precisely this piling up of cases one upon the other that gives the *Acts and Monuments* its compelling power. Each victim, one by one, testifies against his persecutors. Each martyr casts his vote against the Catholic church. Taken one by one, these voices are impressive. But taken together they form a chorus of united protest that no impartial reader can lightly brush aside: doctrines defended by such devilish means must be devilish.

In terms of cold logic, the Marian persecutions were a disastrous mistake. They not only turned people against the Catholic church; they also drove into exile the moderate Protestant leaders. Many of the young men who had left England as lukewarm Protestants returned at Mary's death as fiery Calvinists. Ironically, Mary became not the restorer of the Catholic past but the mother of English Puritanism.

As if it were not enough that Pole saw his work undone by the excessive zeal of the queen, he had to contend as well with the jealousy of his old rival, Carafa, who had been elected as Pope Paul IV. The pope accused Pole of heresy to the queen and proposed to revoke his legatine status. His move was delayed by Mary, who argued that Pole's continued presence in England was essential for the program of Catholic reform and restoration. However, before the matter could be brought to a successful conclusion, death intervened. On November 17, 1558, Mary passed away. A few hours later on the same day, her cousin followed her.

No man loved England, that other Eden, more than Pole. And yet he lost her twice, first to Henry's wrath and then to Mary's piety. With the death of Mary, England fell to the Protestant daughter of Anne Boleyn. Pole, who thought he was the first of a new line of Roman Catholic archbishops of Canterbury, proved instead to be the last.

II

The Lutheran Tradition

6

PHILIP MELANCHTHON

(1497–1560)

Return to Method

THE CREATIVE WORK OF Luther and Zwingli, often diffuse and disorganized, needed to be systematized and brought into some order, especially if Protestantism hoped to withstand the threat of a resurgent Roman Catholic church. For the Lutherans, this work of systematization was begun by Philip Melanchthon, the only humanist for whom Luther had an enduring, almost unexplainable respect. In a canny, though highly inaccurate, estimate of his contemporaries, Luther once remarked: "Res et verba Melanchthon; verba sine re Erasmus; res sine verbis Lutherus; nec res nec verba Carlostadius" (Substance and words, Melanchthon; words without substance, Erasmus; substance without words, Luther; neither substance nor words, Carlstadt).[1] Even the old Luther, who was not notably slow to take offense at deviations from what he considered to be the correct understanding of the gospel, praised the *Loci Communes* with the kind of unqualified language he did not think proper to employ in recommending his own favorite works, *The Bondage of the Will* and the *Commentary on Galatians*.[2]

Nevertheless, the friendship between Luther and Melanchthon was not without its difficulties.[3] Melanchthon was in many ways a bewildering combination of contradictory qualities. He was a gentle and irenic man[4] who won not only the respect but even the firm friendship of his students. But he also had a terrible temper and could unleash a tempest to rage and crackle around the ears of a dullard who had spent the evening in a tavern rather than at his books.[5] He was a shrewd and tireless scholar, a master of many subjects, who was himself the best proof of that aphorism of Aristotle that a human being is that creature who desires by nature to know. At the same time he displayed what Luther regarded as a naive trust in astrology[6] and refused to accept a call to England because of a prophecy that he would die by drowning if he went on a sea voyage to the north.

The differences between Luther and Melanchthon, however, were more fundamental than differences of temperament. Luther was amused by Melanchthon's fearfulness[7] and annoyed by his readiness to make concessions for the sake of harmony.[8] But neither Melanchthon's timidity nor his diplomacy threatened to disrupt their relationship. The strain in their friendship, when it finally came, was caused—as one might have expected—by differences in theological approach. These differences, though they never led to a breach between the two men, are so significant that Franz Hildebrandt in his book on Melanchthon raised the question whether Melanchthon should be regarded from the standpoint of the Lutheran reformation as an alien or an ally.[9] It is a nice question, and one that is not easily answered.

Melanchthon was born in Bretten in southwestern Germany, a nephew of the famous German humanist Johannes Reuchlin.[10] His family name was Schwartzert, and his father was an armorer for the elector. Melanchthon, in accordance with the common practice of the humanists, translated his rather ordinary German name into the more elegant Greek name Melanchthon.

On October 14, 1509, Melanchthon began his university career at Heidelberg, where he studied for his baccalaureate. There is no evidence that he studied theology at Heidelberg, though he did compose a poem in memory of Geiler von Kaysersberg, who died in 1510. In 1512 Melanchthon transferred to Tübingen, where two years later he received his master's degree. At Tübingen Melanchthon read Erasmus, as well as some theology, especially Jean Gerson and Wessel Gansfort, whom Reuchlin recommended highly. But for the most part Melanchthon concentrated on the study of the classics, delivering lectures on Virgil and Cicero and preparing a new edition of the works of Terence. In 1518 at the age of twenty-one he accepted the call to become professor of Greek at the University of Wittenberg.

Melanchthon had not been drawn to Wittenberg because of his interest in the new theology being developed there or because of any fascination with the person of Luther. Like many of the humanists, his interests were primarily philological and literary, though he was not disinterested in ethical problems.[11] While comparing the Latin translation of Aristotle with the Greek original, Melanchthon came to the conclusion that medieval scholasticism had not only perverted the gospel but also misunderstood ancient philosophy. Melanchthon went to Wittenberg with the intention of purifying Aristotle of the absurd opinions of the medieval Aristotelians.

However, at Wittenberg Melanchthon came under the influence of Luther, who persuaded him to give up his plans for the study and publication of Aristotle and to devote himself to the study of theology instead. Luther admired Melanchthon's vast classical erudition and his ability for careful and precise definition. Melanchthon chose to remain a layman, though he did yield to Luther's persistent urging to earn at least the first theological degree. He refused, however, in the face of Luther's subtlest blandishments, to earn a theological doctorate.

When Melanchthon first began to lecture on the Bible, he repudiated philosophy with, if anything, a more radical antiphilosophical zeal than Luther himself had shown. He attempted to interpret Scripture by employing the philological methods used by the humanists in interpreting ancient literary texts. In his return to Scripture and his devaluation of tradition and philosophy, Melanchthon developed a radically biblicistic ethic, arguing that Scripture was the norm of civil law as well as the schoolmaster that leads to Christ. His radical rejection of philosophy proved to be temporary, and in 1527 he returned to his original project by publishing a new edition of the *Nicomachean Ethics* of Aristotle.

In 1521 Melanchthon published the first edition of what became his most important theological book, the *Loci Communes*. Translated literally, *loci communes* means "common places"—though a less literal and better translation would render it "basic concepts." This book was a discussion of Lutheran theology, ordered by topics. It was a rather simple manual of the fundamental principles of Luther's thought. Only those doctrines that touched directly on the life of the believer were discussed.

Melanchthon wished to be true to Luther throughout the *Loci Communes*. He did not attempt to walk his own independent way, at least not at first. For Luther the subject of theology was not, as the medieval scholastics had argued, God in himself, and not, as Feuerbach later thought, human beings in themselves. Those were topics for philosophical speculation, perhaps, but not for theology. Theology is an ellipse with two foci. It is concerned with God in his relation to sinners and sinners in their relation to God. The subject of theology is not a neutral knowledge of God—as if such a neutral knowledge of God were even possible! The subject of theology is God in his dealings in judgment and grace with fallen humanity. Thus Melanchthon, in harmony with Luther, wrote:

> I do not see how I can call that man a Christian who is ignorant of the remaining topics such as the power of sin, the law and grace. For by them is Christ properly known, if indeed this is to know Christ, to wit, to know his benefits and not as they teach, to perceive his natures and the mode of his incarnation. Unless one knows why Christ took upon himself human flesh and was crucified, what advantage would accrue from having learned his life's history? . . . Precisely this is Christian knowledge, to know what the law demands, whence you may seek the power to discharge the injunctions of the law, whence you may seek pardon for sin, how you may arouse a wavering mind against the Devil, the flesh and the world, and finally how you may console a dejected conscience. Of course the Scholastics teach such things, do they not? In the Epistle to the Romans, when he drew up a compendium of Christian

doctrine, did Paul the author philosophize about the mysteries of the Trinity, the mode of the Incarnation, or about "creation active and passive?" On the contrary, what does Paul do? He reasons most certainly about the Law, Sin and Grace. Topics, I say, on which alone the knowledge of Christ depends.[12]

Yet one can see from the very beginning that there are differences between Luther and Melanchthon. Melanchthon's interest in education and pedagogy, to take an easy example, is apparent in the earliest edition of the *Loci Communes*. Melanchthon wished by precise definition to safeguard the truth of Luther's ideas against misconception, since misunderstanding of ideas often leads to perversions in practice. This concern with accuracy of conception is not characteristic of Luther and foreshadows the concerns of Lutheran Orthodoxy.

Furthermore, Melanchthon had an interest in ethics that was different from Luther's interest. The justified sinner, the man or woman united to Christ, was for Luther a transformed person. Christians have no need of the law or of rule books to tell them what to do. A good tree bears good fruit automatically. One does not need to read a botany book to an apple tree to save it from possible confusion in the spring. The law is irrelevant for Christian ethics. The only demand laid on Christians is the demand of love. Christian ethics is the response of love to the situation of human need that confronts it. It is even permissible to speak of Luther's teaching as situation ethics, so long as it is clear that it is the new person in Christ and not the old Adam who has the right to live in such perfect freedom. It is Mr. Greatheart and not Mr. Carnality who was unleashed by Luther.

Melanchthon was very chary of this situational approach to ethics. He valued casuistry and was careful to spell out in some detail the place and province of the law. The Christian life is a holy life. There is no place for "lawlessness" in it. Therefore, the Christian's ethical responsibility needs to be clarified and elucidated.

Still another difference emerges when one examines the approach of Luther and Melanchthon to Scripture. Melanchthon did not appear to distinguish between the Word of God and Holy Scripture. Luther insisted that Scripture had a center from which it must be understood and that not all parts could be considered of equal authority. Melanchthon did not elucidate a doctrine of Holy Scripture in these early *Loci*, but he did quote and use Scripture as if it were all of equal authority. Scripture was not interpreted from a center, but all parts were viewed as having the same weight as far as their claim to truth is concerned.

In the later editions of the *Loci* these deviations from Luther became even more pronounced. The philosophy of Aristotle regained a position of prominence.[13] In spite of his early antiphilosophical bias, Melanchthon was not bashful to talk about final cause, proximate and instrumental causes, undistributed middles, and unproved minors. Where Luther in his insistence on a theology of the cross was opposed to all philosophical theology, Melanchthon took up the tools of philosophy to ground, clarify, and order the biblical theology of Luther.

Furthermore, the scope of the subjects discussed by Melanchthon is broadened. For Luther, theology focused on God in his dealings in judgment and grace with human beings. Now for Melanchthon in the 1530s the doctrine of God's Unity and Trinity, the two natures of Christ, the mode of the incarnation—all subjects purposefully omitted from the earliest *Loci*—were taken up and treated at some length. A doctrine is important because of its place in the overall system. No doctrine should be omitted if the truth in its wholeness is to be understood. Theology becomes, from Luther's point of view, less existential and more speculative.

Philosophy was not only used by Melanchthon to order the teaching of Luther. It now had a propaedeutic value. Philosophy is a device that leads men and women to the gospel. Faith is not for Melanchthon, as it sometimes appears to be for Luther, simply the committal of the self unreservedly to God; not merely the total response of the total human being to the divine initiative. Faith is also agreement with a set of revealed truths.[14] Christians need philosophy therefore to make the mind certain of what it believes. Philosophy helps to produce certitude.[15] It serves an important function as an instrument of pastoral care.

Furthermore, miracles became for Melanchthon a means of validating the gospel. It sometimes appears that he argued that miracles recounted in the Bible are true; hence, the gospel is true. Proofs for the existence of God, valueless for Luther and only *adminicula* ("little helps for our weakness") at best for Calvin, were given greater prominence by Melanchthon. A theologian cannot operate without the aid of Aristotle.[16] The radical and abrasive insight of Luther, that one cannot be a theologian with Aristotle but only without him, is turned on its head. Philosophical theology becomes a necessary activity for the Christian theologian.

Melanchthon's interest in education (he is called the *praeceptor Germaniae* for his role in improving the educational methods of the schools in Germany) was also shaped and dominated by the influence of Aristotle. Whereas for contemporary men and women knowledge is fragmentary and one has, at best, only an eschatological vision of the unity of all knowledge, Melanchthon began with the whole, with the totality of knowledge, and divided it into parts. The categories of Aristotle enabled Melanchthon to break knowledge into manageable parts for pedagogical purposes.

Not only was faith as assent to doctrine increasingly emphasized by Melanchthon, but the scope of the doctrines to be believed was increasingly widened by him. One is to believe the whole Bible understood in the light of the three ecumenical creeds and the teaching of Luther.[17]

The ideas that truth is propositional and that faith is assent to those propositions represent a shift in the message of the Reformation as conceived by

Luther and dominate Orthodox teaching until the time of the Enlightenment, when they are increasingly eroded away. The idea that the gospel is a message of divine judgment and grace, so clearly elucidated in the first edition of the *Loci*, is at least partially obscured. The gospel is a system of truths that it is our duty to accept. Sound doctrine becomes one of the marks of the church. The church is composed of "those who hold pure doctrine and agree in it."[18]

Melanchthon tended to lose Luther's sharp and antithetical distinction between law and gospel. Human beings come to know the law by the exercise of their natural reason. The gospel they come to know through revelation. Natural reason is not abolished by but is rather supplemented by revelation. In the same way, the law is not abrogated by the gospel but is supplemented by it. This means, of course, that the law is binding on believers as well as unbelievers. To be sure, the Christian is justified by faith alone. But this must be followed by regeneration through the indwelling Spirit. Only as the Spirit takes possession of the justified man and woman and enables them to keep the law are they truly saved. The ethical interest, which I noted before, becomes prominent once again in this context.

In spite of the differences between Luther and Melanchthon, which became more pronounced as the years pass, the fates of the two men were inextricably bound together. Melanchthon was Luther's companion and coworker at the Leipzig disputation in 1519 and the Marburg colloquy in 1529. Though he made a greater effort than Luther to effect a rapprochement with the Reformed, he loyally defended the Lutheran position. When Luther was an outlaw under the ban of the empire, it was Melanchthon who represented the Lutherans at the Diet at Augsburg and who wrote the Augsburg Confession, one of the fundamental confessional documents of the Protestant Reformation. Though Luther was impatient with what he regarded as Melanchthon's diplomatic equivocations at Augsburg, he nevertheless approved of the Augsburg Confession. Indeed, the confession itself, as Wilhelm Maurer has observed,[19] is built on an earlier personal confession of faith written by Luther. Though Melanchthon in a later edition of the confession, called the *Variata*, amended it to conform to his changing theological ideas, it is nevertheless clear that Melanchthon always understood himself as a disciple of Luther, even if not a slavish one.

Melanchthon's theological development, if it made Luther nervous, managed to infuriate some of Luther's other disciples, the strict or Gnesio-Lutherans, of whom Nikolaus von Amsdorf and Matthias Flacius Illyricus were among the most influential leaders. These men by innuendo and direct attack attempted to drive a wedge between Luther and Melanchthon. Though they did fan the fires of Luther's suspicion, they did not succeed in persuading him to break with Melanchthon or to denounce his theology. Luther and Melanchthon remained friends until Luther's death.

With Luther gone, the Gnesio-Lutherans sprang once more to the attack. In the first edition of the *Loci*, Melanchthon had taught a doctrine of predestina-

The Lutheran Tradition

tion and had agreed with Luther's teaching on the bondage of the will. Later on, Melanchthon rejected predestination, which seemed to him only another form of the Stoic doctrine of fate, and reintroduced a certain freedom of the will.[20] The human will has an active part in conversion. Though it follows rather than leads and can do little more than not resist the gospel, nevertheless it is a third factor in conversion, in addition to the Holy Spirit and the Word of God.[21]

This conception was sharply attacked by Amsdorf. Fallen human beings are only able to resist the grace of God, only able to be saved against themselves. Sinners need to have a new will. They are like the inert clay molded by the potter, like a stone carved by God. In defending Luther's teaching, however, Amsdorf shifted the basis of his argument from a theological to an anthropological foundation. Luther's point in describing the bondage of the will is to describe the human situation before God. It is not a description of human nature as such apart from that situation. The bondage of the will meant for Luther that human beings cannot reconstitute their broken relationship with God. The fundamental question that he asks is, "Who are we in the presence of God?" For Amsdorf the bondage of the will was a formal definition of human capacities, abstracted from the experience of faith. The fundamental question that he asks is, "Who are we in ourselves?" It is clear that Melanchthon, by denying the bondage of the will, had broken with Luther. But so had Amsdorf, in a far more subtle way, by affirming it.

A second attack on Melanchthon was launched by Osiander, who was not a member of the strict Lutheran party. Nevertheless, he felt that the doctrine of justification Melanchthon taught in the *Loci* was not a faithful and accurate representation of Luther's position. Melanchthon had stressed the forensic character of justification as an act of divine imputation.[22] But he had neglected, Osiander felt, Luther's emphasis on the real transformation of human beings in faith. The doctrine of Christ for us was stressed by Melanchthon at the expense of the doctrine of Christ in us. Osiander, on the other hand, wished to emphasize that a human being was made genuinely righteous in faith. But by stressing this side of Luther's thought Osiander lost the tension in Luther's thought between *iustus et peccator simul*. Luther did not mean by imputation that Christians were not to some degree actually righteous. But he denied that any human being could stand before God on the basis of this actual righteousness. Human destiny before God rested on imputation.

A third attack centered on Melanchthon's understanding of the Lord's Supper. The Gnesio-Lutherans felt that Melanchthon and his disciples had abandoned the teaching of Luther on the Lord's Supper and had stated a doctrine of the Eucharist only barely distinguishable from that of John Calvin.[23] To be sure, Calvin and Melanchthon were not gross sacramentarians like the Zwinglians, who held a purely symbolic view of the Eucharist and maintained that only bread and wine are present on the altar. They were crafty sacramentarians, who spoke of spiritual presence but who believed that the body and blood are in heaven and who ascend to heaven by faith to feed on Christ there. Luther, the strict Lutherans delighted in pointing out, believed that the bread and wine left over from the celebration of the Eucharist should be treated sacramentally, while Melanchthon argued that when the Lord's Supper is over, it is over. Furthermore, whereas Luther had stressed that there is a real communication of attributes between the two natures of Christ, so that the humanity is not subject to the limitations of space and time and can be present on the altar of the church, Melanchthon sided with the Reformed in denying an actual communication of attributes. In the light of these differences, which are clear and can be documented, the Gnesio-Lutherans repudiated Melanchthon's understanding of the Lord's Supper as crypto-Calvinistic.

The final attack focused on the so-called *adiaphora*, or indifferent matters. This was a criticism of Melanchthon, who had sanctioned the Leipzig Interim, which permitted Protestant theology but required the use of the entire Roman ritual. Are there indifferent rites in which a Christian may participate or from which he may abstain without touching in either case the heart of the gospel? The opponents of Melanchthon argued that in times of conflict Christians may not yield to opponents in matters that in other, more peaceful times might be regarded as *adiaphora*. There are, in other words, junctures in history at which indifferent matters cease to be indifferent. And the publication of the Leipzig Interim was one such crucial juncture.

Melanchthon faced up to the attacks with a weary resignation. He had not wished to become a theologian in the first place. He was, after all, a professor of Greek and the classics. The whole world seemed to be seized with madness, and he prayed for deliverance from the "fury of the theologians." On April 19, 1560, he died peacefully in his home in Wittenberg.

How one answers the question whether Melanchthon was an alien or an ally will depend in the last analysis on the stance one takes with respect to the teaching of Luther. If the final test of fidelity to the Reformation is absolute agreement with the teaching of Luther,[24] then Melanchthon, however clearly indebted he is to Luther for much of the substance of his thought, must plead guilty to the charge of Ritschl that he is a corrupter of the Lutheran reformation—though it must be pointed out that the teaching of Luther was fragmented in the hands of the opponents of Melanchthon as well as by Melanchthon himself.

If, on the other hand, it is possible to believe that the Reformation took a plurality of legitimate forms, then it must be noted that Melanchthon performed a variety of important services for the Lutheran camp. Melanchthon kept alive among the Lutherans an ecumenical concern and vision for the unity of the church of Christ, which was often obscured by other Lutherans in the scramble for confessional purity. Furthermore, he listened to the teaching of the

Fathers and tried to incorporate their insights into the teaching of the Lutheran church. Finally, he made room for the claims of reason and philosophy, which could be shunted aside for a time by a prophetic figure like Luther but which would eventually—perhaps at the hands of far less capable theologians—have reasserted their importance for the church.

7

JOHANNES BUGENHAGEN
(1485–1558)
Structures of the Church

JOHANNES BUGENHAGEN LOVED TO preach and was reluctant to quit. His long-windedness, though it was well intentioned and generally tolerated, got to be something of a joke in Wittenberg. Luther in his *Table Talk* told about a man who came home from church on Sunday, expecting to find a hot meal waiting for him.[1] When his wife hurriedly put a half-cooked meal on the table before him, he was outraged and demanded an explanation. "Well," his wife said, somewhat flustered, "I thought Dr. Pommer [Bugenhagen's nickname] was going to preach today."

If it had been anyone but Bugenhagen, the joke might have had a bitter edge. But Bugenhagen was so widely respected that his penchant for preaching long sermons was overlooked as the one regrettable weakness in an otherwise splendid pastor. Bugenhagen was the minister of the city church in Wittenberg, the translator of the Bible into Low German, and Luther's spiritual adviser. If he had been nothing more than Luther's pastor, that very fact would have been enough to merit him a paragraph in subsequent history books. But he earned a place in history in his own right by his composition of liturgies and church orders. He was, above all else, the one man in Luther's entourage in Wittenberg who was able to translate the insights and principles of Luther's theology into the forms and structures of congregational life.[2]

Bugenhagen was born at Wollin near Stettin in Pomerania on June 24, 1485.[3] He studied classics at the University of Greifswald and in 1504 became rector of the school in Treptow on the Rega. Though he had not studied theology at the university, he was nevertheless ordained to the priesthood in 1509. Like many of the other Protestant reformers, he was influenced by Erasmus to undertake a deeper study of the Bible and the Church Fathers. Unlike Luther he had no real background in late medieval scholastic theology.

In 1517 he was appointed as lecturer on the Bible at the cloister school of

Belbuck. The same year he was commissioned by the duke to write a history of Pomerania. Though he completed the book in a very reasonable period of time, it was not published until many years after his death (1728). The book was important mainly for its collection of rare documentary materials and for its criticisms of the life of the late medieval German church.

While still at the cloister of Belbuck, Bugenhagen read the first writings of Luther to be published in Germany. Luther's criticisms of the medieval Catholic theology of the sacraments in his "Babylonian Captivity of the Church" shocked Bugenhagen at first but eventually persuaded him. He began to correspond with Luther and to discuss the questions Luther's searching attack on the medieval church had forced to the surface. Finally Bugenhagen was convinced of the truth of Luther's interpretation of the gospel and set out for Wittenberg in order to learn more from Luther himself. He arrived in 1521, shortly before Luther departed for his fateful confrontation with Charles V at the Diet of Worms.

Bugenhagen matriculated at the University of Wittenberg, where he made friends with Melanchthon. He began to lecture in private on the Bible, continuing in Wittenberg the courses he had taught at Belbuck. He lectured on the Psalms and on the letters of Paul. Luther was quick to see that a man of unusual talent had come to Wittenberg and cast about to find a place where he could make the best use of him. He settled on the city church, whose pulpit had recently fallen vacant, and over the protests of the chapter, which felt its rights were being violated, succeeded in installing Bugenhagen there. From 1523 through the turbulent years that followed Bugenhagen remained as the pastor of the city church.

Of all the reformers in Wittenberg, Bugenhagen was the first to marry. In 1522, after courting briefly one woman, he married another instead. When Luther in 1525 decided to follow Bugenhagen's example, it was Bugenhagen who performed the ceremony and who defended the marriage of Christian clergy in print. In a very real sense it was Bugenhagen and not Luther who founded the Lutheran manse.

Bugenhagen was the great popularizer of the Lutheran reformation. Like Geiler von Kaysersberg he had the common touch, a gift for making difficult ideas clear and understandable to people who lacked the ability to follow an intricate argument or to distinguish subtle shades of difference. The lectern in the university was the proper place to juggle a paradox or balance a conundrum, not the pulpit. The preacher who missed his audience proved not that he had superior ammunition but only that he had bad aim.

Bugenhagen's gifts for popularization won him recognition far outside the city limits of Wittenberg. His commentaries on Scripture as well as his translation (1524) of Luther's New Testament into Low German gained him the favorable attention of Protestants in Hamburg, who wished to call him to the pulpit of the Church of Saint Nicholas. The city council, however, balked at the appointment of Bugenhagen and the proposal came to nothing. Bugenhagen was not bitter at the rebuff and even wrote for the Lutherans in Hamburg one of his most important works, *Von dem Christenloven und rechten guden Werken*, a lucid and popular explanation of the main points of Lutheran theology.

Luther always regarded Bugenhagen (or Pomeranus, as he liked to call himself) as one of the most capable theologians he knew. In part this admiration for Bugenhagen grew out of the fact that Bugenhagen agreed with him on every chief point of doctrine. No one was more faithful to Luther in the quarrels that troubled the church than Pomeranus. He stood with Luther against Zwingli when the question was the Lord's Supper[4] and against Johannes Agricola when the question was the nature of Christian freedom.

But Bugenhagen was not simply an echo chamber in which the ideas of Martin Luther could reverberate with a minimum of static interference. He was a gifted organizer who translated the theology of Luther into the structures of congregational life and who, by doing so, actually carried Luther's reformation one step further. Luther did not begin, as Calvin did, with the doctrine of the church and then move from there to a consideration of the status of the individual believer. Rather, his doctrine of the church and his concept of the believer developed together.

Luther stressed the personal and intensely individual character of the act of faith. Everyone, as Luther pungently put it, must do his own believing, just as everyone must do his own dying. However, people of faith find, when they believe, that they are not alone. They belong to a great company of people who have experienced the wrath and mercy of God. The church is the communion of believers, created and nurtured by the Word of God. It is by the proclamation of the gospel and the administration of the sacraments in this company that faith is kindled and nurtured. For Luther both sides of the paradox must stand: without faith no church; without church no faith.

Just as faith does not rest on any human institution, so too the church is independent of its various institutional forms. Catholics are wrong to insist that the hierarchy and the visible, juridical structures of the church are in any sense necessary to salvation. Similarly, Anabaptists are wrong to insist that their voluntary associations are the only genuine structures for the authentic existence of the true church of Christ. The church of Christ is pluriform and can thrive in a wide variety of ecclesiastical structures.

Because faith is invisible, the true church is a scattered and invisible fellowship as well. That does not mean that there are no distinguishing marks by which the church may be differentiated from other human communities. After all, while faith is invisible, love is not. The church is invisible in its faith but visible in its works.

Luther could list as many as seven marks of the church, though he generally preferred to settle on the two principal marks, the preaching of the Word and the administration of the sacraments. And yet, though Luther could list marks of the church, his attitude toward visible institutions was still ambiguous. The marks do not prove that the true church is present; they mark out the space in which the event of the church takes place. They are like the signs ornithologists may post around a valley to indicate that a rare bird is in the habit of nesting there. They do not mean to imply that every moose one may meet in that valley is a robin. Where the Word of God is preached and the sacraments are administered, one may dare to believe that the true church is to be found. That does not mean that the true church is simply identifiable with the local congregation—though on occasion it may be.

The local congregation does not have the right to be called a church, in the strictest sense of the term, because it is not filled with true believers to the exclusion of all unbelievers. Or, to make that judgment even sharper, since the line between faith and unbelief runs through believers and not simply between believers and unbelievers, the congregation does not have the right to be called a church because it is not a place of unmixed faith. Even the believers are just and sinful at the same time. The congregation is called a church because the true church is hidden in it. The congregation contains believers as a penny contains some copper. But the alloy in the penny is not copper, just as the unbelievers are not members of the church, even though they are part of the congregation.

Luther was opposed to any attempt to separate the true believers from the rest of the congregation, the invisible community of faith from the visible institution. The Anabaptists with their voluntary associations of true believers failed to understand that the revelation of God is always hidden under the form of its opposite. It is not evident to the eye that Jesus Christ is really the Messiah, that the church is really the body of Christ, or that Christians are really just. The evidence the eye sees is always ambiguous. If this were not so, then the church would have nothing to do with this world. Ambiguity may be dissolved in heaven; it is certainly not dissolved on earth. Even the greatest people of faith are still sinners. Their justice before God (*coram Deo*), which is real, is hidden before other human beings (*coram hominibus*) under the ambiguity of their sin.

Insofar as the church is a human institution, it must have some constitution or form of church order. That was for Luther simply a matter of common sense. But he attributed no special theological significance to the order or constitution chosen. If the church, however structured, is free to preach the word and administer the sacraments, then it may have whatever form of government it chooses. Luther would not even be opposed to the papacy if the pope were willing to restore freedom to the church. Liberty to preach the gospel and administer the sacraments is the essential thing. All else is theologically indifferent.

Bugenhagen perceived, as Luther did not, that the freedom of the congregation cannot be taken for granted but must be preserved by the judicious use of institutional forms. It is not simply the case that Reformation theology has consequences for the institutional life of the congregation that cannot be ignored (e.g., a Protestant liturgy can no longer speak of the Eucharist as a representation of the sacrifice of Christ for the sins of the people) but, just as importantly, the freedom of the congregation to act for itself in matters truly indifferent must be preserved in the constitution and structure of the church. A freedom that is unguarded is swiftly lost. Therefore, Bugenhagen could use the language of obligation and necessity in describing the polity and liturgy of Lutheran congregations—language that would have sounded strange had it come from Luther.

Bugenhagen became for the Lutherans, as Bucer and Calvin did for the Reformed, the theoretician of ecclesiastical life. He wrote church orders, liturgies, and instructions for various church bodies throughout northern Germany: for Braunschweig (1528),[5] Hamburg (1529), Lübeck (1531), Pomerania (1534), Denmark (1537), Holstein (1542), Braunschweig-Wolfenbüttel (1543), and Hildesheim (1544). His command of Low German made him the obvious choice to travel throughout northern Germany on behalf of the other Wittenberg reformers who, like Luther, were Thuringians or Saxons or, like Melanchthon, South Germans. He assisted in the coronation of the Danish king Christian III and ordained superintendents to take the place of the Catholic bishops who had been deposed. Though he later declined an invitation to become a professor at the University of Copenhagen, he did assist in the reorganization of that center of learning.

In 1533 Bugenhagen earned his doctorate at the University of Wittenberg, and two years later he became a professor. In spite of his role as professor at the university and various calls to become a Lutheran bishop (from Schleswig and Kammin), he retained his position as pastor of the city church. In 1539 he assisted Luther in his revision of the German Bible and in 1544 published his own great commentary on the Psalms. His chief contribution, however, lay in his composition of church orders. These orders shaped the character of Lutheranism in northern Germany and in Denmark.

Two characteristics of Bugenhagen's church orders deserve special mention. The first is his persistent attempt to give as much autonomy as possible to the local congregation; the second is his effort to provide for some supervision through the provision for an office of superintendent. The superintendent was for Bugenhagen the evangelical equivalent of the Roman Catholic bishop. He was to oversee the pastors in his district to make certain that the doctrine they preached was "pure" and that the life they lived conformed to the gospel they preached. One can see in Bugenhagen's description of the task of the superintendent something of the Melanchthonian concern for the church of pure doctrine, which is not quite the same thing as Luther's concern. There is a conserving tendency in the church orders that is different from the more prophetic and pioneering character of Luther's own work.

When Luther died, Bugenhagen gave his funeral address on February 22, 1546. He took the death of Luther harder than some of the other men in Wittenberg and seemed to age more rapidly after that. Nevertheless, he remained by his post, even when the city was besieged and fell to the emperor. The emperor treated Bugenhagen with considerable respect, as did his ally Moritz of Saxony. Because Bugenhagen wished to remain at the university and in the city church, where he felt he was still needed, he adjusted to the terms of the Leipzig Interim with what seemed to many other Lutherans disgraceful ease. Both Duke Albert of Prussia and the deposed elector became alienated from Bugenhagen in the last years of his life, and there were even rumors that he had been bought off. The rumors were not true, and Bugenhagen tried to win back his friends with a commentary on Jonah in which he sharply criticized the Catholic church and charged it with the heresy of Montanism. But his effort was not a great success, and his last years were spent under a cloud.

Bugenhagen died on April 20, 1558, and was buried under the altar of the city church in Wittenberg. He had been throughout his life Luther's close friend and adviser. Luther was more than his friend; he was his fate. The whole direction of his life was changed by his encounter with Luther. The same thing, of course, could be said of Melanchthon. But Melanchthon, unlike Bugenhagen, emerged from the shadow cast by Luther to win a place in the sun for himself. There was no place in the sun for Bugenhagen. Yet his contribution was no less significant. Next to Luther he was the formative influence on the Lutheran church in northern Germany. With the regaining of much of South Germany in subsequent years for Roman Catholicism, the importance of his contribution was heightened rather than diminished. He was the one Lutheran reformer who grasped the importance of institutions for the life of faith.

8

ANDREAS OSIANDER
(1498–1552)

The Renewal of Human Life

ANDREAS OSIANDER WAS A gifted but difficult man who had a rare talent for making real enemies out of potential friends. Because of his undeniable abilities, he was sent as a Lutheran delegate to the colloquy at Worms, where he proceeded to make trouble in the camp of his allies. Calvin was offended by his conversation at the dinner table; his Lutheran colleagues by his open and indiscreet criticism of Melanchthon. Though he had planned to take part in the Colloquy of Regensburg after Worms and Hagenau, he was replaced as a delegate and sent indecorously back to Nuremberg by colleagues who had plainly had enough.

The incident in Worms was a miniature of his whole career. Wherever Osiander worked, he was sure to leave a legacy of bad feeling behind him. Though Nuremberg owed him an enormous debt of gratitude for his work as a reformer, he had been such a prickly and difficult man to deal with that very few people were genuinely sorry to see him leave. He had hardly settled into his new post at Königsberg before he managed to alienate the majority of his new coworkers there. In the last years of his life, he sparked a controversy over the nature of justification that generated nearly universal hostility toward him. Melanchthon and the Gnesio-Lutherans, who up to this point had been locked in mortal combat with each other, regrouped and launched a combined attack against their common foe. Calvin, who had lost none of his old aversion for Osiander, passionately refuted his teaching in the *Institutes*. Even the *Formula of Concord*, the official confession of the Lutheran church, rejected his ideas in article 3. Indeed, if it had not been for his enemies, Osiander might very well have been forgotten by succeeding generations.

Osiander was born on December 19, 1498, at Gunzenhausen near the city of Nuremberg. He studied Hebrew at the University of Ingolstadt and, like Hans Denck, whom he was later to oppose, became an accomplished Hebraist. He was ordained to the priesthood in 1520 and took a post in Nuremberg, teaching Hebrew at the cloister of the Austin Friars. This Augustinian cloister was the same one in which four years earlier Staupitz had preached his famous sermons on predestination and Christian discipleship.

Osiander's first project in Nuremberg was the revision of the Latin text of the Vulgate Bible in the light of the original Hebrew. He devoted all his free time to the revision and in 1522 published the results of his work, complete with marginal annotations on the text. The same year the Latin Bible was released for sale, he was called as the pastor of the Church of Saint Lorenz in Nuremberg.

He first caught the public eye by becoming embroiled in the controversy over communion in both kinds. Together with the prior of the Augustinian cloister and several others of the clergy who had been won for the Protestant Reformation, he began to encourage the people of Nuremberg to agitate for the right to receive the cup as well as the bread in communion. The rejection of their request by the bishop of Bamberg, Weigand von Redwitz, did not discourage them from persisting in their demand. Finally in 1523, with Osiander's vehement denunciation of the Roman Antichrist still ringing in their ears, more than three thousand people received the cup from the hands of the Austin Friars. Osiander himself offered communion in both kinds to Queen Isabella of Denmark, the sister of Emperor Charles V. Even the presence of the papal legate Campeggio in the city did not deter him.

Willibald Pirckheimer[1] and several other distinguished humanists gave Osiander a degree of support, moderately enthusiastic at first, hesitant and suspicious somewhat later. Many of the humanists finally opposed the Lutheran reformers, though they were not for a simple restoration of the status quo ante. The humanists were, at best, uncertain allies because they were lured by another vision of ecclesiastical reform and could not reconcile themselves to what they felt were the excesses of the Protestant Reformation.

In 1525, following the example of the other reformers, Osiander married. It was a public declaration of his rejection of Catholic teaching concerning clerical celibacy. His new family obligations, however, did not slow down the pace of his involvement in the reformation in Nuremberg. Together with Lazarus Spengler, he introduced the liturgical and doctrinal reforms that strengthened the position of the Lutheran church vis-à-vis the other parties in Nuremberg. He also engaged in literary polemics, writing in 1525 an attack on the treatise concerning the mass composed by Luther's Franciscan opponent, Kaspar Schatzgeyer. He followed that essay with another in 1527, directed this time against the old enemy of the Reformation, Johann Eck of Ingolstadt.

Though Osiander was not greatly beloved, he had been effective as the reformer of Nuremberg and had merited a place at the tables where the pressing issues of the time were being debated. He attended the colloquy at Marburg, where as a Lutheran he opposed the understanding of the Eucharist defended by Zwingli and Johannes Oecolampadius. But Osiander's support was never unqualified. The following year, after opposing Luther's policy of moderation toward the Catholic estates, he criticized Melanchthon's irenic posture at Augsburg. If Osiander had been in charge of negotiations instead of Melanchthon, he would have rallied the Protestant princes to declare war on the emperor. At Schmalkalden in 1537, he again went on record as a Lutheran dissenter by preaching a sermon critical of Luther. When he continued his criticism of Wittenberg at the colloquies of Hagenau and Worms, he was replaced as a member of the Lutheran delegation and sent home. If Osiander had squandered the capital of goodwill with which he started in Nuremberg, and if he had wearied the Lutheran leaders in other cities of Germany with his incessant—and not always germane—criticisms of Melanchthon, he had not so diminished his influence that he was no longer looked to for guidance and assistance. In 1542 he was invited by Count Ottheinrich of Neuburg to help in establishing the Lutheran reformation in the Palatinate. A year later he was asked by Nicholas Copernicus to take part in the publication of his important new book, *De Revolutionibus Orbium Caelestium*.[2]

Osiander realized that the book was sure to be opposed by the defenders of the Aristotelian position. He attempted, therefore, to disarm the opponents of the Copernican theory by writing an anonymous preface to the book, without either the knowledge or the permission of the author. In the preface he called the theories in the book hypotheses. It was traditional in the Middle Ages to propound new theories as hypotheses, whose truth remained to be tested in the public forum. Though Osiander had acted arbitrarily in writing the preface, it is difficult to see, as Johann Kepler later charged, that he had done anything to undercut confidence in the thesis of the book. While Osiander believed that the only realm of absolute truth is the realm of revelation, he had, nevertheless, a vigorous interest in science and in the work of Copernicus. At most he was guilty of an error of judgment, though even that is subject to debate.

With the publication of the Leipzig Interim, Osiander joined the ranks of the reformers who felt bound by conscience to leave their homes rather than abide by the terms of the Interim. He went first to Breslau and then to Königsberg, where in 1549 he was made a pastor and professor on the theological faculty by Duke Albert of Prussia, his longtime and unfailing admirer. At the disputation that marked his inauguration as professor, he attacked the Melanchthonian doctrine of justification in the name of Luther's teaching. His opponent, Martin Chemnitz, was unconvinced. So were his colleagues on the theological faculty. Only the duke and a few friends stood by him in the controversy that now erupted.

Osiander's chief opponent in Prussia was Joachim Mörlin, who not only rejected Osiander's theology but even denied him the sacrament. The Prussians were joined in their attack both by the Lutherans in other parts of Germany and by the Swiss Reformed. The sound of battle stirred the old veteran to buckle on his armor and sharpen his sword. He loved nothing so much as a good fight, and he launched a counterattack with all the pugnacity and fervor he could muster. The pages of his anti-Melanchthonian polemic were hot to the touch. Unfortunately, he did not live to see the resolution of the conflict. He died suddenly on October 17, 1552, while the controversy was still at its height.

Osiander was opposed to what he regarded as the cold doctrine of forensic justification.[3] Melanchthon, above all, had stressed the idea that justification is a judicial act in which God for Christ's sake freely forgives sinners on no other ground than faith alone and imputes to them the righteousness of Christ. Justification is distinguished from regeneration (which is human renewal by the Holy Spirit) and sanctification (which is gradual growth in Christlikeness).

Osiander came down hard on the Melanchthonian understanding of justification as a forensic act. He maintained—rightly, as it happens—that Luther included the renewal of the human being in justification and understood it as a personal union with Christ. He was wrong, however, to assert that Melanchthon's understanding of forensic justification was unfaithful to Luther's intention. Luther, even the mature Luther, understood justification as both union with Christ and pardon for the sake of Christ. There is no forgiveness where there is no union, but neither is the union the ground of the pardon.

Under the banner of the restoration of Luther's teaching, Osiander put forward a new understanding of justification, one that owed as much to Reuchlin[4] and Pico della Mirandola as to Luther. There is a strong parallel in Osiander's teaching between the incarnation of the Logos, the justification of the Christian, and the celebration of the Eucharist. In each case the divine Word, the Second Person of the Trinity, unites himself to creaturely elements, though not in the same way.

Osiander returned to the teaching of Scotus that God would have become incarnate even if human beings had not fallen. God had determined to create men and women in the image of Jesus Christ and had therefore decided to become incarnate in Jesus Christ to demonstrate in him the fullness of his creative intention. The human fall, however, altered the purpose of the incarnation. God no longer wishes merely to demonstrate his intention but to restore sinners to it.

Human beings were created in the image of God. That is to say, they were created in the image of Jesus Christ, who is himself the image of God. The creation of humankind is in anticipation of the incarnation. As created, human beings possess original righteousness. Adam is an anticipatory model of the man Jesus Christ, who has not yet become incarnate but who exists in the intention of God.

The incarnation demonstrates, as the fall of Adam had tended to discredit, that human flesh is capable of holiness. Sinners cannot, however, attain this holiness by their own efforts to reform themselves or to model their lives on the pattern of the life of Jesus. Sinners can only be redeemed by the gracious act through which God communicates himself through external things. As the flesh of Jesus was the bearer of the Logos, so now the spoken word of the preacher is the bearer of the divine Word that is received by faith alone. When the Word is grasped by faith, it indwells human beings and unites with them. Where the Word is present it transforms sinners and renews them in the image of God. Sinners are justified not because their works are now holy but because Christ indwells them. The indwelling Christ is the basis of human acceptance and not the renewal as such, though where Christ is present sinners are renewed in the image of God.

The human nature of Christ is only important as a bearer of the divine nature. It is not the human nature that saves sinners and with which they are united but only the divine nature. Nevertheless, the divine nature is not accessible apart from the human. The human nature is the essential means by which the divine nature is communicated to men and women—no incarnation, no salvation; no preaching, no reception in faith. Osiander does not intend to lapse into the spiritualism of a man like Hans Denck. External elements are the channels by which the divine Word is mediated.

When the New Testament declares that Christ is "our righteousness," it does not mean, as Melanchthon appears to think, that Christ is the basis on which God by a forensic act declares human beings righteous. The text must be interpreted in the light of 2 Peter, which affirms that Christians have become partakers of the divine nature. The Word of God—that is, the divine nature of Jesus Christ—is the Christians' essential righteousness, when Christians receive that Word in faith as it is proclaimed. There is a sense, then, in which Christians, by receiving the indwelling Word and participating in the divine nature, become themselves Jesus Christ. Having been restored to the image of God through him and in constant dependence on him, they are like him in every important respect. He is the original, and they are the carbon copies. Their full destiny as human beings is first realized in union with Jesus Christ. It is their true humanity that is restored through the divinity of Jesus Christ. It is not the case, as some of Osiander's enemies charged, that he does away with pardon. Sinners must be forgiven their sins before the divine Word can indwell them. But the pardon is not the justification itself but only a kind of preparatory stage. Justification is Jesus Christ, period! Whoever has him has the whole Godhead and is righteous.

Parallel to the incarnation is the union of the Word with the elements of bread and wine in the Lord's Supper. There occurs through the words of institution a kind of hypostatic union between the bread and wine and the body and blood of Christ. Osiander's doctrine of the Lord's Supper is called impanation and is only his way of asserting in the strongest possible terms the mystery of the real presence. Just as he rejects the teaching of the Zwinglians, who deny the real presence in the elements, so too he rejects as an extension of Zwinglian principle the teaching of those who deny his doctrine of the essential union of Christ with the believer.

No one was satisfied with Osiander's theory of justification. Only Johannes Brenz, of all the prominent Lutheran theologians, gave it a sympathetic hearing. Though Osiander was aware of the danger of mysticism and was as hostile as any Lutheran to the spiritualism of Denck, his teaching veered too close to the danger it sought to avoid to satisfy either Melanchthon or Amsdorf. Osiander's emphasis on the divine nature of Christ tended to devaluate, without eliminating completely, the significance of his humanity as a crucial element in human redemption. Furthermore, if there was anything on which the Lutherans were clear, it was that the forgiveness of sins is central to human justification and cannot be shunted aside as merely a presupposition for God's justifying act. Finally, lest anyone should overlook it, Calvin pointed out the fact that Osiander had tended to confuse regeneration and justification. Unless justification is (at the very least!) a forensic act, human beings cannot have assurance of salvation in this life.

The controversies that surrounded Osiander have tended to obscure the fact that he was a creative and independent theologian and that he had grasped certain important elements in the teaching of Luther that had not faithfully been retained by other disciples of Luther. Perhaps if he himself had been less polemical and more willing to talk in terms of the "hypotheses" with which he introduced the radical theses of Copernicus he might have received a more sympathetic hearing. But he was not irenic by nature, and his opponents had— quite apart from the question of justification—many old scores to settle with him. Besides, it was not an age noted for its patience with dissent, especially when an important issue was on the table. The question whether he might, under certain circumstances, have received a more favorable hearing is therefore largely gratuitous. The fact is that he did not. Like the crusty old warrior that he was, he asked no quarter and he gave none.

9

NIKOLAUS VON AMSDORF
(1483–1565)
Set for the Defense of the Gospel

THE ROLE OF A religious conservative is rarely a popular one, especially when this conservatism is combined with an intolerance of all theological innovation. There is something pinched and one-sided about the mentality that holds that a decisive theological breakthrough has taken place in the past but denies (or is at least distrustful of) the possibility of new and original insights in the present. That the church has been led into truth in the past does not exclude the possibility of the discovery of new truth in the present, even if the new insight is only a deepened participation in the meaning of the old.

The conservative, however, while often unpopular, is nevertheless a necessary fellow. The natural tendency of any parish is toward heresy. Unless the church is willing to lose its treasure without a struggle, there is a need for watchmen to sound the alarm and remind the church that the gospel it is preaching is not the gospel it has preached. It may well be that the church may decide that its new understanding represents a growth in insight rather than a relapse. But it needs to be reminded in any case that it has changed its course, so that it may consult its charts and compass and come to a conscious decision concerning the advisability of its new direction.

Amsdorf was the conservative gadfly of the Lutheran reformation. He was born on December 3, 1483, at Torgau, the second among six brothers.[1] He began his university studies at Leipzig in 1500 but quickly transferred to Wittenberg in 1502, where his uncle, Johannes von Staupitz, was professor of Bible and dean of the theological faculty. Nikolaus was a good, though not brilliant, student and received his licentiate in theology in 1511. Three years earlier, in 1508, he had been made a canon of All Saints, the university church. He was a skilled debater and an uncompromising opponent in theological disputations.

When Luther challenged the medieval theology of penance in the Ninety-five Theses, Amsdorf became an immediate convert to his cause. He accompanied Luther to the Leipzig Disputation with Eck in 1519 and did everything in his power to assist Luther in the reform of the theological curriculum at Wittenberg. Luther was appreciative of the loyalty of Amsdorf and dedicated his *Appeal to the Ruling Class* of 1520 to his friend and coworker. Indeed, Amsdorf was such a close friend and trusted adviser of Luther that he was one of the very few men who knew that the elector was hiding Luther in the Wartburg Castle following the Diet of Worms. And it was Amsdorf and Melanchthon who dealt in Luther's absence with the challenge of the Zwickau prophets.

In 1524 Amsdorf moved to Magdeburg, where he became the pastor of Saint Ulrich's and the first Protestant superintendent. In Magdeburg he opposed the teaching of a Catholic preacher by the name of Cubito at the cathedral and carried through the work of the Lutheran reformation, modeling the Magdeburg liturgy on the liturgy used in Wittenberg. He also founded a Protestant Latin school at Saint John's, to which Caspar Cruciger and later George Major were called as rectors.

His work in Magdeburg was so well regarded that he was called to assist in the work of establishing the Reformation in several cities in Lower Saxony, especially Goslar (1528, 1531) and Einbeck (1534). He also gained a reputation as a defender of the faith through his determined opposition not only to Radical reformers like Melchior Hoffman but to all attempts on the part of fellow Lutherans to dilute or weaken the theological position of the Lutheran movement. Accordingly he opposed the Wittenberg Concord, which attempted to draw together the positions of the Lutherans and the Reformed on the Eucharist, and the Colloquy of Regensburg, which attempted to heal the divisions between Protestants and Catholics. If the truth had come to light in the teaching of Dr. Luther, as Amsdorf believed it had, then no purpose could be served in arriving at a compromise except the re-obscuring of the truth.

When the bishop of Naumburg/Zeitz died on January 6, 1541, the chapter of the cathedral in Naumburg elected Julius von Pflug, a distinguished Catholic cleric, to be his successor.[2] However, the elector, Johann Friedrich, who regarded the approval of a successor as his feudal right, rejected the candidate chosen by the chapter and named Amsdorf, the Lutheran superintendent in Magdeburg, to the post instead. This highhanded action flew in the face of custom and of canon law and left Amsdorf to rule a diocese unreconciled to his presence and only barely civil. Nevertheless, he was installed as bishop of Naumburg by Luther, who broke with Catholic custom by laying on of hands without the use of chrism.

Scarcely in the history of the world was there ever chosen a more reluctant and unhappy prelate. Caught between the prince on the one hand, who regarded the bishop as his servant in no way distinct from the men employed in his civil service, and a chapter headed by the unlucky candidate von Pflug, who resisted his every wish and tried to fight his reform efforts to a standstill, Amsdorf felt himself hemmed in by the unreasonable demands of an impossible job. He found it difficult to write, and what he did compose was marked by a certain bitterness.

Though Amsdorf was able to make some progress in his attempts to reform Naumburg, it was almost with a sense of relief that he saw the forces gather that compelled him to flee. The outbreak of the Schmalkaldic War and the success of Moritz of Saxony against the Protestants drove Amsdorf out of Naumburg and into Weimar. In his absence, von Pflug claimed and was granted the diocese of Naumburg. The Lutheran hold on the bishopric of Naumburg was brought to an end, and Amsdorf entered a period of exile from his diocese.

During the years that followed, Amsdorf served as the adviser of elector Johann Friedrich and then, at the elector's death, of his sons. He helped to found the new University of Jena in opposition to Wittenberg, where the teaching of Melanchthon was in vogue, and was instrumental in having Flacius called to its faculty. He assisted in the production of the so-called Jena edition of Luther's works, which was designed to correct the errors in the Wittenberg edition. He opposed the Leipzig Interim from his headquarters in Magdeburg and flayed in the press the Adiaphorists Melanchthon and Bugenhagen, who were prepared to abide by its terms. He stopped his quarrel with Melanchthon only long enough to join forces with the Philippists in opposing the teaching of Osiander.

When Magdeburg was relinquished to Duke Moritz of Saxony, Amsdorf, breathing fire and threats against the duke, left Magdeburg for Eisenach, where he became in fact, though not in title, the leader of the Lutheran reformation there. In 1554 he became embroiled in a conflict with the superintendent in Gotha, Justus Menius, who refused to reject the teaching of Major that good works are necessary to salvation. In opposing the teaching of Menius and Major, Amsdorf defended the often misunderstood thesis that good works are harmful to salvation. He meant by this to exclude good works from the order of salvation, where they automatically become merits, but not from the Christian life, where they are the fruits of faith.

Though Amsdorf had taken the side of Flacius in the controversies that swirled around him, he was not in total agreement with his ally. He rejected, for example, the teaching of Flacius that original sin is the substance of fallen man and could not understand why Flacius refused to accept his teaching that good works are harmful to salvation. Because there were differences between Flacius and Amsdorf and because Amsdorf had rendered service to the Lutheran reformation from the very earliest days, he was spared when Flacius and his followers were expelled from the city of Jena.

Amsdorf may have hoped to be restored to the diocese of Naumburg at the death of von Pflug in 1564, though he made no mention of that fact in his *Testament*. Since he had remained celibate all his life, even after his conversion to Protantism, he could not be disqualified on the grounds of a clerical marriage. At any rate, whether he entertained such hopes or not, they did not have time to come to fruition. He died in Eisenach on May 14, 1565, and was buried before the altar in Saint George's Church.

Amsdorf's theology must be regarded as a clumsy approximation of Luther's.[3] He did not, of course, intend to be original. Originality that deviated from the norm of Luther's theology was in fact what he intended at all costs to avoid. But he was less apt at expressing himself than the circumstances warranted. Certainly he had none of the precision of definition that characterized Melanchthon's thought. As a result he confused his enemies when he wanted to confound them. Even the thesis that alienated his friends—namely, that good works are harmful to salvation—is a perfectly acceptable idea from Luther, expressed in Amsdorf's own bumbling Pickwickian way.

Luther had rejected the doctrine of merit by stressing the difference between the relationship of human beings before God (*coram deo*) and toward their neighbors. Luther's teaching resulted in a radical secularization of good works. Good works are taken out of the order of salvation and are offered to human beings in their need rather than to God. As God in his overflowing bounty has perfectly justified and accepted sinners because of Christ, so Christians, in gratitude for all that they have received from God, do works of love for their neighbors. In their relationship to God (*coram deo*), Christians bring nothing but open hands to receive whatever God has to give them. Faith is what counts in the relationship to God, not works. Christians commit themselves in trust to God and receive all that they have and are *sola gratia* from the hand of God.

If works are removed from the order of salvation, they are not removed from the Christian life. In the relationship to the neighbor (*coram hominibus*), it is not faith but works of love that count. To refuse to give to one's neighbors what they need, when one has something to give them, and to say that instead of responding to such need one will pray that God will meet their need from some other source, is false piety. In the relationship between God and human beings (*coram deo*), Christians are recipients, never givers. In the relationship between one human being and another (*coram hominibus*), Christians give gladly to their neighbors what they have received from God. All doctrines of human merit are excluded from this framework of thought.

By affirming that good works are harmful to salvation, all Amsdorf wanted to do was to reaffirm the main lines of Luther's teaching concerning merit.[4] He did not mean to preach antinomianism, the idea that Christians may do whatever immoral acts they please since they are not justified by the law. He believed, fully as much as his opponents, that faith would issue in works of love toward the neighbor. But when Major and Menius argued that good works are necessary to salvation, that meant to Amsdorf that they were reintroducing good works into the order of salvation. Works become the partial ground on which men and women are accepted by God. It is not necessary to call these works merits, but that is what in fact they are. Such works are harmful to faith because they delude people into believing that they can gain salvation by means of them. To say that works are necessary to salvation is to say that they are necessary *coram deo*. To admit that is to renounce the Reformation on the key issue of justification by faith.

Amsdorf agreed with Melanchthon that the church of Jesus Christ must be a church of pure doctrine. But he understood pure doctrine somewhat differently from Melanchthon. For Melanchthon philosophy is a schoolmaster to lead sinners to Christ, an essential tool for the clarifying of doctrine so that it may be pure. Philosophy clarifies belief so that faith may be certain of what it believes. The purity Melanchthon envisions is a conceptual purity.

Not so for Amsdorf. There are for him three enemies of pure doctrine: logic, mysticism, and speculation. Philosophy does not help to ground faith but rather introduces the worldly wisdom that unsettles it.[5] Pure faith is obedient recognition of the Word of God;[6] it is a wholehearted embracing of the gospel against the objections of reason. Reality is, finally, not rational; it does not neatly conform to the categories of Aristotle. The gospel has the irregular and unexpected shape of things that are true. Pure doctrine is doctrine that clings to the revelation of God in Scripture against the witness of reason and conscience.

Furthermore, the Word of God and Scripture are to be identified.[7] Amsdorf applies to Scripture a principle derived from Luther's doctrine of the Eucharist. The elements do not symbolize (*significat*) the body and blood of Christ; they are (*est*) the body and blood of Christ. Amsdorf applies the eucharistic *est* to Scripture. The word of God is not symbolized by Scripture or contained in Scripture. The *est* of identity excludes the spiritualistic understanding of the Bible of people like Caspar Schwenckfeld or Sebastian Franck just as it excludes the eucharistic theology of Zwingli or Melanchthon.[8]

This Scripture contains both law and gospel. The law does not offer the road to justification; only the gospel does. The humanists and the mystics want to see the law as the expression of the possibilities of the human situation, as the summary of the ideals that humans are summoned to emulate. However, the Bible makes clear that no keeping of the law except a perfect one will suffice for salvation.[9] This means, of course, to anyone who is honest with himself or herself that the law uncovers the impossibility of the human situation, not its unfulfilled possibility. The law belongs to the order of salvation only in the sense that it has been perfectly fulfilled in Jesus and, as such, belongs to the gospel.[10] The law drives men and women to Christ. Only in Christ is the law salvific.

The human will is bound and cannot turn to Christ. Amsdorf rejects Melanchthon's thesis that the will is a third factor in conversion along with the Holy Spirit and the Word of God. He argues, rather, that human beings are like stones and as incapable of response to God as a stone would be.[11] He hastily adds, of course, that the analogy is imperfect. Sinners are not passive like a

The Lutheran Tradition

stone but resist God with every resource at their command.[12] But the activity is all negative. The will is free to resist but not to respond, which means that the only freedom fallen human nature knows is bondage. Faith is not a human possibility[13] and cannot be cultivated or brought into existence by employing the right method of speaking or hearing. Faith is not a matter of method. Faith is an event for which the Holy Spirit alone is responsible in conjunction with the Word.[14]

Amsdorf's writings are almost all tracts for the times. There are no biblical commentaries, no leisurely treatises on systematic theology in the corpus of writings he composed. This means, of course, that his essays were for the most part short, journalistic editorials, written in the heat of anger and with the sense of shocked outrage still fresh in their pages. The polemical nature of these essays and their uncompromising character tend to obscure the fact that Amsdorf was fighting to defend some important insights that were in danger of being obscured.

That is not to say that Amsdorf was simply a repristination of Luther. It is clear that Luther's thought was fragmented in his hands as well as in the hands of Osiander or Melanchthon. But there were important issues at stake that Amsdorf was correct to defend. His intolerance, so distressing to the modern mind yet so commonplace in the sixteenth century, grew out of his and his contemporaries' conviction of the seriousness of the matters that were being considered. If Christianity were for them only one worldview among others, one possible option among many equally attractive options, then, of course, intolerance would be unforgivable. They were convinced, however, they were dealing with truth as such, with the narrow way that leads to salvation. One does not call a doctor intolerant who insists on submitting an inflamed appendix to surgery and who is rigorous in the surgical procedures he or she follows. In their view a physician of souls cannot afford to be less rigorous. Commenting on the tepid religious convictions of the early twentieth century, G. K. Chesterton once observed that tolerance can be the easy virtue of people who do not believe anything in particular. Still it is preferable to the uncharitable and suspicion-laden atmosphere of the sixteenth century.

The distressing thing about Amsdorf is not the sharpness of his invective— even the irenic Erasmus could be far more inventive in composing a studied insult than the direct and plain-spoken Amsdorf—but the clumsiness of his exposition. His treatment of his opponents is often superficial and his formulation of his own opinions imprecise. Nevertheless, he did manage to stimulate the Lutheran church to examine its teaching on justification and to formulate its own position on the question of the place of good works. Forced to a decision between ecumenical openness and confessional purity, Amsdorf chose confessional purity. One can only regret that he saw as antithetical what ought to be regarded as complementary. By making this choice, Amsdorf became one of the principal fathers of confessional Lutheranism.

IO

JOHANNES BRENZ
(1499–1570)
The Authority of the State

NOT ALL MEN AND WOMEN who innovate do so in the same way. Some, like
Luther, are able to break through to fundamental new insights that cause a revolution in thought. Others, like Brenz, are able to draw out the implications of
the insights of someone else or to put them together in a combination un-
dreamed of by their inventor. While it is more exciting to discover a new world
than to settle it, it is in the long run not more essential. The world depends on
both the adventurer and the colonist and could not last long without either.

Johannes Brenz was born into the family of a baker, on June 24, 1499, in
Weilderstadt near Stuttgart. He studied at the University of Heidelberg, where
he became the master of a house of study in 1518. At Heidelberg he lectured
on the Gospel of Matthew as well as on philology and philosophy. Like Bucer,
Brenz also attended the Heidelberg Disputation in April 1518, at which Luther
presided. He found Luther's rejection of Aristotle and of medieval scholasticism persuasive and was motivated by him to turn to the study of Augustine
and Paul. His conversion to Luther's thought, however, was more thoroughgoing than Bucer's, whose indebtedness to Luther did not inhibit his own independence in developing somewhat different solutions to Luther's questions.
While Brenz was a first-class theologian and not lacking in theological intu-
itions of his own, he remained (or at least attempted to remain) faithful to
Luther's thought throughout his life.[1]

He accepted a call to the parish of Schwäbisch-Hall with considerable relief
when it became apparent that he would be forced to endure a heresy trial if he
remained in Heidelberg. He served as pastor in Hall from 1522 to 1548. He was
in many ways the model pastor. As prudent and cautious as Carlstadt was rash
and impetuous, he introduced the Reformation gradually into the city of Hall,
quietly dropping the Corpus Christi Feast in 1524, transforming a monastery
into a school in the same year with as little fanfare as possible. By the time he

celebrated a Lutheran Communion instead of the Mass on Christmas of 1525, the ground had been carefully cultivated to receive the innovation gratefully.

The year 1525 brought the Peasants' Revolt, an uprising on which Brenz cast a jaundiced eye. He agreed with Luther that the peasants had resorted to fleshly means to advance spiritual goals and that they should have relied rather on the Word. But he could not agree with Luther when he exhorted the princes to crush the uprising with all the force at their disposal. Subjects have no right to rebel against their overlords, but neither should magistrates rule without mercy.

When the eucharistic controversy broke out between Zurich and Wittenberg, Brenz unhesitatingly took the side of Luther and the Wittenberg theologians. In 1525 Brenz, together with thirteen other theologians, issued the *Syngramma Suevicum*, in which they attacked the eucharistic theology of Oecolampadius and insisted on the real presence of Christ in the sacrament. The argument was Lutheran and not original with Brenz. If there is any point at which Brenz gave the doctrine of the Lord's Supper a twist of his own it is probably in his insistence, even more forceful than Luther's, that it is the Word and not the elements that mediate the presence of Christ.

Brenz was interested in the problem of Christian education and in 1527–1528 prepared a Lutheran catechism—a full year before Luther prepared his own Large and Small Catechisms. Even though Luther's catechisms were widely used, they did not replace Brenz's *Questions on the Christian Faith*. In fact, the second edition of Brenz's book was incorporated in 1536 into the church order for the duchy of Württemberg, mute testimony to the esteem with which it was regarded.

Brenz swiftly became the foremost spokesman for Lutheranism in South Germany, almost as important for the course of the Reformation in Nuremberg as he was for Swabia. The first church order, which he composed in 1526, made provision both for synods and for the role of the magistrate in governing the church. He attended Marburg in 1529 and Augsburg in 1530 as a representative of the Lutherans of South Germany. In 1532 he assisted in the composition of church orders for both Brandenburg and Nuremberg. In 1536 he was invited by Duke Ulrich of Württemberg to advise him in establishing the Reformation throughout his territory and to aid in the reorganization of the University of Tübingen. He also took part in the Reformation of Brandenburg-Ansbach, Dinkelsbühl, and Heilbronn. He attended the meeting of the League of Schmalkalden in 1537, though his reluctance to take arms against the emperor and his desire to let the Word of God effect the religious transformation of Europe inclined him to view the plans of the league with frosty detachment. In September 1537 he attended a conference called at Urach to discuss the usefulness of images in the worship of the church and spoke forcefully for their abolition. When the emperor called a series of colloquies between Protestants and Roman Catholics, first at Hagenau and then at Worms and at Regensburg, Brenz was also present. In short, there was scarcely an event in the 1520s and 1530s at which Brenz was not in attendance, either as a participant or as an observer.

Brenz's activity in other parts of Germany did not mean that he neglected his pastoral duties at home. His exegetical sermons were famous for their thoroughness and the depth of their penetration into the biblical text. Feeding into his sermons, and also to some extent growing out of them, were his extensive commentaries on twenty books of the Bible. These commentaries and sermons had a formative influence on the church in Württemberg. Many a Swabian pastor learned how to expound the Bible to his people by taking the sermons of Johannes Brenz as his model.

Brenz did not remain in Hall because he had no invitations to go elsewhere. On the contrary, churches in cities far more prominent than Hall extended invitations to him to become their pastor. Leipzig issued a call in 1542, Tübingen in 1543, and Strasbourg in 1548. But in spite of tempting offers to leave Hall, Brenz declined all invitations and remained at his post.

He was never easy, however, about the adherence of Hall to the Protestant League of Schmalkalden. His uneasiness about the formation of a league to oppose the emperor was traceable to his conviction, already mentioned, that the Reformation should be furthered by spiritual means alone and that it was impermissible for Christians to foment rebellion against the rulers set in authority over them. He opposed the entry of Hall into the league until 1538, when the implacable attitude of the emperor finally persuaded him to yield to the arguments of those who pled the necessity of a military alliance against the Habsburgs.

Brenz's attitude toward the state has always been a subject for considerable discussion.[2] On the one hand, he went beyond Luther in giving the state a role in the internal affairs of the church; on the other hand, he opposed Melanchthon by rejecting the Augustinian idea that the state could compel people against their conscience to subscribe to theological orthodoxy.[3] He enlarged at one and the same time the authority of the state and the freedom of the dissenting conscience.

Luther argued that the welfare of the Christian congregation rests equally on all members of that congregation. The prince has responsibility for the welfare of the church only as a member of the community of faith. He has no office in the church by reason of his office in the state. Where the welfare of the church is concerned, he is a Christian who happens also to be a prince. His responsibility for the church resides in his person as a Christian rather than in his office as a prince. The local butcher or baker contributes to the welfare of the church with the means at his disposal and the prince with the means at his disposal. That the prince can do more for the church than other Christians who lack his position and power is purely accidental.

There is, of course, one exception to this general rule. In a time of crisis in the church, when the ordinary bishops refuse or neglect to fulfill their proper function in the reform of the church, the prince has the right to assume a *temporary* office as emergency bishop (*Notbischof*) to fulfill the functions neglected by the regular ecclesiastical officials. Luther understood this office, however, as a merely temporary one. When the crisis is past, the princes surrender their emergency powers to the bishops and resume their role as Christian laymen.

The princes understood the call of Luther to assume the role of *Notbischöfe* with ears conditioned by the church-state struggles of the later Middle Ages. For centuries the princes had been trying to assume the rights, privileges, and powers of the church within their own domains. They understood the administration of the church as a subdivision of their general governing power over the state. The state is absolute and total. It has responsibility for everything which happens within it. A prince who provides for the bodily needs of his subjects but who neglects their spiritual welfare is a poor specimen of a prince, scarcely fit to rule. The administration and reform of the church are duties of the Christian prince like collecting taxes or building roads.

This, of course, was not Luther's understanding of the state at all. The only spiritual function the state has is its right and obligation to prevent the public blasphemy of God within its domain. Apart from that duty, the prince has only the temporary office as emergency bishop and the permanent duty toward the church that he shares with all other laymen who are not princes. As far as possible the independence and autonomy of the local congregation must be preserved. It must have the right to govern its own affairs independently of the state and, if necessary, with the state's active disapproval.

Brenz did not accept the absolutist doctrine of the state embraced by the German princes, but neither did he agree in toto with Luther. The Christian magistrate has a responsibility for the church by reason of his office as prince and not simply as an expression of the common priesthood of all believers. The princes are called by God to establish peace and order within their kingdoms. Since the preaching of the gospel contributes to that peace within the realm of the state, the Christian magistrate as magistrate (and not simply as Christian) has a responsibility to further and promote it.

That does not mean that all power in the church is delegated to the prince. Nevertheless, the powers he does have by virtue of his office make an impressive list. He may appoint pastors to the churches within his realm with the approval of the congregations. This, of course, runs contrary to the ideas of Luther, who defended the right of each congregation to call its own pastor. Furthermore, the administration of finances should not be left to the discretion of the local congregations but should be handled by a central office of the state, which will pay the salaries of the ministers and administer benevolences. The local congregation also has no right to determine the ceremonies it will observe. Since ceremonies are *adiaphora*, the princes of the various principalities are within the bounds of their authority when they determine the liturgy to be followed by the congregations within their realms. The old rural deans are to be abolished, and superintendents appointed by the prince will visit the congregations and oversee their work. Finally, the local church and its pastor may not excommunicate a wayward member. Excommunications will be imposed by a committee appointed by the prince, which, because it is disinterested, can render impartial judgment.

It is clear, however, that the prince does not have the right to define the faith of the church or to determine the content of its confessional standards. Furthermore, he cannot compel belief by torture or execution. Brenz, like Luther, opposed the execution of Anabaptists or other dissenters within the state. Persecution only tends to harden heretics in their beliefs and may in fact contribute to the conversion of others to false belief. The Word of God alone can correct the errors of the heretics, and the proper strategy for dealing with them is the provision of instruction. Nevertheless, Brenz was not an advocate of tolerance in the modern sense. The state has the right to forbid heretics from preaching and may even compel the children of Anabaptists to be baptized against the express wishes of their parents. A conscience not instructed by the Word of God and indwelt by the Holy Spirit is not worthy of respect. One cannot, however, force men and women to faith by reliance on the heavy-handed methods of the state. True faith is a free response to the gospel, not a hypocritical confession wrung out of a peasant terrified for his life. Since the prince has the right to punish open blasphemy, he would have a right to punish the Anabaptists, if that were their crime. But it is not. The Anabaptists are guilty of a sin not against the law but against the gospel. And only the gospel can convert them.

The state, in other words, has a right to intervene with its police and its penal codes only when the peace of the commonwealth is in jeopardy. God has not made the prince, however, a judge of theological orthodoxy. He cannot punish men and women for holding wrong opinions but only for undermining the well-being of the state. Furthermore, princes have a difficult time realizing that God is praised through the heterodoxy of unbelievers and heretics. God has, for reasons best known to him, decreed that the kingdom of Christ in this world will be a mixed one to the end of time, with wheat and tares growing side by side until the final judgment. Princes, like overzealous gardeners, want to yank out all the weeds in the church, but they will succeed only in causing more damage than the weeds themselves could possibly inflict. The duty of a Christian prince is not to execute Anabaptists but to instruct them by providing a learned ministry that can truly expound the Word of God. God himself will do the weeding, now by the Word of God, later by his judgment.

Brenz was not a spokesman for the absolutist doctrine of the state. The duties of the Christian prince for the proper administration of the church are numerous, but they are not unlimited nor are they unrestricted. The prince is bound in his dealings with the church by the very law and prophets that it is his duty to have rightly expounded in his kingdom. The prince is not above the law of God. And the Christian preacher, though he may be dependent in many matters on the central administration of the state, is nevertheless free to declare the whole counsel of God to the prince as to any member of the body of Christ.

With the defeat of the League of Schmalkalden by the emperor and the imposition of the Augsburg Interim, Brenz fled Hall on June 24, 1548. Duke Ulrich gave him refuge in the castle of Hohenwittlingen, where, under the pseudonym Joannes Witlingius, he wrote an interpretation of Psalm 93 and Psalm 130. Since the emperor was looking for Brenz in every likely hiding place, Ulrich helped him to escape to Basel, where he wrote a commentary on the prophecy of Isaiah. In January 1549 he was called by Duke Christopher to Montbéliard, where he learned for the first time the distressing news that his wife had died in his absence. In order to care for his children, he attempted to return to his home. He was forced, however, to spend eighteen months in hiding in the castle of Hornberg near Gutach, under the pseudonym Huldrich Engster.

The talents of the reformer of Hall had not been forgotten by Protestants outside Swabia. He received calls to Magdeburg, Königsberg, and England, even though he declined them. In August 1549 he went to Urach, where his old friend Isenmann was pastor. There in the fall of 1550 he married for the second time; his new wife was Catherine Isenmann, the eldest daughter of his oldest friend.

In the same year he married, Brenz was commissioned by Duke Christopher to draw up the *Confessio Virtembergica*, a confession of faith intended to explain the Lutheran position to the Catholic fathers at the Council of Trent. Brenz even went to Trent in 1552 but was given no opportunity to interpret this document.

With the abolition of the Interim, Brenz was appointed provost of the cathedral in Stuttgart in 1553 and visitor-general of the cloisters in 1557. In his new position as provost, he was in fact the head of the Lutheran church in Württemberg. He cooperated with Duke Christopher in consolidating the Lutheran reformation in South Germany. His work was summarized in the great church order of 1559, which molded ecclesiastical life in Württemberg for centuries to come as the work of Bugenhagen shaped congregational structures in the North.

His last years were spent in controversy, though grudgingly. He felt the attacks on Osiander were nothing more than a frivolous war of words. He engaged in discussions with Jan Laski and with the Anabaptists, especially at Frankenthal and Worms. Controversies with Schwenckfeld and with the Dominican Peter de Soto, who attacked the *Confessio Virtembergica*, also absorbed his time. But the principal controversy was with the Reformed in South Germany and Switzerland, who denied the Lutheran understanding of real presence. Brenz repeated the Lutheran arguments for the ubiquity of the body of Christ, but he moved them in a new direction when he argued on the basis of the union of the divine and human natures for a ubiquity that began with the incarnation and not with the resurrection or ascension. If South Germany remained Lutheran rather than Reformed, Brenz deserves a large measure of the credit for that fact. Without his influence the balance might have swung the other way.

When Brenz died on September 11, 1570, he was occupied with the dream of uniting the various Lutheran groups throughout northern Europe. It was typical of the man that he died with a project still on his desk. He did not retire; he simply wore out in his work. He was not as original in his theology as Melanchthon or Osiander, though certainly he was more imaginative than Bugenhagen. Like Bugenhagen, however, he had a gift for embedding the Reformation in the lives of the people. Though he did not embrace the absolutist theory of the state, he did, nevertheless, by his stress on the role of the prince in the administration of the church and by his preference for centralization, pave the way for the dominance of the church by the state that marked much of the later history of Lutheranism within Germany. But the negative results of his work should not be allowed to cloud his positive contributions. He was, without a doubt, one of the most remarkable figures of the sixteenth century.

III

The Reformed Tradition

II

MARTIN BUCER

(1491–1551)

The Church and the Social Order

THOUGH MARTIN BUCER was the reformer of the city of Strasbourg and, next to Luther and Melanchthon, the most important leader of Protestantism in Germany, his role in the crucial events of his time has, until recent years, been overlooked by the vast majority of Protestants, who acknowledge Luther, Calvin, or Menno Simons as their spiritual father but who have no recollection of the significance of Martin Bucer in the formation of the Reformed tradition or, to a lesser extent, the Anglican. Yet in his own lifetime Bucer was one of the most influential religious figures on the continent of Europe. He was instrumental in bringing Luther and Zwingli together for their fateful confrontation at Marburg. He took a leading role in the colloquies between Protestants and Roman Catholics held at Worms and Regensburg. He was, one might say, the principal spokesman for the moderate Protestants in Europe, those who sought ecumenical solutions in a time of confessional conflict and tension.

Bucer was born in Schlettstadt near Strasbourg on November 11, 1491.[1] Though his father was only a poor cobbler, Martin received an excellent education in the Latin school in his hometown, where in 1506 at the age of fifteen he entered the Dominican cloister. As a Dominican postulant he was given a thorough introduction to scholastic thought, especially to the theology of Thomas Aquinas. In 1516 he was transferred to the cloister of the Blackfriars in Heidelberg, where he continued his education, studying Greek with Johannes Brenz and reading the works of Erasmus, whom he very much admired.

When Luther came to Heidelberg in April 1518 to preside at a disputation during a meeting of the Augustinian order, Bucer went out of curiosity to hear him. He was deeply impressed with the new theology that Luther defended against the traditions of medieval scholasticism. Further conversation with Luther only served to reinforce that first favorable impression. Captivated by Luther's thought, Bucer, though a member of Johann Tetzel's order, sprang to

Luther's defense. His ecclesiastical superiors took a dim view of his new enthusiasm and attempted to dissuade him from his avowed intention of withdrawing from the Dominican order. Finally, in 1521 he was able to leave the cloister at Heidelberg and assume the duties of parish priest at Landstuhl, a parish belonging to Franz von Sickingen. While still the pastor at Landstuhl, Bucer took the daring step of marrying Elizabeth Silbereisen, a young nun from the cloister of Lobenfeld.

Meanwhile, von Sickingen was defeated in his disastrous campaign against the elector of Trier. This turn of events made it necessary for Bucer to resign his post at Landstuhl in order to join Luther in Wittenberg. He resolved, however, to take his wife to safety in Strasbourg, where he had relatives. The road to Strasbourg passed through the city of Weissenburg. Heinrich Motherer, the pastor of Saint John's Church, had already initiated the work of reform in Weissenburg and prevailed on Bucer to stay and assist him in that work. Bucer agreed and preached a series of sermons in Saint John's on the First Letter of Peter and the Gospel of Matthew. However, before the series on Matthew was completed the political situation again became dangerous for Bucer. In the spring of 1523 the princes returned to the offensive against von Sickingen. By the middle of May the fighting had moved to the neighborhood of Weissenburg. The fact that Bucer had served von Sickingen in the past, a fact that was generally known to all, placed Weissenburg in a tenuous position so far as von Sickingen's enemies were concerned. The town council, therefore, urged both Bucer and Motherer to leave the city. The two men reluctantly agreed and on May 10, 1523, slipped quietly out of the city.

The *Summary*, which Bucer wrote immediately after his arrival in Strasbourg, contained a short explanation to the citizens of Weissenburg concerning the circumstances surrounding his sudden and mysterious departure from their town.[2] It also contained a digest of the main ideas he had preached in Saint John's during the preceding Advent and Epiphany seasons. This early treatise makes it clear both that Bucer was Luther's disciple and that from the very first he was independent of him.[3]

Bucer opened the first section of his treatise with an address to the people of Weissenburg, celebrating the fact that the gospel had been preached fruitfully among them to the evident discomfiture of the Antichrist, a name applied pejoratively by Bucer to everyone who denies the Lutheran teaching that men and women are justified by faith alone apart from all consideration of merit. A human being who cannot trust Christ alone, but must buttress the finished work of Jesus Christ with human contributions, and proclaims this patchwork redemption as the pure Christian gospel, that person, Bucer insists, is the Antichrist. The people of Weissenburg were not in bondage to the heretical message of the Antichrist but had been privileged to hear the gospel in all its clarity and simplicity. And this, Bucer felt, could only be a matter of immense satisfaction to every true believer.

Bucer then struck what remained a dominant motif in his theology through-out his life; namely, the cruciality of the work of the Spirit. The Holy Spirit has been given to Christians in order to guide them in their understanding of Scripture. Anyone who does not have the Spirit is blind and unable to under-stand the message of the Bible. Insight into Scripture is given only to persons who have the Spirit, and the Spirit is given only to persons who have faith in Jesus Christ. The Word, therefore, divorced from the Spirit and from faith—and ultimately from Jesus Christ—is not profitable for salvation. The Word and the Spirit must be conjoined for the edification of the church, an emphasis later taken up by Bucer's illustrious friend and coworker John Calvin.[4]

Bucer's stress on the Holy Spirit, however, did not issue in a kind of vague spiritualism, a subjectivism that dissolves objective standards of doctrine in a miasma of undifferentiated experience. If the Word must never be interpreted apart from the Holy Spirit, neither must spiritual experience be accorded va-lidity apart from the objective check of the inscripturated Word. For a doctrine to be believed it must agree with the teaching of Scripture.

Sinners who are justified *sola fide* and given the gift of the Holy Spirit are en-abled to perform works of love. Such works do not justify sinners, though they are the fruit of justification. Bucer would have agreed with the scholastic doc-tors, such as Aquinas, that a living faith is a faith that works by love. But he would have denied that the works so produced were meritorious. Men and women are justified on the basis of the meritorious activity of Christ alone. Good works contribute nothing to this justification.

Justified people, however, do not live an undisciplined, self-serving life. Bucer retained the moral emphasis of humanists like Erasmus (*bene beateque vivere*). Christians have been called to a life of discipleship, an active life of struggling against the downward pull of the flesh. They have been given the Holy Spirit who gives them the power to bear their cross and who transforms human weakness into the power of Christ. The trials and troubles of this life serve to further the sanctification of Christians by teaching them to put their reliance in God alone and not in his gifts, however good they may be. Fasting and other forms of spiritual discipline have their rightful place within the Christian life. However, they must never be used to destroy Christian freedom. Christians must do only what Scripture commands; namely, love God and their neighbors. To observe fasts or feast days may be helpful in the disciplining of the flesh, but the regulations governing them are human regulations and do not carry the weight of divine authority. Anyone who raises all such matters to the level of divine command—and by *anyone* Bucer means particularly monks and nuns—strikes a blow against Christian freedom.

These ideas were, of course, not wholly original with Bucer. The influence of both Luther and Erasmus can certainly be discerned, Luther in the teaching of *sola fide* and of the theological primacy of Scripture over tradition, and Erasmus in his reading of the Pauline contrast between flesh and the spirit and the necessity for the discipline of the one by the other. But the balanced statement, which unites Luther and Erasmus, can only be regarded as Bucer's own.

In Strasbourg, Bucer swiftly moved to the leadership of the reform movement, serving as pastor of Saint Aurelia's from 1524 to 1531 and Saint Thomas's from 1531 to 1540. He wrote a new, evangelical liturgy for worship in Strasbourg a full year before Luther composed the *Deutsche Messe* for Saxony.[5] He wrote three catechisms and in 1539 reinstituted the rite of confirmation as a means of furthering Christian education. In 1529 he succeeded in persuading the town council to abolish the Mass. Together with Johannes Sturm he founded two educational institutions in the city of Strasbourg, the preparatory school in 1538 and the seminary in 1544. In 1534 he introduced the office of lay presbyter into the church government. He was not able, however, to convince the magistrates of Strasbourg that a vigorous program of discipline was essential to the wellbeing of the church. Finally, in desperation he suggested in 1546 that small groups be organized in the congregations of the city, composed of people willing to submit on a voluntary basis to strict discipline. This suggestion of the formation of small, disciplined groups within the state church (as a partial answer to the Anabaptist groups formed outside it) served as an inspiration to Philip Spener and the Pietists, who also at a later date attempted to organize *ecclesiolae in ecclesia*, little ecclesial groups within the larger church, more or less on Bucer's model.

Bucer's work took him outside the walls of Strasbourg. He participated, to a greater or lesser extent, in the introduction of the Reformation in Hanau-Lichtenberg, Baden, Württemberg, and Hesse. When Calvin was expelled from Geneva, he found refuge with Bucer in Strasbourg. Though the exact degree of Bucer's influence on Calvin has yet to be determined, it is clear nonetheless that Bucer was one of the more important figures in Calvin's theological development. Even Belgium, Italy, and France were not untouched by the impact of Bucer's thought.

In 1529 Bucer attempted, with the aid of Philip of Hesse, to unite the Swiss and the German reformers on the question of the meaning of the Lord's Supper.[6] Bucer tried to take a mediating position between Luther and Zwingli. Until 1524 Bucer had been a Lutheran in his doctrine of the Eucharist. Then, under the influence of Zwingli and Carlstadt, he was led little by little to embrace a more symbolic interpretation of the sacrament. From the very first he could never stomach Luther's doctrine of the ubiquity of the body of Christ. He agreed with Zwingli that the body of Christ was in heaven at the right hand of the Father and that the sacrament is not, properly speaking, a means of grace. Gradually, however, he moved back to an intermediate position, agreeing with the Swiss that the body of Christ is in heaven but accepting the idea, promoted by the Lutherans, that the Lord's Supper is an objective means by which God graciously feeds and nourishes his church. While the humanity is in heaven, the divinity is present, both in the sacrament and in the hearts of believers.

The Reformed Tradition

In 1529/30 Bucer composed a formula he thought might put an end to the bitter hostilities between Luther and Zwingli. Bread and wine, body and blood form a sacramental union, which is different from every other union we know. Under the banner of the *unio sacramentalis* the warring parties were free to believe pretty much what they wished to. The Wittenberg Concord of 1536, for example, unites Bucer's formula with Lutheran concepts. This successful marriage of Bucer's language with Luther's ideas is due at least in part to the fact that Bucer had himself moved away from a strict Zwinglian position to one closer to, but by no means identical with, Luther's. The humanity is in heaven, but the sacrament is, nevertheless, a means of grace. This is the direction in which Calvin's thought also moved—whether under the guidance of Bucer is difficult to say.

Under Bucer's leadership Strasbourg became one of the few oases of tolerance in the sixteenth century. Only Wolfgang Capito, who after all was also a Strasbourg reformer, was more tolerant in his attitude toward the Radical reformers than Bucer. Though Bucer tried to convert the Anabaptists by reasonable arguments and even agreed in the early 1530s to a harsher policy of expulsion from the city for dissenters, he opposed the death penalty employed by the Swiss.

In 1540 Bucer took part in a series of colloquies aimed at reuniting Protestants and Catholics by resolving the theological issues between them. Though Melanchthon and Eck were the chief negotiators at Worms and at Regensburg, Bucer and Gropper composed the articles they debated in the *Regensburg Book*. This book contained, among other things, the famous article 5 on the doctrine of double justification.

Initially, Bucer had followed Luther's teaching on justification very closely, though he combined Luther's thought with certain Erasmian motifs. As the years passed, however, Bucer diverged more and more from Luther as he increasingly emphasized the work of the Holy Spirit. Melanchthon had laid heavy stress on justification as a forensic declaration, preserving its formal character as a forgiveness of sins. Unlike Melanchthon, Luther had also stressed justification as the transforming work of the Holy Spirit that really slays the sinful impulses and tendencies of the old Adam. Bucer could not decide between the two possibilities, so he chose rather to unite them and to make two steps out of them. Justification is both a forensic declaration and a real making just, though Bucer understood by that formulation something different from what Luther meant when he spoke of justification as both an imputation and a human transformation.

There are for Bucer, as there are not for Luther, two steps or gradations in justification. In the first stage, human beings are justified through the forgiveness of sins. On the basis of this forgiveness, sinners are granted the Holy Spirit. On the foundation of the gift of the Spirit, a second justification is built. The first justification is without any merit whatever on the part of men and women.

Sinners are forgiven by grace alone on the basis of God's redeeming act in Christ. In the second stage, Christians are justified on the basis of the fact that as new persons in Christ they have begun to perform works of love. There is a certain sense in which Christians are rewarded for the works the Holy Spirit performs in and through them.

In defending this point of view, Bucer appeals to the scholastic distinction between first and second causes. That God as a First Cause works in men and women through his grace in no way excludes their own free activity as second causes. Second causes are not automatons dangling from the strings of a heavenly puppeteer.

There is, in other words, a double justification: the justification of the ungodly, which takes place by grace alone, and a justification of the just, which is based on human renewal by the Holy Spirit. In fact, if one wants to press the point, it is even possible to speak of a triple justification, since the first justifying act of God is his pretemporal act of election, in which some persons, though not others, are chosen for faith. But the second and third steps are the really decisive ones.

It is fairly clear that Bucer's doctrine of double justification is different from the teaching of Gropper and Contarini, though Bucer's mediating position made it rather easy for him to empathize with their attempts to spell out a Catholic doctrine of double justice. One could not reconcile this doctrine, however, with Luther's thought. It represented from Luther's point of view an impossible union of Erasmian moralism with a Lutheran religion of grace. Furthermore, this second stage of justification (*justificatio legis*) opened the door for theological developments in the direction of perfectionism. Bucer is in many ways the spiritual, if not the direct, ancestor of Wesley. Indeed, Bucer's mediating position, with its stress on discipline, visibility, and the justification of the just, was not without its effect on the development of Reformed theology, generally. Puritans could with good reason consider Bucer one of their seminal thinkers, even though he himself favored the moderate Anglican position.

Though the colloquy at Regensburg came to a disappointing conclusion, not everyone saw the lesson of Regensburg clearly. There were still prominent churchmen like Archbishop Hermann von Wied of Cologne who saw the Christian world divided solely between those who favored reform and those who opposed it. Following Regensburg, however, he began to associate himself more clearly with the Lutheran reform party and asked Bucer to assist him in the work of reforming his diocese. To that end he appointed him preacher in Bonn. Gropper, who had worked with Bucer on the *Regensburg Book*, opposed him as the archbishop's adviser.[7] The ensuing struggle of the two reformers over the nature of the reform to be undertaken in the archdiocese of Cologne was finally won by Gropper. Cologne was not to fall into the hands of the Protestants.

When Charles V after the defeat of the Protestant League of Schmalkalden issued the Augsburg Interim, the city of Strasbourg found itself compelled to accept a document favorable to the teachings and practices of the Catholic church. Though the document permitted Protestant ministers to marry and allowed communion in both kinds, it was unacceptable to Bucer. When Cranmer invited Bucer to England, he readily accepted the invitation.[8] He arrived in London in 1549 and in January 1550 began to lecture at the University of Cambridge. He assisted Cranmer in the revision of the Book of Common Prayer and as a present for the king composed his most famous treatise, *De Regno Christi*. The book represented Bucer's attempt to explain the nature of the kingdom of Christ and to suggest in what way that kingdom might be realized in England.

Bucer defined the church as the community of the elect under the heavenly king, Jesus Christ. The contrast between the visible and invisible church, sharply preserved in the teaching of some of the reformers, is blurred in Bucer's thought. The spiritual life cannot be nurtured in a vacuum. There must be concrete forms and structures to nurture and protect the faith of the flock of Christ. The concrete community of the church in its disciplined life together provides these necessary structures. Bucer was the great theoretician of ecclesiastical discipline prior to Calvin, though unlike Calvin he made discipline one of the marks of the church. Calvin, in part because of his desire to preserve good ecumenical relations with the Lutherans, was unwilling to go quite that far in his emphasis on discipline.

Ecclesiastical, political, and social tasks overlap for Bucer, who drew no sharp distinction between the spheres of church and state. He spoke again and again of the responsibility of the total Christian community for the care of the poor and rejected the idea that they should be dependent on haphazard, private charity. The Christian community as a whole is directly responsible for its suffering members and may not shirk that duty under the guise of a higher piety.

All civil and political duties are viewed by Bucer in the light of his understanding of the kingdom of God. The state, no less than the church, is an instrument of the kingdom of God. The state in its very character as a state is also a Christian instrumentality. God is doing his work in the world through secular agencies as well as through the preaching of the gospel and the administration of the sacraments. One finds, thus, in Bucer a kind of social gospel, even if aspects of that gospel reflect as well some of the nationalism of Tudor England.

The decisive factor for both Bucer's doctrine of the church and of the Holy Spirit is his doctrine of double predestination. Only the elect have the Holy Spirit. Therefore, he concluded, those who bear the fruit of the Spirit, especially love, must by the same token be the elect. Saints are, so to say, visible. This was a theme that Bucer's students of a more or less Puritan disposition at Cambridge did not miss.

The Spirit also makes ministers fit to discharge the office of the preaching of the gospel. At least, that was Bucer's original point of view. Later he had a change of heart, feeling that his position on the charismatic qualifications for preaching was too close to the views espoused by the Radical reformers. In his mature thought he placed more weight on the scriptural character of the office of preacher as such and its role in the government of the church and less weight on the possession of the Spirit (evident in the fruits of faith) in the life of the preacher. He saw preaching more in terms of office and institution and less in terms of individual charisma. Nevertheless, his writings abound with rich descriptions of the work of the Spirit in the life of the church. Indeed, his doctrines of church and Spirit are the two strongest themes in his entire theology.

King Edward VI was delighted with the *De Regno Christi* and indicated his pleasure to Bucer, who was awarded a doctor of divinity degree by the University of Cambridge. Shortly after writing this book, however, Bucer became seriously ill; he died on February 28 or March 1, 1551. He was buried in Great Saint Mary's Church in Cambridge. In 1556 Queen Mary had Bucer's body exhumed and his bones burned in public. When Mary's Protestant half sister, Elizabeth, ascended to the throne, she attempted to make amends for the Tudor family by honoring Bucer in an official ceremony of state.

Bucer was, one may say, an extremely important reformer. His direct influence, however, was lessened through the misfortune caused by the Interim. When Bucer went into exile in England, the vacuum he left behind him was filled by Lutheranism and by Calvin. His principal importance lies in the field of ecclesiastical politics and practical theology. His ideas on church discipline and on confirmation, and his social teaching, were very fruitful in later Reformed thought.

12

HEINRICH BULLINGER
(1504–1575)

Covenant and the Continuity
of Salvation History

THE SHOCK OF THE tragic death of Zwingli at the Battle of Kappel left Zurich and the Protestant cantons of Switzerland dazed and thoroughly demoralized. None of the ministers in Zurich, not even Zwingli's close friend Leo Jud, had the gifts to rally the people in the face of what seemed to them to be an unredeemable disaster. When Zurich finally found a new pastor to succeed Zwingli, it turned to a twenty-seven-year-old refugee from Bremgarten, who had been forced out of his own parish by the defeat of the Protestants at Kappel.

The new pastor, Heinrich Bullinger, was born in Bremgarten on July 18, 1504.[1] His father, also named Heinrich, was a parish priest. Since priests were under the rule of celibacy, they were forbidden to marry. But it was not uncommon in the later Middle Ages for priests to enter into an "arrangement" that had all the stability, if not the official sanction, of marriage. Though Heinrich was technically born out of wedlock, he was not the product of a casual affair. Indeed, in 1529, after his father was converted to the Protestant cause, his parents legitimated their arrangement by entering into marriage.

Heinrich received his earliest education in Bremgarten. In 1516 his father sent him to a Latin school in Emmerich, where his older brother had already studied. At one time it was believed that Heinrich had come under the influence of the Brethren of the Common Life at Emmerich, though since the research of Fritz Blanke this is no longer affirmed. In 1519, the year of Zwingli's conversion to the Protestant cause, Bullinger matriculated at the University of Cologne.

The theological faculty at Cologne was dominated by Thomists and Scotists. If Bullinger had devoted his time to the study of theology rather than the arts, he would have been exposed to a scholastic theology quite different in its presuppositions from the scholastic theology to which Luther had been subjected. Bullinger, however, was not deeply immersed in scholastic thought. He had come to Cologne to study the humanities. To be sure, he read Peter Lombard and Gratian, the two principal textbooks in theology and canon law. But this limited reading in medieval theology only served to sharpen his appetite for the study of the Fathers. Origen, Augustine, Chrysostom, and Ambrose, rather than Scotus, Ockham, and Biel, became his daily fare.

While still a student in Cologne, Bullinger broke with the medieval Catholic church. Although he soon became an ally and coworker of Zwingli, it was not Zwingli who led him to throw in his lot with the Protestants. He seems to have come to his decision somewhat independently. He read Luther and Melanchthon and concluded that their position was more in harmony with the teaching of the Bible and of the Fathers than was the doctrine of the Catholic church in which he had been raised. It was a careful reading of the sources of the faith and not the personal influence of some gifted teacher that led to his conversion in 1522.

Bullinger had intended to enter a Carthusian cloister. His conversion to Protestantism made that course of action impossible. It was not impossible, however, for him to teach the Bible and classics at the Cistercian monastery at Kappel, provided that the abbot was willing to allow him to remain a layman. Though Bullinger's refusal to enter the Cistercian order caused a good many eyebrows to be raised, the abbot knew a gifted teacher when he found one and agreed to Bullinger's terms. The abbot got more than he bargained for in the young humanist scholar. Bullinger not only taught the brothers, as the terms of his contract stipulated; he persuaded them to embrace the evangelical faith. In 1527, four years after Bullinger first began to teach in Kappel, the monastery was dissolved as a monastic establishment and transformed into a Protestant parish. Bullinger stayed on for two more years as the pastor.

Bullinger first met Zwingli in 1523. Despite the difference in their ages, the two men became good friends. Zwingli, who was more meteoric and intuitive than Bullinger, clearly became the dominant partner in their relationship. Nevertheless, Zwingli valued highly the contribution of his somewhat more sober and pedantic ally. Bullinger aided Zwingli in his controversy with the Anabaptists in 1525 and accompanied him to the disputation in Bern in 1528. The controversy with the Anabaptists revolved around the problem of the covenant.[2]

The Anabaptists in Zurich regarded the church as a covenant community. So, of course, did Zwingli. But there the similarities end and the differences begin to multiply. For the Anabaptists the church was a covenant community because it was constituted by a voluntary agreement among believing adults. Since infants do not have faith and cannot enter into a voluntary contractual agreement, they may not be baptized.

This view of the nature of the church led the Anabaptists to an understanding of history marked by discontinuity. There is a discontinuity between the Old Testament and the New with respect to the sacraments. Baptism and circumcision are quite different ceremonies. Though all the children of Abraham were circumcised, they were not all believers, nor did they all stand in a

The Reformed Tradition

covenant of grace. Baptism, on the other hand, can only be administered where faith and grace are already present. If circumcision is a sacrament at all, it is a sacrament clearly inferior to the ordinance of adult baptism.

Zwingli understood covenant quite differently. For Zwingli the fundamental covenant was the covenant God concluded with Adam. Because the covenant was made with Adam, it was made with the benefit of the entire human race in view. Later this covenant was renewed with Abraham for the people of Israel. But the Adamic covenant, no matter how many times it has been renewed, is still the same covenant. The appearance of Jesus Christ in history represents not the abrogation but the fulfillment of the covenant with Adam and Abraham. Abraham anticipated God's saving act in Jesus Christ; the church remembers and celebrates it. But the faith of Abraham and the faith of the church are essentially the same. Both are heirs of the same covenant. Indeed, the abolition of the ceremonies of Israel and the undertaking of the Gentile mission by the early church are only a reaffirmation of the universal character of the original covenant made with Adam.

With this view of the unity of the covenant and the continuity of the history of salvation, Zwingli found the analogy between circumcision and baptism inescapable. Since children were included in the Abrahamic covenant through circumcision before they believed, it was perfectly in order for the children of Christian parents to be included in the church before they believed through the rite of infant baptism. This was not the only basis on which Zwingli argued for the propriety of infant baptism, but it is certainly fundamental to his thought.

Bullinger took Zwingli's idea of the covenant and of the unity of salvation history and carried it still further. While Zwingli only dealt with the idea of covenant incidentally in the context of the discussion of infant baptism, Bullinger broadened the idea of covenant and used it as a constitutive dogmatic principle. Bullinger was opposed to any vision of history marked by radical discontinuity. Though there are differences between Israel and the church, those differences should be interpreted within a larger framework of continuity. The history of salvation is only correctly understood when it is perceived to be the history of God's dealing with one covenant people.

According to Bullinger the starting point of the history of salvation is the eternal covenant concluded with Abraham.[3] To be sure, Bullinger, like Zwingli, spoke of a covenant antedating the covenant with Abraham. The fathers who preceded Abraham were not excluded from the sphere of redemption but were saved by faith in the promise made to Adam in the garden of Eden. The earliest proclamation of the gospel was the so-called Protoevangelium of Genesis 3:15. Bullinger also gave some attention to the covenant God made with Noah after the waters of the flood had receded from the earth. But Bullinger's principal emphasis fell on the covenant made between God and Abraham that is reported in Genesis 17. Bullinger singled out four elements in this covenant for special mention. (1) When God concludes the covenant with Abraham, he reveals himself as El Shaddai; that is, as God Almighty. (2) The covenant is not simply for the benefit of the Jews but is directed from the very first toward all human beings, Jews and Gentiles alike. God says to Abraham: "In you shall all the nations of the earth be blessed." In other words, the covenant brings the promise not only of an earthly home for the Jews but also of a heavenly Canaan for all humankind. (3) There is a condition laid on Abraham: "Walk before me and be blameless." (4) Finally, circumcision is introduced as the sacrament of this covenant.

The New Covenant in Christ is nothing other than the fulfillment of the covenant with Abraham. The eternal covenant of God with human beings is established in and through the Person and work of the Redeemer. Indeed, the saving act of God in Christ can only be understood when it is put in the framework of the Abrahamic covenant. For Bullinger, as Joachim Staedke has quite rightly noted, the primacy of the Abrahamic covenant leads to the hermeneutical principle that the Old Covenant is the interpreter of the New.[4] The significance of the passion narratives in the gospels cannot be rightly assessed until those narratives are seen against the background of Genesis 17.

The Abrahamic covenant, moreover, is brought to fruition at every point in the event of Jesus Christ. (1) Jesus Christ is Emmanuel, God with us, the fullness of the revelation of El Shaddai. (2) The entire work of the Redeemer is the fulfillment of the promise to Abraham: "In you shall all the nations of the earth be blessed." Redemption is given through Christ to Jew and Gentile alike. The universal note present in Zwingli's understanding of the covenant is also present in Bullinger. (3) Christ fulfills the ethical demand of the condition of the covenant: "Walk before me and be blameless." By his word and deeds he leaves an example for the church, which it, too, is called to emulate. (4) The meaning of this renewed covenant is summed up in the sacraments of baptism and the Lord's Supper, just as the meaning of the covenant with Abraham was contained in the sacrament of circumcision.

If the entire drama of redemption can be understood from the standpoint of the two moments, Abraham and Christ, then the role of Moses and the function of the moral and ceremonial law of Israel is placed in question. Bullinger explained the giving of the law as a concession to human weakness. Abraham's descendants were adversely affected by the idolatry of Egypt and so the law was given to strengthen and undergird the original covenant relation. Because the Israelites continued to be faithless and unbelieving, God further disciplined them by adding the requirements of the cultic ceremonies. The law and its ceremonies were given to strengthen the covenant, not to replace or alter it. The fathers who lived before the law was given were saved by the covenant, apart from the law and the ceremonies. The covenant was written on their hearts, not on tablets of stone.

In short, the distinction between the Old and New Testaments does not touch the substance of the covenant, but only its accidents. Both Testaments witness to the same redemption in Christ. The Old Testament witnesses by promise and type; the New Testament points to the reality which was prefigured. To the extent that the ceremonies of the Old Testament are fulfilled in the New Testament, the New Testament is really new. But the New Testament is not new in its demands. Like the Old Testament it demands faith and love from us. Through his saving act Jesus Christ does not destroy but rather restores the innermost meaning of the law.

It is clear that Bullinger, like Zwingli before him, directed many of his remarks against the Anabaptists, who tended to denigrate the Old Testament and who rejected infant baptism. On the question of infant baptism Bullinger made the identical point Zwingli made; namely, that children were not excluded from the Old Covenant and therefore ought not to be excluded from the New. Baptism in the New Covenant corresponds to circumcision in the Old.

Bullinger could make the same point as Zwingli because he shared with Zwingli the same belief in the unity of the two testaments. Abraham anticipated Christ by faith and was justified through him. The Christian religion is in reality the oldest religion because all believers in the Old Testament from the time of Abraham to the advent of John the Baptist are in fact Christians. They share in the same covenant in which the church shares. Both Jews and Gentiles are children of Abraham by faith.

In 1529 Bullinger left Kappel and succeeded his father as the pastor of Bremgarten, which had by now been converted to the Protestant cause. The year before Bullinger accepted the call to Bremgarten he married a former nun, Anna Adlischweiler. He would have married sooner, but his prospective mother-in-law was opposed to the union and fought against it.

On November 20, 1531, after the defeat of the Protestants at Kappel, Bullinger was forced to flee at night from Bremgarten to Zurich. Shortly after his arrival in Zurich, he was chosen to succeed Zwingli at the Great Minster. On December 9, 1531, he stepped for the first time into the pulpit Zwingli had occupied with such distinction. Before he finished his first sermon, people realized that they had called a worthy successor to assume the leadership of the church in Zurich.

Like Zwingli, Bullinger felt obliged to touch on political issues in his sermons, though unlike Zwingli he tended to regard church and state as coordinate and independent spheres of influence. He preached six to eight times a week until 1542, when his preaching load was reduced to two sermons, one on Sunday and one on Friday. Like Zwingli he preached through books of the Bible rather than on pericopes arranged according to the church year. Fifty of his sermons, called variously the *Decades* or the *Hausbuch* and organized by theological topic rather than by biblical text, were printed and widely circulated, not only in German-speaking countries but also in Holland and England. The sermons were written in Latin and were meant to be a discussion, in homiletical form, of all the central doctrines of the Christian faith. This book was extremely influential, not only for its content but also for its method. Against the tendency to write systematic theological treatises by the *Loci* method, arranging all doctrines according to the logical categories of Aristotle, Bullinger helped to preserve within the Reformed tradition a homiletical approach to theology, in which biblical categories and the history of salvation are more important organizing principles than the categories of Aristotle.[5]

Bullinger rallied the Protestant communities of Switzerland and helped them to recover from the defeat at Kappel. Indeed, Bullinger was so successful in his efforts to recoup the Protestant losses that the Catholic cantons were never able to reap all the fruits to which their victory over Zwingli had entitled them. In the forty-four years during which Bullinger was the *antistes*, or chief minister, of Zurich, the Reformed church experienced a rapid growth unparalleled in its earlier history. Zwingli had presided over the introduction of the fundamental reforms. Bullinger consolidated and refined them.

The intellectual leadership of the Reformed movement shifted gradually from Zurich to Geneva; after the death of Zwingli, Calvin became the leading theologian of the Reformed church. That does not mean, however, that Bullinger's theological influence ceased to be felt. In 1549 Bullinger and Calvin were able to unite the Zwinglian and the Calvinist factions in the Reformed church on the question of the Lord's Supper. To be sure, the *Consensus Tigurinus* of 1549 represented a movement of the German-speaking churches toward the position of Calvin. Nevertheless, Bullinger was able in this document to preserve certain important Zwinglian insights.

Even more important than the *Consensus Tigurinus* for the theological formation of the Reformed movement was the *Second Helvetic Confession*, written by Bullinger as a personal testament of faith and issued in 1566, when the historical circumstances in the Palatinate justified its release.[6] All the churches of Switzerland, except Basel, embraced this confession. But the confession found acceptance far beyond the boundaries of Switzerland. The Reformed churches in France, Hungary, and Scotland adopted it as an official statement of faith. While the Reformed churches in Germany, Holland, and England did not take the step of formal adoption, they nevertheless commended the confession and made use of it. Of all the Reformed confessions of faith, the *Second Helvetic Confession* was the most widely recognized. It alone of all the Reformed confessions could claim to be universal.

While the intellectual leadership of the Reformed movement shifted to Geneva, the pastoral leadership did not. Bullinger was the friend and adviser of many of the important figures in church and in state throughout Europe. His extant correspondence, which is voluminous, numbers over twelve thousand items. Many of these letters were written to English bishops, such as John Hooper and John Jewel, who had been forced by the turbulence of Tudor politics to spend a brief exile in Zurich. Others were written to such political figures as Francis II of France, Henry VIII of England, Christian of Denmark, Philip of Hesse, and Frederick III of the Palatinate. His pastoral counsel was widely sought, and the degree of his influence on the course of the Reformation outside his native Switzerland has not yet been adequately assessed.[7]

Bullinger also became significant as a historian. He wrote a general history of Switzerland; its three volumes on the Reformation are an important source of information about the career of Zwingli. He composed a history of the Anabaptist movement and propounded a theory concerning its origin, which has remained influential.[8]

When Bullinger died in 1575, he could look back on a long career, marked not so much by brilliant innovation as by prudent consolidation. He conserved the gains made by Zwingli and built on them. Certain theological motifs, such as Zwingli's idea of the nature of the covenant, Bullinger developed further. But Bullinger is less important for his originality than for his wisdom. He was the humane and compassionate *pastor pastorum*, whose learning and gifts were modestly put at the service of others. Precisely because he was less innovative than either Zwingli or Calvin, he was better able than either to state in a way that transcended factional differences the hard lines of the faith of the Reformed church. Without Zwingli there would have been no Reformation in Zurich; without Bullinger it would not have lasted.

13

JOHN HOOPER
(1495–1555)
The Birth of the Puritan Spirit

JOHN HOOPER WAS NOT an easy man to reason with. He had an angular personality, fiercely stubborn and unwilling to compromise. Though his friends admired his gift for administration and his zeal for reform, they found him nevertheless a frustrating colleague to deal with. It is not surprising that Archbishop Cranmer, having exhausted all reasonable methods of persuading Hooper to change his mind, committed him in exasperation to the Fleet; or that Mary, in her desire to destroy Protestantism "root and branch" throughout her realm, included Hooper in that select band of bishops who were martyred for their faith. Hooper was no Broad Churchman who served jolly doses of Christianity-and-water to the phlegmatic and self-satisfied communicants of a sleepy Tudor diocese. He was a volcano of energy, who shook the indifferent out of their self-satisfaction and who let the ignorant and the slothful catch a sobering whiff of brimstone. Hooper was one of the earliest embodiments of the Puritan spirit, which was increasingly to dominate English church life over the course of the next century.

To call Hooper a Puritan is to raise as many problems as it solves.[1] One of the most difficult things about Puritanism is to say exactly what it was. It has been used, of course, as an unflattering epithet to describe a Christian piety gone sour, an unlovely legalism more interested in enforcing a series of rules than in commending the love of God. And yet, if there is anything characteristic of Puritanism, it is the intensity and depth of its religious experience. Puritanism is an experiential, or "experimental," religion, and the Puritan is a person who claims to have had a living experience of the God of wrath and redemptive love, however set and logical the formulae may be that are used to describe this experience. John Bunyan claimed to preach "what I felt, what I smartingly did feel."

Furthermore, while it is true that Puritanism valued Christian discipline and demanded fairly rigorous moral achievement on the part of its followers, it was in certain matters less rigorous than the frontier revivalism that followed it in North America. Puritans, for example, no more thought of doing without their glass of ale or bottle of port than they thought of doing without a rifle or plow or New Testament. Drunkenness was forbidden, not alcohol; and the model for the Christian was temperance, not abstinence.

One thing the Puritans had in common was dissatisfaction with Tudor religious policies. The Tudors (with the exception of Mary, who for obvious reasons differed with the policies of her father) viewed church and state as two aspects of the same thing. The king of England was head not only of the British state but also of the English church. Together with Parliament he had power to make pronouncements in matters theological. Defining doctrine was a function of government that did not differ in any significant way from the right of the state to establish weights and measures.

Although the Tudors claimed wide powers in theory, in practice they proceeded more cautiously. Henry threw into the caldron of public opinion here a pinch of Protestantism and there a jigger of Rome to flavor it as political necessities dictated. Elizabeth, who was required to be a Protestant if she wished to secure her right to the succession, did not flirt with transubstantiation as her father had but viewed the break with Rome as final. However, she did not wish to prescribe theology too closely. The government was only interested in preserving good order in a Christian state. It felt, therefore, that its obligations were satisfactorily discharged when it provided a form for worship—the modified Prayer Book of Edward VI—a church, and a trained ministry. One cannot compel belief by law, but one can prescribe a decent conformity in outward worship. The Tudors moved slowly but inexorably in the direction of a broadly based church that could embrace all Christians within the realm (with the exception of Roman Catholics and Anabaptists), whatever their theological persuasions.

This policy of the Tudors was unsatisfactory to the Puritans, who wished to see a Reformation in England along the lines of the Reformation in Zurich and Geneva. Theological issues, they reasoned, can only be determined through an exegesis of Holy Scripture; they can never be settled by a whimpering appeal to tradition and the Crown. If the necessities of national policy stand in the way of a thoroughgoing Reformation according to the Word of God, so much the worse for national policy!

The defenders of the Tudor religious settlement might have been perfectly right when they argued that the polity and discipline of the Church of England were not forbidden by Holy Scripture. But this shaky affirmation was not sufficient to satisfy the Puritans. The Puritans did not take the attitude that what is not forbidden is permitted. They adhered to the far more stringent principle that what is not commanded is forbidden. The conclusion the Puritans drew from this premise was clear and uncompromising: the polity and liturgical practices of the Church of England as well as its theological convictions must be scrutinized and amended in the light of Holy Scripture. Tradition and reason are admissible as theological witnesses only when their testimony tends to confirm the affirmations of Scripture. In any conflict among the three, it is Scripture alone that must prevail.

This conviction about the absolute priority of Scripture rested on the Puritan's vision of the totality of the sovereignty of God. God lays claim through Scripture to the whole of life, not merely to some areas or compartments. An appeal to tradition that overrides or invalidates Scripture is nothing less than the interposition of an obstacle to that total claim of God. The opposition to vestments, candles, and ecclesiastical offices not prescribed in Scripture was an outgrowth of the Puritan's understanding of the absolute sovereignty of God.

Hooper, whose career was a classic example of the Puritan opposition to what other reformers called *adiaphora,* or "indifferent matters," was born in Somerset, probably in 1495.[2] He studied at Merton College, Oxford, where he received his baccalaureate in 1519. Though a good deal of mystery surrounds his early life, it seems probable that he became a Cistercian monk and resided in Cleeve Abbey in Somerset until Henry VIII dissolved the monasteries in 1536. He returned to Oxford for further study and then served in London as the steward of Thomas Arundel. His studies in Scripture as well as in the writings of the Protestant reformers, especially Zwingli and Bullinger, led to his conversion to Protestantism in the early 1540s. Thomas Arundel attempted to persuade Hooper of the error of his ways by arranging an interview with one of the most competent defenders of the old way in England, Bishop Stephen Gardiner, but to no purpose. Gardiner found, as Cranmer discovered later, that once the mind of John Hooper was made up it was not swiftly unmade.

The Six Articles Act forced Hooper to flee to Paris and from Paris to Strasbourg. In Strasbourg, he met the woman he was later to marry. He returned briefly to England to claim against his father's opposition the inheritance he felt was rightly his. In spite of the dangers of the road (Hooper was thrown into prison twice on the way), he was able to make his way back to Strasbourg and to the woman he loved. In March 1547 he married and settled, not in Strasbourg, where the Interim was soon to go into effect, but in Zurich. At Zurich Hooper came under the influence of Bullinger, with whom he lived and studied. There, too, he wrote his first works, *A Declaration of Christ and His Office,* which he dedicated to Somerset, the Lord Protector of England, and *An Answer unto My Lord of Winchester's Book,* in which he attempted to refute the eucharistic theology of his erstwhile tutor Stephen Gardiner.

When Edward became king of England, it was safe for Hooper to return. Shortly after the birth of his child, he set out for an England hospitable as it had never been before to the voice of the Continental Reformation. Foxe (whose testimony in such matters is never wholly reliable) reports in his *Acts and Monuments* that Hooper, in his last meeting with Bullinger, predicted that he

The Reformed Tradition

would be burned at the stake. While the wild fluctuation of the religious situation in the sixteenth century would make any such prediction less a miracle of clairvoyance than a sober statement of historic probability, Foxe's report must still be taken with a grain of salt. Once again in England, Hooper became the chaplain to Somerset, preaching as often as twice a day. In Lent of 1550 he was commanded by the king to preach before him on the seven Wednesdays of that season. He chose for his text the book of Jonah from the Old Testament. Ignoring the advice of Aristotle that a drama has a beginning, a middle, and an end, Hooper was less concerned in his sermons to shape them according to aesthetic principles than to be responsive to the content of the text. Though the sermons are aesthetically flawed, they are a powerful statement of theological convictions. The king was impressed and offered Hooper the bishopric of Gloucester. For once Hooper was speechless. He had not expected to be offered a diocese. Nevertheless, though he was surprised, he was not reluctant to accept the bishopric, on the condition that he be consecrated without the vestments and the traditional oath required of bishops. If the vestments were mandatory, then he could not accept it.

Hooper's refusal to wear vestments or to be consecrated in the normal way quickly inflated into a *cause célèbre*. The controversy swirled around the theological status of *adiaphora*, or "indifferent matters." These indifferent matters were, for the most part, questions of ecclesiastical ceremonies and polity, issues on which there were sharp differences of opinion among people who, in the central matters of Christian doctrine, held remarkably similar theological positions. Nicholas Ridley, and those who shared his point of view, regarded these indifferent matters as theologically neutral, as a kind of no-man's-land between the fronts in which there could be legitimate differences of opinion without endangering the substance of the Christian faith. Hooper and those later Puritan divines who shared his convictions were thoroughly convinced that what is not commanded in Scripture ought not to be instituted in the church. Hooper did not deny outright the category of *adiaphora* but astutely observed that things regarded by one generation as indifferent are quickly hallowed by time and usage and regarded by the next generation as things essential to the life and well-being of the church.[3] The only way to combat that metamorphosis is to choke it off at birth.

There was division in the camp of the reformers over Hooper's stand. Most of the reformers, however, including Bucer and Peter Martyr, took the side of Hooper's opponent, Nicholas Ridley. The Bible may not command the minister officiating at the Lord's Supper to wear vestments, but it does command the minister to obey the prince set in authority over him. If one admits, as Hooper was willing to do in principle, that vestments belong to the *adiaphora*, then one is obliged to obey the state when it rules that vestments shall be worn. As far as Ridley was concerned, Hooper's arguments were invalidated by Romans 13.

Pressed by Ridley, Hooper shifted ground and denied that vestments were indifferent matters. Liturgical vestments and ceremonies are theologically grounded. They are part of a total vision of the relationship between God and humankind. One cannot alter that vision, as the Protestants have done, and leave the vestments intact. The proclamation of that church is contradicted by its liturgical life, which, from the standpoint of pastoral care, is a very serious thing indeed! Ordinary parishioners have every right to be confused when, like Isaac in the Old Testament, they are confronted with the voice of Jacob and the hands of Esau. The liturgical life of the church must express its theological convictions; it cannot be exempted from modification.

The controversy swiftly developed a personal and ad hominem character. Edwardian England was slowly moving in the direction of greater simplicity in liturgical matters. Other men had been consecrated with a minimum of ceremony. There was no reason why Hooper's wishes could not have been honored.[4] But his intemperate attack on vestments evoked an intemperate and irrational hostility, determined at all costs to consecrate Hooper with the maximum of pomp and circumstance. Finally, after a term in prison, Hooper was persuaded to give ground to his opponents and to be consecrated in the ordinary way.

He soon proved to be an exemplary bishop. Immediately on assuming office, he made an inspection tour of his diocese.[5] The results were unnerving. Ten of his priests were unfamiliar with the Lord's Prayer; twenty-seven were unable to tell who had composed it. Hooper set about with customary zeal to reform the diocese. He uprooted heresy, exposed inefficiency, and made provision for the correction of ignorance. Like the Swiss, he appointed superintendents rather than the customary archdeacons and rural deans. He established quarterly meetings with the diocesan clergy to discuss any problems that had arisen in the Gloucester parishes. He provided meals for the poor and even attempted to stir the government in London to do something about the burden of high prices. His administration of Gloucester was so admired by his superiors that he was given charge of the Diocese of Worcester as well. Other bishops were more conciliatory, some were more learned, but none was better at his task than John Hooper.

With the death of Edward VI and the succession of Mary, the political climate in England chilled for Protestants who had been prominent in the reform movement encouraged by Mary's half brother. In September 1553 Hooper wrote to Bullinger that he was now in prison and that the prospects for Protestants in England were, to say the least, bleak. In March 1554 he was deprived of his post as bishop of Gloucester because of his refusal to put away his wife or to subscribe to a Roman Catholic understanding of the Eucharist. A year later he was stripped of rank and honors and sent to Gloucester for execution. The fire the executioners set was made of green wood and refused to burn properly. For forty-five minutes Hooper suffered as the flames flared up about him and then subsided. The third fire, however, succeeded where the others had failed, and Hooper bravely died in it. Hooper's death only served to reinforce in the minds of the succeeding generation the forceful impact of his personality. He was not the most theologically astute of the martyrs who died in the fires which Mary kindled, but he was certainly one of the bravest. Reasons of state and arguments from political expediency had never moved him when the issues at stake were matters of conscience. Loyalty to the Word of God was more important than life itself. His example of uncompromising fidelity to the principles of the Protestant Reformation was not forgotten by the Puritans who followed him.

14

PETER MARTYR VERMIGLI
(1499–1562)

The Eucharistic Sacrifice

THE PENETRATION OF Protestantism into the countries of southern Europe was more successfully resisted by the Roman Catholic church than was its advance to the north and west. That is not to say that there were no Protestant leaders in Italy and Spain who made a lasting impact on the church, but most of them belonged to the left wing of Protestantism rather than its center, a fact that tended to limit their influence in northern Europe, where the center and not the extremes held sway. Yet some exiles from the south did manage to shape the Reformation in the north and not merely to criticize it. Among these exiles must certainly be counted the most learned of all the Italian refugees, Peter Martyr Vermigli, the Regius Professor of Divinity at the University of Oxford from 1547 to 1553.

Peter Martyr was born in Florence on September 8, 1499, to Stephano Vermigli, a wealthy shoemaker who had greatly admired the work of Savonarola and who revered his memory.[1] Though Peter was christened Piero Mariano, he took the name Peter Martyr when he entered the Order of the Canons Regular of Saint Augustine. Peter Martyr of Verona had been an inquisitor in the thirteenth century who was brought to an untimely end by Patarene heretics in Barlassina near Milan. It was not uncommon to take the name of a saint when entering a religious order.

Peter Martyr was taught at first by his mother and later by Marcello Virgilio, who was the secretary of the Florentine Republic. In 1514 he entered the monastery of San Bartolomeo di Fiesole, which belonged to the Lateran Congregation of the Austin Canons, to begin a novitiate that culminated in his profession sometime in the early part of 1518. From Fiesole he went to Padua, where he distinguished himself both as a scholar and as a preacher. Of the scholastic doctors, he was most familiar with the works of Thomas Aquinas and Gregory of Rimini. But he found himself driven beyond the medieval doctors to the early Fathers and behind the Fathers to Scripture itself. In order to master the Old Testament as well as the New, he studied Hebrew with a Jewish physician in Bologna. His work did not pass unnoticed or unrewarded. He was made abbot of Spoleto and in 1537 was promoted to the important post of prior at the monastery of Saint Peter ad Aram in Naples.

Naples marked a turning point for Peter Martyr. The man who left Naples in the spring of 1540 for Ravenna was not the same man who had taken charge at Saint Peter's in 1537. In Naples he read for the first time the writings of the Protestant reformers, especially Zwingli, Bucer, and Melanchthon. He also met and was influenced by Juan de Valdès, who, though he remained a Catholic, nevertheless taught ideas that were not greatly different from themes prominent in Protestant thought, especially his stress on justification by faith.[2] Other evangelical Catholics, such as the Capuchin Bernardino Ochino,[3] and the friend of Cardinal Pole, the poet Marcantonio Flaminio, gathered around Valdès in Naples. Valdès's lectures on 1 Corinthians stimulated Peter Martyr to give lectures of his own on that epistle at the monastery.

Martyr's new theological orientation and his immersion in the writings of Paul were developments not universally hailed by the citizens of Naples. The Theatines, with the support of Rebiba, the future cardinal of Pisa, registered complaints against the abbot of Saint Peter's. His exegesis of 1 Corinthians 3:11–13, which suggested that Paul did not have purgatory in mind when he used the image of salvation by fire, so angered his enemies that he was forbidden to preach by the viceroy, Don Pedro de Toledo. Martyr appealed, naturally enough, to Rome, where he had powerful friends such as Contarini and Pole, who persuaded the pope to lift the ban.

In 1540 Martyr was chosen by the Austin Canons to serve as a visitor and was given wide powers to reform the order in Italy. His broom, as many Augustinians discovered to their dismay, swept clean. He even took part in the movement, eventually successful, to have the former rector general of the order banished—though not, as older scholarship thought, during his year as visitor.

In May 1541 Martyr was elected prior of Saint Frediano in Lucca, one of the most desirable appointments under the control of the Lateran Congregation. The prior of Saint Frediano's not only ruled over an important cloister but also exercised a kind of episcopal authority over half of the city of Lucca. Though, as a Florentine, Martyr had every reason to be apprehensive about an appointment to the rival city of Lucca, he soon won the hearts of his new colleagues by his zeal for reform. His reform efforts were not limited to morals and education, however, but extended to doctrine as well. It became increasingly clear that his theological sympathies were with Calvin, Zwingli, Bucer, and Melanchthon. It was only a matter of time before those sympathies would become apparent to the Inquisition as well. Finally, in 1542, after a prolonged crisis of conscience that extended over the summer months, Peter Martyr left Italy for Zurich.

Martyr stayed only briefly in Switzerland. In December 1542 he was selected through the good offices of Martin Bucer to succeed Capito as professor of theology in the city of Strasbourg. In Strasbourg, Martyr lectured on the Minor Prophets and the Pentateuch, illuminating his exegetical comments with insights from the Fathers. His careful method and his precise use of language made him a popular teacher. Though he was clearly influenced by Bucer in his views, he could never adopt Bucer's point of view that the road to Christian unity lay in the composition of ambiguous and imprecise theological formulae to which people of varying theological persuasions could subscribe. He did follow Bucer's example, however, when he married a former nun, Catherine Dammartin from Metz.

Martyr served as professor of Hebrew and Old Testament in Strasbourg from 1542 to 1547. The threat of the Interim, which later drove Bucer to leave Strasbourg for Cambridge, prompted Martyr to accept the invitation of Cranmer to come to England. In England he was appointed Regius Professor of Divinity at Oxford and made a canon of Christ Church. At Oxford he was swept into the controversies raging over the Lord's Supper, taking part in a famous disputation in 1549 with Tresham, Chedsey, and Phillips.[4]

Though there were still significant differences between the Lutherans and the Reformed on the Continent, there were nevertheless certain points on which both parties were able to agree over against the common enemy in Rome. The Protestant reformers agreed, for example, that the Lord's Supper is not a sacrifice.[5] It is not something that the church offers to God. It is something God offers to the church. To talk about re-sacrifice or unbloody re-presentation of the sacrifice of Christ to the Father seemed to the Protestants to undercut the once-for-allness of the cross. In the Lord's Supper, as in justification, the Christian is one who receives, not one who offers.

The reformers were also able to agree that there is no transformation of the elements into the body and blood of Christ. The doctrine of transubstantiation is categorically denied, by Lutherans as well as by Zwinglians. Nevertheless, there is some doctrine of real presence, even for Zwingli. The Lord's Supper is not simply a memorial meal, in which the church celebrates and reflects on a past event. It is an event itself. Christ the host is present, either by his Spirit (the Reformed tradition) or in his post-Easter body (the Lutheran tradition). Nevertheless, the bread remains bread, the wine, wine.

Furthermore, the Protestants stressed the importance of living faith. Faith does not make Christ objectively present, as if faith could conjure him into existence in the elements. Christ is truly offered to the church together with the elements for Zwingli, in and through the elements for Luther, Melanchthon, Bucer, Calvin, and Martyr. This offering takes place whether one believes or not. Nevertheless, if one does not receive the elements in living faith, the consequences of that unbelief rob one, at the very least, of all benefit from participation. For Luther unbelievers eat and drink the body and blood of Christ, but they do so to their own damnation. God does his strange, rather than his proper, work in the faithless. For Calvin and Peter Martyr there is a difference between offering and receiving. Christ is offered to the church in the Eucharist, but only faith receives him.

Finally, the Protestants reinterpreted the Lord's Supper in view of their new understanding of the centrality of the Word of God. The Eucharist is a *verbum visibile*, a visible Word of God. There is really for the Protestants only one means of grace, the Word. But this Word takes many forms, in Scripture, in preaching, and in the Eucharist. The Eucharist does not offer the church something that the church does not have when it trusts the Word of God in Scripture and proclamation, but it offers the church another mode or form of participation in that Word. The Eucharist is another form of the personal encounter with God in his Word. What is mediated to the Christian is not a substance or power but simply Christ himself.

Still there were disagreements between the Lutherans and Reformed parties in Europe. These differences may, for the most part, be traced to differences in Christology; that is, to different views of Jesus Christ. The classic statement of the disagreements between the Lutheran and the Reformed was hammered out during the course of the colloquy between Luther and Zwingli at Marburg in 1529. Though the importance of this confrontation must not be minimized, it must also not be exaggerated. Increasingly, after the death of Zwingli, the Reformed tradition moved in the direction of the middle ground first occupied by Bucer and later defended by Calvin and Peter Martyr.

There were six issues that surfaced at Marburg. There was disagreement, first of all, over the meaning of the verb *is* in the words of institution, "this is my body." For Zwingli, spokesman of the Reformed, *is* means "signifies" and indicates that the words of institution should be understood metaphorically.[6] There are many such metaphors in the Bible. When Jesus says that he is the Good Shepherd, the Vine, the Door of the sheepfold, he is clearly employing metaphorical language. Luther did not deny, of course, that the Bible sometimes uses *is* in a metaphorical sense.[7] He challenged the Reformed, however, to demonstrate not the possibility but the necessity of a metaphorical interpretation in the context of the words of institution. Possibility and necessity are not the same thing, and until the Reformed can demonstrate the necessity of a metaphorical interpretation, Luther was content to abide by the word *is*, which safeguards, as the verb *signifies* does not, the mystery of the real presence.

The second disagreement revolved around the interpretation of John 6, especially the words "the flesh profits nothing." Zwingli was very much influenced by a Neoplatonic view of human beings, which divided them into a higher "soul" or "spirit" and a lower "body" or "flesh." He read the words "the flesh profits nothing" with these Platonic spectacles and concluded that external or physical things have no effect on the higher nature of men and women. The Holy Spirit must act directly on that higher nature and cannot be mediated by physical elements. Therefore, the Lord's Supper cannot be a means of grace but belongs rather to the response of the church to the grace given to it immediately by the Spirit. Luther rejected this Neoplatonic reading of John and concluded that John meant by flesh very much what Paul meant. It is a description of the self-centered self, which stubbornly refuses to commit itself in absolute dependence to its Creator. Therefore, John 6 is irrelevant for discussions of the Lord's Supper and cannot be used as an argument against the mediation of grace by physical realities.

The Lutheran and the Reformed also found it impossible to agree on the meaning of the phrase "the right hand of the Father" in the Apostles' Creed. Here Luther and Zwingli exchanged roles, Luther defending a metaphorical interpretation of this article of the creed and Zwingli doggedly pumping for a literal understanding. Though the Reformed do not presume to suggest where heaven is, they believe that the right hand of the Father is a place in it. That is where the body of Christ is after the ascension. Because the body of Christ is a genuinely human body, and therefore finite, it cannot be at the right hand of the Father and on the altar of the church at the same time. Luther, however, drawing on his knowledge of the Old Testament, argued that the right hand of the Father is a metaphorical way of saying "wherever the Father reigns." Since the sovereignty of God is universal, that means that the right hand of the Father is everywhere.

This disagreement led to still another. If the right hand of the Father is everywhere, then the risen Christ is no longer subject to the categories of space and time. To confess that the body is at the right hand of the Father is to affirm that it is ubiquitous. It shares in the attribute of omnipresence that belongs to divinity. For Zwingli (and Calvin[8] and Martyr who follow him) the divine nature is free from the limitations of space and time, but not the human nature. This means that even when the body of Christ is in one place, his divine nature may be in many places at once, doing all the things that deity normally does. The Lutherans rejected this idea, summarized in the formula of Calvin that *etiam extra carnem*, "also outside the flesh," the divine nature of Jesus Christ was at work.[9] The Lutherans called this teaching the *extra Calvinisticum*,[10] the Calvinist "outside," though they might just as well have called it the *extra Zwinglianum*, since Zwingli taught it first.

That is not to say that Calvin or Peter Martyr believed that Christ was present in the Lord's Supper only in his divine nature. It was the flesh, after all, that was crucified and raised for human salvation and that must be present, in some way, if faith is to be nourished. Calvin could affirm—with the agreement of Peter Martyr—that Christ was substantially present in the Lord's Supper. But he reinterpreted the word *substance* in that affirmation. The substance of the humanity is its *virtus*, its power and effect for human salvation. That power and effect is present, even if the body itself is at the right hand of the Father. It is made present for the church by the divine Spirit.

Luther and Zwingli could not agree whether unbelievers eat the body and blood of Christ. Luther said yes. Unbelievers eat the body and blood of Christ, though they eat and drink to their own damnation. Zwingli and Calvin said no. Without faith there is no participation in the body and blood.

Peter Martyr attempted to make the Reformed position clear by appealing to the doctrine of the *duplex os,* or "twofold mouth." This doctrine rests on the distinction between the sacrament and the thing of the sacrament, or, put more simply, between the sign and the thing signified. The sign in the sacrament of the Eucharist is the bread and wine; the thing signified is the body and blood of Christ. A physical mouth is all one needs to eat bread and wine. An unbeliever—or even a mouse—has the ability to eat bread and wine. But to eat the body and blood of Christ one needs another kind of mouth, namely faith. Unbelievers eat the bread and wine, but they do not eat the body and blood, because they lack the faculty of reception. More is needed to participate in Christ than teeth and a tongue. There is no communion where there is no faith.

A final disagreement between Zwingli and Luther centered on the question whether the church or the elements should be regarded as the true subject of the Lord's Supper. For Luther the answer was clear: the subject of the Lord's Supper is the elements of bread and wine. The body of Christ is present in, with, and under the elements of bread and wine, though the elements themselves are not transubstantiated. For Zwingli, however, the real subject was the church. There is a transubstantiation of the gathered community. Through the action of the Holy Spirit, the congregation that has assembled to celebrate the Lord's Supper undergoes a transubstantiation. It is transformed by the Holy Spirit into the body of Christ. In response to this act of divine grace, the community gives public thanks by participating in the Lord's Supper. As a joyful celebration of grace already given, as the response of faith to the gracious act of God, the Lord's Supper is most appropriately called a Eucharist (or Thanksgiving). The body of Christ is localized, not in the bread and wine, but in the congregation gathered around the elements. By participating in this sacrament, the church takes part in a feast that is an anticipation of the heavenly banquet to be celebrated in the kingdom of heaven at the end of time, and so proclaims the Lord's death until he comes. Interpreters have always stressed the past dimension of the Lord's Supper as the crucial one for Zwingli, who wanted to stress the once-for-allness of the cross—though memory is not so much an escape into the past as it is the faculty for making the past an aspect or dimension of the present, as real as the neighbor sitting next to one in the pew. But the future was equally important for him. The Lord's Supper is the sacrament of those who have, and who long for the fullness they do not yet have.

Peter Martyr, in agreement with Zwingli, kept the emphasis on the transformation of the congregation, which is brought into union with Christ through the sacrament. However, he broke with Zwingli's parallelism, which made the bestowal of grace a thing that happens alongside the celebration of the Eucharist rather than through it. By stressing the reality of physical elements as channels of grace, Bucer, Calvin, and Martyr demonstrated their indebtedness to Luther and their independence of Zwingli.

Peter Martyr is important for his rehabilitation of the idea of sacrifice within the framework of a Reformed doctrine of the Lord's Supper. He agreed with the other Reformers in rejecting the idea that the Lord's Supper is a sacrifice in the Roman Catholic sense, that it is an unbloody re-presentation to the Father of the sacrifice of Jesus Christ for the renewal of the forgiveness of sins. That is a propitiatory sacrifice, and all such propitiatory sacrifices have been rendered obsolete and ineffective by the unique and unrepeatable event of Calvary. Nevertheless, though Christians do not sacrifice Jesus Christ anew but simply receive him as a divine benefit, they are called on to sacrifice themselves in the response of faith. The letter to the Hebrews exists side by side in the New Testament with Romans 12:1. There is, in other words, a distinction to be made between eucharistic and propitiatory sacrifices. When the church, in response to divine grace and in dependence on it, gives alms, offers praise and thanksgiving, disciplines itself or loses itself in the service of men and women, it is offering God not a meritorious service that can expiate sin but a eucharistic sacrifice of praise and thanksgiving. The once-for-allness of the cross does not exclude such eucharistic sacrifices. On the contrary, it evokes them.

Along with Bucer, who was Regius Professor of Divinity at Cambridge, Martyr attempted to assist the course of the Reformation in England, advising Hooper about the place of vestments and Cranmer about the revision of the Book of Common Prayer. When Mary ascended the throne in 1553, Martyr resigned his post at Oxford and returned to Strasbourg. In his absence, however, the Lutherans had gained an influence in the city that they had not exercised prior to the publication of the Interim. He found himself in almost constant theological dispute with them, especially over the doctrine of the ubiquity of the body of Christ. His chief opponent among the Lutherans during the last years of his life was Johannes Brenz.

Finally, in 1556, he accepted an invitation from Bullinger to become professor of Hebrew in Zurich, a citadel the Lutherans had not yet penetrated. During the years he lived in Strasbourg, he had provided a refuge for exiles from the England of Mary Tudor. And so it was not surprising that when he moved to Zurich he took an important Marian exile, John Jewel, later bishop of Salisbury, with him. When Elizabeth replaced Mary on the throne of England in 1558, the exiles were free to return to their homeland. Martyr, however, maintained a correspondence with them and advised the Elizabethan clergy as he had earlier advised the Edwardian. He never yielded to the temptation to return to England, though he was invited to do so. To travel from Zurich to London was an arduous journey for a young man, much less for an old professor of Hebrew.

Peter Martyr did leave Zurich once. In 1561 he attended the colloquy between

Protestants and Roman Catholics held at Poissy under the sponsorship of the queen mother of France, Catherine de Medici. Poissy was not a success, and the toll the long trip had taken weakened his health still further. Shortly thereafter, on December 12, 1562, Peter Martyr Vermigli died, an exile in a foreign land. He was more important to his generation as a mediator than as an innovator. He mediated to the English Reformation the mature Reformed understanding of the Lord's Supper, born in Strasbourg and nurtured in Geneva. As a refugee himself, he formed an exiled generation of English clergy in the Calvinist tradition.

15

THEODORE BEZA
(1519–1605)

Eternal Predestination and
Divine Sovereignty

STRICTLY SPEAKING, Theodore Beza should be regarded as one of the third generation of Protestant reformers. He was born ten years after Calvin, the most eminent of the second-generation reformers, and lived into the middle of the first decade of the seventeenth century. Yet Beza, though he was a contemporary of such later Lutheran reformers as Flacius and Chemnitz, in a very real sense antedates them. There are two reasons for this.

In the first place, Beza's rise to prominence in the French Reformed movement was so rapid that he must be regarded as Calvin's coworker and contemporary and not merely successor. Though Beza lived for forty years beyond the death of Calvin, many of his most important contributions to the Reformed cause took place before Calvin's death, not the least of which was his participation in the famous colloquy at Poissy.

In the second place, the French Reformation blossomed somewhat later than the German. That is not to say that there were no French Protestants in the 1520s and 1530s. The Affair of the Placards, which jolted the French king out of his complacency concerning the growth of Protestantism in his dominions, decisively undercuts any such thesis. Nevertheless, the greatest burst of growth of Protestantism in France stretches from 1540 to 1572, when French Protestantism found in Calvin an intellectual leader who was the equal of the German theologians and in Geneva a protected center for the dissemination throughout France of a new theology.

Theodore Beza (or de Bèze) was born on June 24, 1519, at Vézelay in Burgundy into a family of the lesser nobility.[1] Beza's uncle, Nicholas, who was a member of the Parlement in Paris, was so taken with his nephew that he obtained the parents' permission to bring him to Paris in order to further his education. In 1528 Theodore left Paris for Orléans, where he studied with Melchior Wolmar, who is also famous as the teacher of Calvin. Though

Wolmar was a Protestant, he did not succeed in converting his brilliant young student from Burgundy. Nevertheless, when Wolmar accepted an invitation to Bourges, Beza followed him there.

In 1534, in the wake of the Affair of the Placards, Wolmar left Bourges in order to return to his native Germany. With Wolmar gone, Beza (like Calvin before him) yielded to the request of his father to study law and enrolled with the faculty of law at Orléans, where he spent the next four years. He had no particular interest in law, though he regarded it as a useful way to make a living. His real passion was literature, especially the Latin poets. After receiving his law degree on August 11, 1539, he returned to Paris, where in cooperation with his uncle he began his legal practice.

The years in Paris were happy ones. While he was busy as a lawyer, the legal profession was not such a jealous mistress that there was no time for literature. Furthermore, his family had arranged for him to receive the proceeds from two benefices amounting to seven hundred golden crowns a year, a tidy sum that provided a financial floor under his law practice. Freed from financial worry, he could take time when he wished to compose Latin poems of his own. In 1548, he published a collection of Latin poems, the *Juvenilia*, which won him a solid reputation as a Latin poet of considerable ability. Though he later composed many of the French paraphrases of the Psalms that, together with the French Psalms of Clément Marot, made up the text of the Huguenot Psalter,[2] he was always regarded as a greater stylist in Latin than in French.

In 1544 he became secretly engaged to Claudine Denosse, a young woman whose station in life was lower than his own. He promised to make the engagement public as soon as it was possible to do so. Beza was true to his promise and later took Claudine as his wife. They remained childless, however, and after Claudine died in 1588, Beza married again. His second wife, Geneviève del Piano, was the widow of a refugee from Genoa.

There is a remarkable similarity between Beza's conversion to Protestantism and the spiritual awakening of Huldrych Zwingli. Both became aware of their spiritual needs when suddenly struck down by a physical disability. Beza's conversion to Protestantism can be dated fairly accurately in 1548, following an attack of a serious illness. When Beza recovered, he broke off his law practice in Paris and emigrated with his fiancee Claudine to Geneva, where he was welcomed by Calvin, whom he had come to know when he was a student in the home of Melchior Wolmar.

Beza's abilities as an exegete and theologian were instantly made use of by the Protestant reformers in the French-speaking regions of Geneva and Lausanne. Pierre Viret saw to it that Beza was called to Lausanne as professor of Greek at the Lausanne Academy in 1549, the year following his flight to Geneva. Geneva, however, was not content to lose the services of such a promising young man and in 1559 called him as professor of theology at the Geneva Academy. He remained in Geneva until his death, serving as professor of theology from 1559 until 1599 and as rector from 1559 to 1563. He also became a pastor of the church in Geneva (1559–1605) and the moderator of its company of pastors at the death of Calvin (1564–80).

While other reformers wrote as much as or more than Beza, few could claim to have such a varied literary corpus. In addition to the Psalms and Latin poems already mentioned, he wrote dramas, satires, polemical treatises, Greek and French grammars, biographies, and political treatises. He even edited an annotated text of the Greek New Testament and bequeathed to Cambridge University one of the most valuable of the ancient manuscripts of the New Testament, the *Codex Bezae*.

Unlike Brenz, Beza was not a tolerant man and took the more stringent attitude of the German Swiss toward the Anabaptists and other left-wing reformers. One of his most famous writings, published in 1554, was the book *De Haereticis a Civili Magistratu Puniendis*, a defense of the execution of the anti-Trinitarian heretic Michael Servetus at Geneva in 1553. Beza also shared the attitude, foreign to Luther and the first generation of magisterial reformers, that Christians may not only resist but even overthrow a tyrannical ruler. His treatise *De Jure Magistratuum*, written at the time of the Saint Bartholomew's Day massacre of Protestants in 1572, was the most explicit statement of the Huguenot belief in the right of revolution for religious reasons.

There seems to be no end to his polemical treatises defending the polity and doctrine of the church in Geneva. Against Morély, who argued for a kind of congregationalist polity, Beza defended the presbyterian polity of Geneva.[3] Against Joachim Westphal and the other Lutherans who attacked the Reformed understanding of the Lord's Supper with its stress on the importance of the doctrine of the ascension, Beza wrote a carefully reasoned apologetic for the Calvinist position. When Sebastian Castellio attacked predestination and Bernardino Ochino the doctrine of the Trinity, their arguments were met and refuted by Beza.

Catholics fared little better in their assault on the theology of Geneva. Beza attacked the eucharistic theology of Claude de Sainte, burlesqued the person as well as the teaching of the heretic-baiter Pierre Lizet, and crossed swords with Johannes Cochlaeus, better known for his scurrilous gossip-mongering attacks on Luther. In view of Beza's gifts for satire, an opponent of the French reformation who wished to attack the teaching of the Calvinist movement hesitated before committing himself to print. There was a very real danger of coming off second best.

Beza's noble family connections and his background in law made him an obvious choice to represent Geneva and the French Protestant movement in the sensitive negotiations that Geneva carried on with the Germans, the Swiss, and the French. The most famous of these negotiations was the Colloquy of Poissy, which was convened on July 31, 1561, and aimed at the peaceful settlement of the religious differences between the Protestants and the Roman Catholics in France. In addition to Beza and the other Protestant delegates from Switzerland, there were eleven Reformed pastors from France, including such important ministers as Augustin Marlorat and Nicholas des Gallars. Opposing the Reformed delegates were the French bishops under the chairmanship of Cardinal de Tournon. The king, who was still scarcely more than a child, and the queen mother, Catherine de Medici, were present at the debate.

The colloquy was not a success. The Protestants were not given seats but were forced to plead their case while standing behind the bar at one end of the meeting room. The bishops, who had tried to delay the colloquy and who were uneasy about exposing the royal family to Protestant teaching, interrupted the opening address of Beza at that point where he denied the doctrine of transubstantiation. The disturbance, though quelled, was curiously prophetic of the outcome of the negotiations. The negotiations foundered on the doctrine of the Lord's Supper. And the attempt of Beza to show that it was not the fact of real presence but the manner that divided Reformed and Roman Catholic did not receive a sympathetic hearing by the members of the French hierarchy.

Nevertheless, if the colloquy was not a success, it was not a total failure. The Protestants had pled their case before the royal family over the protests and opposition of the French episcopate. The stirring address of Theodore Beza before the French king, an address that was immediately printed, was undeniable evidence of the fact. Furthermore, the colloquy did lead, in January 1562, to the edict that granted the French Protestants recognition and a degree of freedom. Though Beza had not succeeded in bridging the gap between Protestants and Roman Catholics in France, he did not return to Geneva with completely empty hands.

Beza's return to Geneva did not mark the end of his relationship to Protestantism in France. He remained the principal adviser of Gaspard de Coligny and the French princes who led the armies of the Huguenots in the wars of religion that wracked France in the latter half of the sixteenth century. He also played an important role in the intra-ecclesiastical life of France, struggling for a presbyterian form of government against the more congregational polity that marked much of French Protestantism. At La Rochelle he even presided over the last national synod of the French Reformed church held before the traumatic experience of the Saint Bartholomew's Day massacre.

Theologically, Beza was less original than Calvin, whose teaching he attempted faithfully to expound. Beza was not in marked disagreement with Calvin over any theological issue, and there has been a tendency on the part of many scholars to regard Beza's theology as nothing more than an echo of Calvin's. In recent years scholars have debated whether this opinion is justified. Some have argued that there is a sense in which Calvin's theology undergoes a subtle transformation at Beza's hands, a transformation all the more difficult to detect because it was not intended.[4]

Such historians concede that it is not easy to explain how Beza, using the same language and theological formulations as Calvin, nevertheless managed to say something different. There are, of course, some explicit differences that are not difficult to identify. Beza, unlike Calvin, argued that God imputes the guilt of Adam's sin to all of Adam's progeny. It is not a major difference between Beza and Calvin, but it does exist.

From their viewpoint a more serious difference emerged over the doctrine of atonement. Beza, who was somewhat more interested in the logical consistency of an argument than Calvin, who at times preferred simply to follow what he regarded as the surprising logic of Scripture, allowed the doctrine of election to qualify the doctrine of the atonement. According to Beza, Christ died only for the elect.[5] While Calvin may have entertained this idea, only Beza flatly stated it.

A third difference appears to these historians to emerge over the doctrine of justification. Calvin regarded justification as both the forgiveness of sins for the sake of Christ and as imputation, though he laid greater stress on the forgiveness of sins. Beza, however, took up the distinction that he found in the Lutheran theologian Flacius between the active and passive obedience of Christ. The active obedience refers to Christ's whole life of choosing and performing the will of God as an obedient Son in his Father's house. Passive obedience, on the other hand, refers to Christ's willing submission to death on the cross for the sake of sinners. The two parts of justification were tied by Beza to the twofold obedience of Christ. Justification is the forgiveness of sins on the basis of the passive obedience of Christ and the imputation to the sinner of the active obedience.[6] This linking of justification to the twofold obedience of Christ becomes a common position of Reformed theologians in the century that follows.

The heart of the controversy over Beza has centered on alleged differences over the doctrine of predestination. Because the argument over predestination has been very influential, it is useful here to examine the problem in detail. The key to the difference between Calvin and Beza lies not so much in the language they employ as in the larger theological context within which they viewed the doctrine of predestination.

The historians who stress the difference between Calvin and Beza argue that predestination is clearly the nerve center of Beza's theology. For many years it was believed to be the center of Calvin's theology as well, partly because Calvin's theology was read by later generations with the spectacles of Beza. Predestination for Calvin must be seen as a partial doctrine that is not complete in itself but that throws light on other doctrines. It is, in other words, not an independent doctrine but, rather, a subdivision of the doctrines of justification and of the church.

In 1559, in his last and definitive edition of the *Institutes*, Calvin takes the doctrine of predestination out of the context of providence, where it had traditionally been discussed, and moves it to a new location. In this edition of the *Institutes*, predestination follows justification and precedes the doctrine of the church. This is evidence, so some historians argued, that Calvin viewed the doctrine not speculatively but confessionally. It springs out of the surprise of the elect that they believe when many fine people do not. The context of the church, furthermore, establishes the priority of election over reprobation. Calvin was interested in explaining the mystery of faith, not of unbelief. He had no intention of speculating about the fate of the reprobate.

Of course, election and reprobation are of the same weight in the sense that both are acts of the divine will. God actively rejects some men and women; God does not simply permit them to be lost. But election and reprobation are not really of the same weight, when one considers the context in which they appear. Wedged between justification and the church, the positive side of predestination (election) and not the negative side (reprobation) were what was stressed. For Calvin, the context made the difference.

The historians who see sharp differences between Calvin and Beza argue that Beza took the regressive step of moving predestination back into its traditional context of providence.[7] Predestination became thereby a logical and necessary consequence of Beza's doctrine of God. If one knows the attributes of God, one can deduce from them the whole plan of salvation, including the necessity of atonement by the God-man (which historians must concede Beza never does). The drama of redemption stands from first to last under Beza's speculative doctrine of predestination.

In this view the leitmotif of Beza's theology is the doctrine of the sovereign will of God. God has willed everything that comes to pass in human history, including the fall of Adam and Eve into sin (a position that is called supralapsarianism and that runs counter to even the radically Augustinian theology of many medieval Augustinians—but not, historians must again concede, counter to Calvin).[8] Because predestination is no longer treated in the context of justification and the church, election and reprobation become of equal weight in all respects and not merely in some. Since God is glorified by the reprobation of some men and women as well as by the election of others, it becomes almost a matter of indifference to God (so some historians argue) which fate befalls a human being. Divorced from the context of faith and of the surprise of the elect, predestination begins to live a life of its own and is no longer a partial doctrine. Indeed, one sees in the theology of Beza the worst fears of Melanchthon come to pass. Predestination became in the hands of this speculative theologian a form of philosophical determinism, scarcely distinguishable from the Stoic doctrine of fate. It is Beza, therefore, and not Calvin, who becomes the father of the hyper-Calvinism of Reformed Orthodoxy.

Recent studies have tended to undercut the alleged differences between Beza and Calvin, whose eucharistic theology is virtually identical with Beza's and whose doctrine of predestination seems to impartial observers remarkably similar in detail. Even the argument from context has come under searching scrutiny. Indeed, Calvin may have been influenced by Melanchthon to move predestination out of the doctrine of God in Book I of the *Institutes* and to treat it after he had discussed justification in Book III.[9] After all, Paul discussed election in Romans 9 only after he had first discussed justification in Romans 4 and 5. Melanchthon, who was eager to incorporate in his theology the methods of Paul, followed suit in his *Loci Communes*. Calvin in his turn may have emulated Melanchthon by following the *methodus Pauli* in his 1559 edition of the *Institutes*. In fact, on closer inspection almost all of the virtues and weaknesses attributed to Calvin's teaching on election can with equal justice be attributed to Beza's as well. At the hands of each theologian the doctrine of election can be by turns speculative or confessional, comforting or terrifying.

The attack on Beza as a speculative theologian who betrayed the insights of the Reformation is part of a longstanding tendency by Protestant theologians to identify the figures of the later Reformation with the development of Protestant Orthodoxy (a development generally to be deplored) and to describe the figures of the earlier Reformation as creative, flexible, and not yet Orthodox (and therefore generally to be hailed and freshly appropriated by postliberal theologians). The tendency to deplore the return of Protestant thinkers to Aristotelian metaphysics and to regard the introduction of scholasticism into Protestant theology as an abandonment of the insights of the Reformation may, after all, prove to be historically naive and to rest on misconceptions concerning scholasticism and the Reformation itself.

The last years of Beza's life were spent quietly. He sought to promote the cause of unity between Lutherans and Reformed at the Colloquy of Montbéliard in 1586 and defended the doctrine of supralapsarian predestination at the Colloquy of Bern in 1587. He taught at the university and kept up an active correspondence. Much to his disappointment he saw Henry IV, leader of the Huguenots, convert to Catholicism in 1593 in spite of repeated exhortations.

The Catholics had not forgotten their old adversary and tried a new strategy with him. Francis de Sales, promising a pension and financial security, attempted to reconvert Beza to the faith of his ancestors. His attempts, though kindly received, were unsuccessful, in spite of rumors circulated by the Jesuits heralding the return of Beza to the Roman fold.

When Beza died in 1605, he had outlived by many years all the Reformers who had labored to establish the Protestant Reformation in Geneva and France. Calvin, Pierre Viret, William Farel, Bullinger, Bucer, and Peter Martyr were all dead. For most of the citizens in Geneva in 1605, they were only names, not personal memories. Beza was the last living link between the turbulent era of Calvin and Melanchthon and the new age of Protestant Orthodoxy. His death, therefore, signaled more than the close of a chapter in Geneva; it marked the end of an epoch in the history of Europe.

The Reformed Tradition

IV

Radical Reformers

16

ANDREAS BODENSTEIN VON CARLSTADT
(1480–1541)
Reformation without "Tarrying for Anie"

THERE IS PROBABLY NO figure in the sixteenth century more difficult for historians to classify than Luther's onetime colleague at the University of Wittenberg, Andreas Bodenstein von Carlstadt.[1] No label seems to fit him exactly. He
rejected infant baptism, but was not, except in the loosest possible sense of the
term, an Anabaptist. He appropriated mystical terminology and ideas from
the later Middle Ages but managed to filter out from that complex of thought
certain presuppositions about human nature and the act of justification that
could not be reconciled with the insights of the Lutheran Reformation. He
was driven by Luther to the study of Augustine, only to become in certain
respects a more faithful Augustinian than Luther himself. Luther charged
him, not unjustly, with a bent toward legalism and an obscuring of Christian
freedom by an emphasis on the Mosaic codes and by a selective universalizing
of the example of Jesus. At the same time, Carlstadt had a spiritualist streak
that manifested itself in his off-again, on-again opposition to scholarly pur-
suits and his occasional belittling of the "external works" of hearing and reading Scripture.

To complicate the picture still more, Carlstadt could and did in fact undergo
sudden and dramatic changes of mind on important issues, even if it meant re-
versing a position passionately defended sometime before. Nevertheless, the
charges of "instability" and "fanaticism" once leveled against him seem from
the perspective of the twentieth century exaggerated. Carlstadt did not lack
theological acumen or originality. What he seemed to lack most was Anglo-
Saxon common sense, the ability to know when a theological point had been
made and adequately defended without wearing his listener's patience thin
with lengthy quotation and tiresome repetition; a sensitivity to all the colors of
the spectrum between black and white; and a willingness to compromise, if
need be, so that the main point might not be lost in a stubborn battle over

trifles. Because Carlstadt was willing to rush in where the bravest angels were unwilling to tread, even gingerly, and because he pressed for the reform of the Reformation before the Reformation itself was firmly established, he was exiled for the better part of his life to the sidelines, where he watched, rather than guided, the course of events. He became a theological gadfly who stimulated (and on occasion irritated) the major reformers, forcing them to clarify their positions in the light of his critiques or counterproposals.

Carlstadt took his name from the Franconian village in which he was born. He studied at the Universities of Erfurt and Cologne and was called in 1505 as a professor at the newly founded University of Wittenberg. He began his theological career as a Thomist, though he also lectured on Duns Scotus while he was at Wittenberg and was influenced on certain points by him. Unlike Luther, however, Carlstadt was not influenced in any important way by the theology of late medieval nominalism. In 1510 he received his doctorate in theology at Wittenberg and was chosen to be the archdeacon of the castle church. Two years later Carlstadt became the dean of the theological faculty and in one of the more ironic coincidences in history administered the doctoral oath to Martin Luther.

Carlstadt was not satisfied to remain the archdeacon of the castle church but hoped to become its provost as well. To further his ambition, he dropped his duties at the university and the castle church (after making only the most desultory attempt to arrange for a substitute to take his place in his absence) and set out for Italy. In a very short time, he managed to earn a doctorate in both canon and civil law at the University of Siena. But the university and the elector were furious with Carlstadt for his flagrant neglect of his duties and forced him to return by threatening to cut off his stipend.

Luther and Carlstadt clashed for the first time at a disputation held on September 25, 1516, in connection with the promotion of Bartholomew Feldkirchen to the second theological degree, the *Sententiarius*. In the course of the discussion, Luther argued that the treatise on the *True and False Penitence*, which was customarily ascribed to Augustine, was not genuine and must be regarded as pseudo-Augustinian. Carlstadt heatedly contested Luther's opinion, though he was at a distinct disadvantage during the debate. While Carlstadt had studied Aquinas and Scotus, he had never devoted himself to a thorough study of the writings of Augustine. Still smarting from the debate, Carlstadt bought a complete set of Augustine's works while visiting in Leipzig and set about to fill the lacuna in his theological education. Shortly after his purchase of Augustine's writings, he read the strongly Augustinian treatise on predestination, which had just been published by his former colleague at the University of Wittenberg, Johannes von Staupitz.[2] The double impact of his own independent study of Augustine and of the contemporary reinterpretation of Augustine by Staupitz led Carlstadt to a decisive turning point in his theological development.

The first public evidence of Carlstadt's new theological orientation was the issuing of 151 Theses on grace,[3] which were published on April 26, 1517, and in which Carlstadt not only rejected the Pelagianizing tendencies of Scotus and Ockham but even took a more radically Augustinian position than Aquinas and Capreolus had been willing to defend. The 151 Theses were followed in their turn by a commentary on Augustine's *The Spirit and the Letter*,[4] which Carlstadt, interestingly enough, dedicated to Staupitz. The commentary represented a break on several important points with Carlstadt's Thomistic past, though it would not be completely accurate to call it a Lutheran document. Carlstadt was a fellow traveler, rather than a disciple of Luther in a strict sense.

The problem that troubled Carlstadt in his commentary on Augustine is a familiar one in Western theology: How can one fulfill the law of God? It was clear for Carlstadt as it had not been before that the scholastic teaching of a disposition for the reception of grace in which the good works of the sinner are regarded as merits of congruity cannot be reconciled with the theology of Augustine.[5] The fulfillment of the law of God is dependent at every point—not just at certain ones—on the gracious assistance of God by his Spirit. Apart from the infusion of divine love, the law remains impossible of fulfillment. The law must be internalized before it can be kept.

The problem of law and grace, however, shaded rather quickly for Carlstadt into the problem of Word and Spirit.[6] The law kills, not simply because it lays demands on the sinner he cannot fulfill but, even more important, because it is an external code. There is something death-dealing about the external letter as letter. This understanding led Carlstadt to a devaluation of external and visible words such as preaching and the sacraments. Scripture is not, strictly speaking, the Word of God but, rather, a witness to the Word, an outward and visible sign of an inward and spiritual reality. This devaluation of external signs did not prevent Carlstadt from insisting puritanically on the immediate fulfillment in the church of legal prescriptions from the Old Testament or from pounding his theological adversaries into insensibility with a proof-text. Carlstadt was usually careful to test personal experience against the criterion of Holy Scripture,[7] even though he was suspicious of a religion that is excessively bookish. One should know God, as Carlyle once remarked, "otherwise than by hearsay" and should not be forced to prove the genuineness of one's faith by an appeal to the Greek original.

Carlstadt now became Luther's ally in the controversy over indulgences that was sweeping Europe. Never one to wait for others to seize the initiative, Carlstadt composed 380 Theses against the famous professor from Ingolstadt, Johann Eck. Eck responded with a challenge to a debate in Leipzig. Though the invitation was issued to Carlstadt, Eck hoped to draw Luther into the discussion before the disputation was over and to expose his erroneous ideas to public scorn in a face-to-face confrontation.

The Leipzig Disputation was not a great success for Carlstadt. To begin with, the cart in which he was traveling was involved in a small accident at the city gate, and he was unceremoniously dumped on the ground. Though the physician bled him twice, he was clearly shaken by the accident and was not at his best form in the debate. Furthermore, when Carlstadt tried to substantiate his argument by reading lengthy quotations from the Fathers (for which at times he vainly searched until aided by Melanchthon), Eck, who had a prodigious memory and no need to rely on books—or, at least, less need—ridiculed Carlstadt and finally succeeded in getting the regent of the debate to rule against the use of books during the disputation. Eck treated Carlstadt like a sparring partner in a preliminary bout, rather than like a serious contender for the title in the main event. Carlstadt, who was as quick to feel a slight as any man, returned home to write a vitriolic attack on Eck entitled *Against the Dumb Ass and Stupid Little Doctor*. Eck, who was not noted for unusual charity toward his enemies, responded by adding Carlstadt's name to the papal bull directed against Luther.

While Luther was in hiding at the Wartburg after the Diet of Worms, Carlstadt went to Denmark to aid Christian II in establishing the Protestant Reformation in his territories. When his efforts to establish the Reformation there miscarried, Carlstadt beat a hasty retreat to Wittenberg. His return was all the more embarrassing, since he had only been gone for six weeks. His colleagues had scarcely begun to miss him when he reappeared, frustrated and a little out of breath.

For a brief period in his life prior to his temporary exile to the Wartburg, Luther became interested in the teaching of certain late medieval mystics. In 1516 he edited and published a new edition of the *Theologia Deutsch*. He was also appreciative of the mystical elements in the teaching of Johannes von Staupitz and commended his treatise *On the Love of God*, which was published in 1518. The story of the relationship of Luther to late medieval mysticism is a complex one, and not all the threads in that relationship have as yet been unraveled.[8] What it is important to note is that just as Luther and Staupitz introduced Carlstadt to Augustine so also they introduced him to German mysticism.

Like Augustine, Carlstadt pointed to the sovereign will of God as the ordering principle of all reality. But now he began to define the relationship of the human will to that principle in the language of German mysticism. The proper relationship of the human will to the will of God is a relationship of *Gelassenheit*, a total abandonment of the self, a surrender of everything the soul is and has to the divine will.[9] Christ is the example of this self-surrender, which Christians are called to imitate, and he is the means by which the possibility of this imitation is mediated to the committed disciple. Above all, the Christian is summoned to abandon the personal pronouns *I* and *mine*, to surrender self-will, and to yield to the will of God. While for Carlstadt Christ is important as an example and as the atoning Lamb who made discipleship possible, he tends to view Christ functionally in a way more characteristic of Augustine than of Staupitz. The will of God is for Carlstadt the central thing, and the life and death of Jesus Christ are viewed only as means to that end.

Although Carlstadt was profoundly influenced by German mysticism, it is clear that he did not expect an ontological union with the being of God. Mystical union for Carlstadt, as for Staupitz, was limited to a union of wills, not of essences.[10] He did not wish to lose his personal identity, but only to surrender his independence vis-à-vis the will of God.

Carlstadt was also too much under the spell of Augustine to accept the teaching of Eckhart and Tauler about a "spark of the soul," some inner undefiled citadel in the human personality that has escaped the baneful effects of the fall and is the sine qua non for any union of the soul with God in this life or the next. When Carlstadt spoke of some inner flame or spark in the soul, he was speaking not of a human faculty that had mysteriously escaped the fall but of the first infusion of divine love that awakens in the sinner the answering response of love.[11] The spark is a gift of divine grace, not a residual capacity of nature. On this point as well, Staupitz and Carlstadt were in agreement. Carlstadt had not repudiated the scholastic teaching of preparation for grace and merits of congruity only to introduce it all over again under the auspices of the mystics.

In Luther's absence from Wittenberg, the pace of the Reformation began to quicken. Carlstadt, who had at first hung back and urged caution in the enactment of new reforms, suddenly changed his mind and catapulted to the leadership of those who demanded the introduction of more radical measures. In December 1521, he announced his intention of marrying Anna von Mochau, who was at least twenty-five years younger than him. Three weeks later, on Christmas Day, after having been expressly forbidden by the court of the elector to do so, Carlstadt celebrated Communion in both kinds in German, while dressed as a layman. In order to reach the laity more effectively, he began to preach in the city church, where Luther ordinarily preached when he was in Wittenberg—all this in the face of restrictions and prohibitions to the contrary. In a famous treatise *On the Putting Away of Pictures*,[12] Carlstadt demanded the abolition of images from the church and the reform of the poor law. Carlstadt's reformation program was a mixture of wise and overdue plans for reform together with shrill and utopian cries for the immediate restoration of Eden. Christians are bound by the law of Moses, which forbids graven images in worship. The absolute demands of the Old Testament must be put into effect immediately without faithless worrying about the consequences. Carlstadt was not interested in what ethicists call middle axioms, approximations of the absolute under the fallen conditions that obtain in the world, or in stages along the way to the attainment of his ultimate goal. He had no patience with prudent calculations of less and more. He lived under the claim of the absolute and thought, mistakenly, that the absolute is capable of simple historical fulfillment. Carlstadt was aided in his radical reform by the so-called Zwickau prophets Storch and Drechsel, who opposed infant baptism and who claimed to be the recipients of private revelations.

Against the advice of his friends, Luther returned to Wittenberg to counteract the excesses of the Zwickau prophets and the iconoclasm of Carlstadt. Luther was not opposed to serving Communion in both kinds to the laity or to removing the statues of the saints from the church, though he had a pastoral concern that the faith of the weak not be needlessly damaged by the reckless introduction of liturgical changes or by imposing on troubled consciences burdens that God did not require. What Luther opposed was Carlstadt's legalism, his replacement of what Luther and Carlstadt both regarded as unscriptural traditions and obligations of the medieval Catholic church with puritanical prohibitions, destroying in the process the true freedom of the Christian. The dangerous thing is not the physical presence of images in the church but that the heart should trust in them. If the heart trusts in God alone through the gospel and is weaned from any lesser trust, then the presence or absence of images in the church is an indifferent matter. One can be an idolater in a bare room as easily as in a Gothic cathedral. Indeed, iconoclasm can be an even more insidious form of idolatry than the veneration of relics.

Carlstadt knew that he had been rebuked by Luther's *Invocavit* sermons,[13] but he was unrepentant. He put away the academic dress he was entitled to wear as a doctor of theology and of law and donned the simple garment of a peasant. He bought a farm near Wörlitz and is reported to have loaded manure onto a cart along with the other peasants. In 1523 he announced that he would no longer promote students to theological degrees, since Christians were commanded in the Gospels to call no man master. But while Carlstadt gave up the duties of academic life out of religious scruples, he did not give up his salary, a development that provoked unfavorable comment among people not afflicted with similar scruples. Carlstadt found an interim way to reconcile his principles and his pocketbook by taking over the parish of Orlamünde, which was part of his responsibility at the castle church, and replacing the unpopular vicar, Glitzsch. In Orlamünde, he continued the reform program that had been interrupted in Wittenberg and, after a brief interval, wrote a number of his more important treatises. In 1524, Luther undertook a preaching mission in the valley of the Saale to reclaim it for the Wittenberg reformation. The mission met resistance on every hand, and when Luther and Carlstadt confronted each other in the Black Bear Inn at Jena, the meeting ended with Luther's throwing a golden guilder to Carlstadt, thereby serving public notice that the two men were henceforth to be regarded as enemies. The Saxon court had had enough of Carlstadt and, shortly after this confrontation in Jena, banished him from its territories.

In the same year Carlstadt was exiled from Orlamünde he wrote a dialogue on the sacrament of the Eucharist.[14] Like Zwingli and the Anabaptists, Carlstadt felt that the uniqueness of the atoning death of Jesus Christ could only be preserved by opposing both the Roman Catholic and the Lutheran understanding of the real presence and by viewing the Lord's Supper as a proclamation and reminder of a historical event that had taken place in the past.[15] But the theory he adopted to justify this understanding of the Eucharist was never widely adopted by other theologians and remained something of an oddity. Carlstadt argued that the pronoun *this* in the formula "this is my body" referred to the body of Jesus then present at the table rather than to the bread.[16] Similarly, when Jesus said "this is my blood" he was referring not to the cup before him on the table but to the crucifixion that was yet to take place and that had been promised by Moses and the prophets. By an unconvincing appeal to grammar, Carlstadt tried to sketch in the stage directions he felt were missing from the text of the Gospels. The theological point was an important one, defended by many other significant figures, but the argument supporting it was strained and lacked convincing power.

When the Peasants' War broke out in 1525, Carlstadt found refuge in the city of Rothenburg ob der Tauber. He was not an active participant in the rebellion, but his friendship for Thomas Müntzer and his unhappy custom of keeping company with rebels brought him under suspicion of the authorities. He was able to save his skin only through the intervention of Luther, who felt he had decisively answered Carlstadt's view of the law and the sacraments in his treatise *Against the Heavenly Prophets* but who had no desire to see him executed. Carlstadt was allowed to return to Saxony on the condition that he would keep a discreet silence. He managed to keep his promise for a while, but only for a while. He left Saxony for East Frisia, where he allied himself for a short time with Melchior Hoffman, the Anabaptist. In 1529 he tried without success to wangle an invitation to the Marburg colloquy.

His last years were spent in Switzerland. Zwingli appointed him to serve as the vicar of Altstatt, and in 1534 he was called to the chair of Old Testament in the University of Basel, once more exercising the calling he had repudiated ten years before. In alliance with the humanist Amerbach, Carlstadt threw himself into the battle for university reform. The university opposed the growing clericalism that reigned in Basel and sought to offset it. Carlstadt proposed a solution that not only reversed his earlier position on the validity of academic degrees but subordinated the pastoral ministry of the church to its teaching ministry. All clergy should become members of the faculty of the university and be subject to its discipline. Furthermore, teachers—and that included Myconius, who had succeeded Oecolampadius as the reformer of Basel—should take their doctoral degrees under him. Needless to say, this demand did not endear Carlstadt to Myconius. The controversy between Carlstadt and the Basel clergy came to an unexpected end in 1541 when Carlstadt contracted the plague. He died on Christmas Eve in the same year. He had sought to carry out a thoroughgoing reform of the Reformation without—to use Robert

Browne's phrase—"tarrying for anie." There is little doubt that his writings exercised an important influence on the early Anabaptist movement. Yet the dominant impression he has left on history is that of a man who, like Lear, "hath known himself but slenderly" and who therefore found it difficult to guard against those rash and impetuous acts that, ironically enough, thwarted his own ambitions and made his aspirations for reform even more difficult to attain.

17

CASPAR SCHWENCKFELD
(1489–1561)

The Renunciation of Structure

THERE WAS NOTHING IN Caspar Schwenckfeld's background or training to lead one to anticipate his decision to become a religious reformer. By education and experience he was a career diplomat rather than a theologian. Yet in spite of his unlikely qualifications he became one of the most vigorous and widely published representatives of the Protestant Reformation. His writings were so numerous that Melanchthon, with a touch of envy, once called him a *centimanus*, a man with a hundred hands.[1]

Schwenckfeld was born in 1489 at Ossig in Silesia to a distinguished German family that had lived in Silesia since the beginning of the thirteenth century. His childhood was spent in his castle home at Ossig, surrounded by gardens and forests of oak, white birch, and fir trees. When he was sixteen, he traveled to the Rhineland for his university education, studying the liberal arts at Cologne and canon law at Frankfurt.

He was a mild-mannered and soft-spoken man, able to keep his temper when others were losing theirs. Not surprisingly, he entered diplomatic service on his return from the university. He accompanied his employers on state visits, drafted official documents, and engaged in a variety of routine and humdrum activities connected with the administration of the political affairs of a small principality. He was a knight of the Teutonic Order and remained faithful to the vows of celibacy which he took, even after his conversion to Protestantism. Deafness put an abrupt end to his diplomatic career in 1523, when his hearing became so impaired that it made court life difficult for him to pursue.

While still an active diplomat, Schwenckfeld read his first book by Luther. Luther's writings intrigued him and drove him to a study of the Bible and the church fathers. Whatever time he could spare from his duties, he devoted to the sermons, pamphlets, and treatises of Luther, Erasmus, Tauler, and Ulrich von Hutten. This concentrated reading soon bore fruit. By 1521 at the latest Schwenckfeld was a committed Lutheran.

Schwenckfeld no sooner embraced the evangelical understanding of the gospel than he set about to convert others to it as well. He immersed himself in the work of a lay evangelist, citing 1 Corinthians 14:30–31 as justification for his audacity in assuming the office of preacher. His evangelistic work was so well received that he contemplated taking up the ministry as a vocation but decided, after devoting some thought to the question, that he could better serve the cause of the gospel by remaining a layman. He insisted that laymen as well as ministers had the right to preach.

His evangelistic preaching led to the conversion of many prominent Silesians, among them Duke Friedrich II of Liegnitz. Friedrich was the most powerful of the Silesian princes, and his conversion lent considerable prestige to the incipient evangelical movement. Schwenckfeld wrote a short treatise in the spring of 1524 criticizing the abuses in the evangelical party and urging the evangelical preachers not to forget to reform themselves in their zeal to reform the land. Duke Friedrich, obviously under the influence of Schwenckfeld, issued a mandate that put in the form of public law the reforms the Silesian reformer had suggested. The duke thus threw his influence behind Schwenckfeld in his attempt to make certain that the gains of the Reformation were not dissipated by an unreformed Protestantism.

These years of evangelistic activity were also years of theological reflection. The Lutheran theory of the Lord's Supper was rejected by Zwingli, who published his own views in 1525 in his *Commentary on the True and False Religion*. Oecolampadius and Bucer were convinced by Zwingli's reasoning and declared themselves in his favor. Johannes Brenz, on the other hand, allied himself with Luther by emphasizing the ubiquity of the body and insisting on the corporeal presence of the risen Christ in the bread and wine. Carlstadt, developing his own theory, argued that the *hoc* ("this") in the sentence *Hoc est corpus meum* ("This is my body") referred to the actual physical body of Jesus, not in the elements but standing beside the table at the Last Supper. According to Carlstadt, when Jesus uttered these words, he pointed to himself. Luther violently disagreed with Carlstadt and opposed him in his treatise *Against the Heavenly Prophets*. In this increasingly tense theological situation, the reformers in Silesia were asked to give their views on the Lord's Supper.

Schwenckfeld had not neglected to study the issues. The crucial passage in the New Testament for understanding the Lord's Supper was, it seemed to him, the sixth chapter of John. Since Schwenckfeld was a disciple of Luther, his first impulse was to ally himself with Luther in his defense of the bodily presence of Jesus Christ "in, with, and under" the sacrament. But Luther's position presented a difficult problem for Schwenckfeld. What about Judas? According to John 6:54, whoever eats the flesh of Christ and drinks his blood has eternal life. But this could hardly apply to Judas, who went directly out from the Lord's

Supper to the high priest in order to betray Jesus. The example of Judas disproves Luther's doctrine of the bodily presence of Christ in the sacrament, unless, of course, one can explain away what seemed to Schwenckfeld the plain meaning of John 6.

Schwenckfeld published his conclusions concerning the bodily presence of Christ in a pamphlet entitled *Twelve Questions or Arguments against Impanation*, and sent a copy to Luther.[2] Valentine Crautwald, the Silesian humanist and biblical scholar, was impressed by this pamphlet and inspired to study the question afresh. After an intense application of his energies to the biblical text, Crautwald came to a unique interpretation of the words of institution that, interestingly enough, he attributed to an act of divine revelation.[3] According to Crautwald, the words of institution should be reversed in the manner of a Hebrew transposition and interpreted pleonastically. That is to say, instead of reading the text in a normal manner as "This is my body," Crautwald read it as "My body is this," namely, the spiritual food and drink of John 6.[4] Schwenckfeld was impressed with Crautwald's interpretation of the text and immediately embraced it as his own. It avoided both a corporeal interpretation of the text, which was the outstanding characteristic of the Lutheran position, and the elision of the verb *is*, which was the outstanding characteristic of the Zwinglian position. It was no longer necessary to read "signifies" for "is" in order to avoid what Schwenckfeld felt to be the pitfalls of Lutheran literalism. One could take all the words of the formula seriously yet interpret the Supper spiritually. Or, as Schwenckfeld himself remarked concerning Crautwald's interpretation, "the *hoc* remains *hoc*, the *est*, *est*, and the *corpus*, *corpus*."[5]

Luther did not respond to the pamphlet Schwenckfeld had sent. Since Schwenckfeld was determined not to let the matter drop, he decided to prepare a new booklet outlining the position of the Silesian brethren and to carry the pamphlet in person to Wittenberg. As a pretext for the journey, Duke Friedrich commissioned Schwenckfeld to transact some business for him with Luther and Bugenhagen. Schwenckfeld set out for Wittenberg and arrived in the little university town on November 30, 1525.

Early the next day Schwenckfeld called on Luther and Bugenhagen in order to attend to the duke's business. During the course of the ensuing conversation, Schwenckfeld led Luther aside to explain the real reason for his visit; namely, to discuss the nature of the Lord's Supper with him. Luther brushed him aside with the brusque comment, "Yes, Zwingli." Schwenckfeld, unruffled by Luther's attitude, continued to speak to him courteously in the manner of a man trained for a life of diplomacy and finally convinced him of the desirability of such a discussion.

The following morning at seven o'clock Schwenckfeld presented himself at Luther's door. The discussion proceeded satisfactorily enough, with Schwenckfeld explaining in detail the Silesian reading of the words of institution. Luther was unconvinced, though he promised to look over the material

Schwenckfeld had brought with him from Silesia. Later that Saturday and again on the following Sunday morning, Schwenckfeld and Bugenhagen discussed the question further. But Bugenhagen was no more amenable to Schwenckfeld's interpretation of the Eucharist than Luther had been. Once again Schwenckfeld returned to Luther to pick up the question where they had broken off. But the discussions with Luther, Bugenhagen, and Justus Jonas failed to shake the Wittenbergers from their settled views. The conversations ended on December 4, 1525, with all the participants defending unaltered positions. Luther characterized Schwenckfeld as the third head of a sacramentarian sect led by Zwingli and Carlstadt.[6]

From Schwenckfeld's point of view, this characterization was highly inaccurate. Schwenckfeld was convinced that Luther on the right and Carlstadt and Zwingli on the left represented extremes Christian theologians should avoid. Schwenckfeld considered himself to be an advocate of a middle way in theology that skirted the Scylla of Lutheran externalism and the Charybdis of sacramentarian memorialism.[7] In order to protest against the externalism into which he felt the evangelical movement had degenerated—since for Schwenckfeld the Lutheran error was always more dangerous than the Zwinglian—he advocated a suspension of the Lord's Supper until agreement could be reached on the meaning of the words of institution. Such a policy was first suggested in a circular letter signed by Schwenckfeld and Crautwald and dated April 21, 1526. This was the so-called *Stillstand*, which was observed by the Schwenckfelders until 1877.

Schwenckfeld was less hostile to Zwingli's view of the Lord's Supper than to Carlstadt's. He appreciated the Swiss reformer's concern to oppose what he also considered to be a crudely corporeal view of Christ's presence in the sacrament, but he saw no warrant for reading the "is" of the formula of institution as "signifies."[8] Moreover, Zwingli did not give sufficient attention to the fact that Christ was, after all, eaten spiritually, if not corporeally. The sixth chapter of John provided ample warrant for this fact.[9]

There was a dualism in Schwenckfeld's view of the Lord's Supper that the Zwinglian system could not adequately support. There was for Schwenckfeld an external celebration of the Eucharist that served as a memorial of Christ's death on the cross and as a symbolic representation of the internal feeding on Christ that is the essence of real communion.[10] The internal feeding, however, was the heart of the eucharistic celebration and could precede, parallel, or follow the external eating.[11] Indeed, the very fact that the internal eating bore no necessary relationship to the external commemoration enabled Schwenckfeld to advocate a suspension of the external ceremony without seriously harming the life of the church. The true believer could still have internal communion with Christ apart from the consecrated elements of bread and wine.[12]

This is not to say that the external ceremony was altogether without value. It is important for the church to commemorate Christ's death and to have a vis-

Radical Reformers

ible representation of its inner bond of communion with Christ. At the very least such a ceremony serves a useful didactic purpose. But the external ceremony is of secondary value and importance compared with the actual feeding on Christ, which is an internal experience. To participate in the external ceremony without the internal experience of drawing spiritual nourishment from Christ is to fail to distinguish the Lord's body and to provoke divine wrath and indignation.[13]

Inner communion with Christ is possible at any time and under any circumstances. Schwenckfeld called this communion an *Erkenntnis Christi*, an immediate apprehension of the exalted Christ in his risen and divinized humanity.[14] "Eating means . . . partaking of the essence of Christ through true faith. The bodily food is transformed into our nature, but the spiritual food changes us into itself, that is, the divine nature, so that we become partakers of it, II Peter 1."[15]

Schwenckfeld's view of the Eucharist was made possible by his understanding of the doctrine of the celestial flesh of Christ. According to Schwenckfeld, the human nature of Jesus is "uncreaturely." There is a tendency in Schwenckfeld's thought to identify creation and fall. Created things are not merely other than God or less than God. They are by very virtue of their creatureliness antithetical to God.[16] Creaturely things are subject to change, decay, death, and the possibility of sinning. Clearly, then, the humanity of Jesus, even though it is real humanity, is from the first moment of its existence "uncreaturely."[17]

Moreover, not only is the humanity of Jesus distinct from the humanity of all other human beings by reason of its uncreatureliness, but it is further set apart by a process of progressive divinization, which begins with the conception of Jesus in the womb of the Virgin Mary and terminates in the glorification of him at the right hand of the Father, following his resurrection and ascension.[18] The incarnation of the divine nature is accompanied by a divinization of the human nature. Yet the two natures are not simply merged. Schwenckfeld struggled to preserve the distinction between the divine and the human natures in Jesus Christ. Just as God becomes human without ceasing to be God, so, too, the humanity becomes divine without ceasing to be human. The incarnation is not a metamorphosis of the divine into the human; neither is divinization a metamorphosis of the human into the divine.[19] Rather, the two natures are "equalized."[20]

This divinized humanity, according to Schwenckfeld, becomes a permanent part of the Second Person of the Trinity. In actual practice, however, the glorified flesh of Jesus performed for Schwenckfeld many of the traditional functions of the Holy Spirit in orthodox Lutheran or Reformed theology. By feeding spiritually on the divinized body of Jesus, believers share in the divine life and are themselves divinized. Redemption is thus thought of primarily as a sanctification of the believer, a kind of deifying process, in which the glorified body of Christ rather than the Holy Spirit is the actual agent of change.[21]

Divinized believers do not lose their being in the Being of God, but they do gain freedom from sin, death, mutability, and all the attendant ills of creatureliness through participation in the divine nature.[22]

Schwenckfeld and his followers had been accused of sacramentarianism by opponents of the Reformation in Silesia, especially by Bishop John Faber. Schwenckfeld had denied the allegation, as well he might, and had sought to clear his name of Faber's charge. In 1528, however, Zwingli printed one of Schwenckfeld's books with a commendatory preface. This publication proved to Schwenckfeld's enemies that he was guilty by association. Duke Friedrich's position was made untenable by this new development. Thus Schwenckfeld, though innocent of the charge against him, entered a voluntary exile from Silesia on April 19, 1529. One month later he arrived at the imperial city of Strasbourg.

Schwenckfeld was welcomed to Strasbourg by Wolfgang Capito and Martin Bucer, to whom he presented a letter of commendation from Crautwald. Capito opened his house to Schwenckfeld, and for two years Schwenckfeld remained with him as a guest. He attended services in the city, standing under the pulpits because of his impaired hearing. He preached on occasion and assisted Matthew Zell at the cathedral. At Capito's house he lectured on the letters of Peter to those who would listen. Even Capito's wife and Catherine Zell, the wife of Matthew, were permitted to attend these lectures. When Capito's wife died in 1531, Schwenckfeld went to live with Jacob and Margaret Engelmann, where he continued the work of lecturing he had begun at Capito's.

Schwenckfeld's steadfast refusal to unite with a Strasbourg congregation became a thorn in the flesh of the Strasbourg reformers. Appealing to the Christ within him as the ground for withdrawal from the visible congregations inside the city, he maintained that Christ had been known to some degree in all the churches but minimized the importance of the visible fellowship of believers.[23]

Schwenckfeld was an antipedobaptist,[24] though he did not subscribe to a rebaptism of believers or actively oppose the ceremony of infant baptism.[25] The quarrel about the proper form for baptism seemed to him largely a fruitless controversy about externals in which none of the antagonists was right since all of them had chosen to focus on the wrong issue. The Anabaptists who denied infant baptism were as bad as the Lutherans who supported it. Both exalted the letter over the spirit. What mattered for Schwenckfeld was the internal presence of Christ, not the particular form of the external rite.[26]

In 1533 the magisterial reformers of Strasbourg organized a territorial synod that attempted to define the position of the magisterial reformers against the radicals and sectarians. The tenth article of the confession that a committee of the synod drew up attacked the notion of Schwenckfeld that the visible communion of the church was unimportant. On June 10, 1533, and again on June 13, Schwenckfeld was summoned before the synod to defend his views. Partly because of the friendship of Matthew and Catherine Zell for Schwenckfeld and partly because the books that Schwenckfeld had submitted to the synod had not been thoroughly studied, the synod was reluctant to act precipitously or to treat Schwenckfeld harshly. Nevertheless, under pressure from Bucer, the council of Strasbourg formally requested Schwenckfeld to leave the city.

Schwenckfeld went first to Ulm, where he soon became embroiled in a christological controversy with the Lutheran pastor Martin Frecht, who accused Schwenckfeld of undermining belief in the real humanity of the Redeemer with his doctrine of the celestial flesh of Christ. The Swiss, led by Vadian of Saint Gall, joined the Lutherans in the attack on Schwenckfeld's Christology. Schwenckfeld defended his understanding of the person and work of Jesus Christ in two monumental treatises, *Vom Fleische Christi* (1540) and *Grosse Confession* (1541). Nevertheless, his christological views were condemned at Schmalkalden in 1540. In addition to these christological controversies, Schwenckfeld also engaged in a lengthy dispute with Pilgram Marpeck over the nature of the church and with Matthias Flacius over the Word of God.

The last years of Schwenckfeld's life were spent in hiding, part of the time in Justingen Castle. While his works were still being published, they were often released under pseudonyms. His followers were not numerous, but they were loyal. They withdrew from organized churches and formed small conventicles of their own, in which they scrupulously observed the *Stillstand*. When Schwenckfeld died in Ulm in 1561, his body was buried secretly by his friends in order to prevent its disinterment by zealots eager to burn the bones of a heretic. His grave has never been found.

18

BALTHASAR HUBMAIER
(1485?–1528)

Free Will and Covenant

A TYPOLOGY CAN BE a useful interpretive tool for cutting through the confusing tangles of historical detail and enabling historians to perceive and, in some cases, to establish orderly relationships in what had appeared at first blush to be a disorganized plethora of unrelated fact. But a typology can also be misleading, if it is taken with undue seriousness and allowed to lead historians away from the very detail it was meant to interpret. When that happens, historical research becomes a genial game of free association, in which generalizations rather than the sources themselves become determinative.

Perhaps no movement has suffered more from typologizing than the Anabaptist movement of the sixteenth century. Roland Bainton at Yale University christened the various groups in the sixteenth century, which were disappointed with the Reformation of Luther and Zwingli and which rejected many of the Lutheran or Reformed doctrines and institutions, "the Left Wing of the Reformation."[1] George H. Williams at Harvard, who prefers to classify these groups under the name of the "Radical Reformation," has further subdivided them into the Anabaptists (represented today by the Mennonites and the Amish); the Spiritualists (represented by the Schwenkfelder church in Pennsylvania); and the Evangelical Rationalists (whose modern spiritual heirs are the Unitarians).[2] Although Professor Williams has worked out the most elaborate and probably the most widely used of the typologies for the Radical Reformation, he is by no means the prisoner of his own generalizations and has been careful to point out the deficiencies in the typology he developed.

What has not been questioned, however, is the adequacy of the term *Radical Reformation* itself. On certain issues, such as pacifism or the establishment of a voluntary church, the Anabaptists do, without a doubt, represent a far more radical break with the customary patterns of the life and thought of the medieval church than the magisterial reformers were willing to make, though it is not, it seems to me, correct to attribute this reluctance on the part of the magisterial reformers to timidity or to a perverse unwillingness to follow their own reformation to its logical conclusion. But on the other questions, such as nature and grace, or free will and predestination, the magisterial reformers represented a far more radical break with the main traditions of the late medieval theology than did the Anabaptists, who rejected the radical Augustinianism of Luther and Zwingli for a view closer to what was taught in the late medieval Catholic church. When the subject under discussion is justification, then it is Luther and not Menno Simons who is the flaming radical.

This typically Anabaptist combination of radical and conservative tendencies in theology is well illustrated by the career of Balthasar Hubmaier, one of the most theologically learned of the early Anabaptist leaders. Because Hubmaier rejected the doctrine of nonresistance embraced by the majority of the Anabaptists, there is a tendency to link him rather with the later English Baptists, though there is absolutely no historical connection between the two.[3] However, since Hubmaier did represent—on the questions of believer's baptism, the voluntary church, grace and free will—the views taught by other Anabaptist leaders, there is no reason to separate him from the Anabaptist movement as a whole. He is an eloquent spokesman for early Anabaptism on all subjects except one.

Hubmaier was born in the early 1480s in the town of Friedberg near Augsburg in South Germany.[4] In 1503 he enrolled as a student in the University of Freiburg im Breisgau, where he studied with Johann Eck, who later became famous as the opponent of Luther at the Leipzig Disputation in 1519 and as a participant in the ill-fated colloquy between Protestants and Roman Catholics held at Regensburg (or Ratisbon) in 1541. Recent scholarship has tended to confirm the belief that Eck was strongly influenced in his theology by the nominalism of Gabriel Biel, especially in his view of justification.[5] Eck thought highly of Hubmaier and, when he was called to the University of Ingolstadt, he arranged for Hubmaier to follow him there. At Ingolstadt, Hubmaier earned his doctorate in theology and became in his own turn a professor at the university. Though no one has studied the degree to which he was influenced by late medieval nominalism, there is evidence in his later writings that he was not untouched by it.

Like Geiler von Kaysersberg, Hubmaier resigned his post at the university in 1516 to become a preacher at the cathedral in Regensburg. Regensburg marks one of the uglier chapters in Hubmaier's life; he became involved in a controversy with the Jews and took the leadership of a movement agitating for their expulsion from the city. When they were finally expelled in 1519, Hubmaier destroyed their former synagogue and erected in its place a chapel dedicated to Mary. Not satisfied with the notoriety gained by his role in the expulsion of the Jews, he claimed that miracles had occurred in the new shrine and submitted a list of fifty-four to the city council. Pilgrims from all over Germany, bearing gifts for the chapel, came to Regensburg to see the shrine where the miracles had occurred. Complications arising from these pilgrimages and from a controversy between the city council of Regensburg and the bishop conspired to make Hubmaier's position in Regensburg untenable. It came as something less than a complete surprise, therefore, when Hubmaier accepted the call to become pastor in Waldshut in the Breisgau, though he claimed in a letter to Sapidus in 1521 that he had left Regensburg to escape the plague, which had broken out late in 1520.[6] Waldshut was at that time under Austrian administration.

Hubmaier, who was influenced by humanism[7] as well as by late medieval nominalism,[8] spent his leisure in Waldshut reading Erasmus, especially his paraphrases on Paul. He also began to read the writings of Luther and Oecolampadius, though he was not an immediate convert to the Protestant cause. In 1522 he was invited to return to Regensburg, since the quarrel between the city council and the bishop had been settled. He agreed to preach in Regensburg as before, without, however, giving up his post in Waldshut. In the winter of 1522 to 1523 he was won over to the Lutheran reformation. As a result of his decision he gave up his post in Regensburg and returned to Waldshut. Soon after his return to Waldshut he came under the influence of Zwingli and the Swiss reformation. The theology of Zwingli proved to be far more decisive for Hubmaier than the theology of Luther. In October 1523, at a disputation held in Zurich, he publicly took sides with Zwingli by opposing the medieval Catholic view of the Eucharist as a sacrifice and by condemning the veneration of images.

Though Hubmaier continued to agree with Zwingli on a wide range of theological issues, he soon came to differ with him on the question of baptism. Zwingli himself had at one point in his theological development come to doubt the wisdom of infant baptism and to entertain the idea that children should not be baptized until they had first been instructed in the Christian faith. Though Zwingli discussed these ideas in private, he never advocated them in public as settled theological convictions. But what Zwingli had discussed in private, Conrad Grebel and the early Anabaptist circle in Zurich began to teach openly. Hubmaier was convinced by the reasoning of Grebel and his friends and on April 15, 1525, submitted to rebaptism by Wilhelm Reublin, thus attesting to the fact that he regarded the baptism which he had received as a child to be invalid. The following day, Easter Sunday, April 16, 1525, Hubmaier baptized three hundred adults in the parish church at Waldshut, using water from a milk pail rather than from the baptismal font. In May 1525 he published his famous treatise, *Von dem Tauf der Gläubigen*, which defended the view that Baptism must follow personal faith and not precede it.

Though Hubmaier was not one of the instigators of the Peasants' Revolt in 1525, he was in general sympathy with it and aided the peasants in revising the Twelve Articles. The Austrian government regarded him as one of the leaders of the rebellion, though he was less concerned with the feudal rights of the

Radical Reformers

peasants than he was with the freedom of Waldshut to remain Protestant. He indicated his willingness to obey the Austrian government, if Austria would grant Waldshut religious toleration. His request was not granted. When Waldshut was occupied by enemy troops on December 5, 1525, Hubmaier was fortunate enough to escape and flee to Zurich. However, while his political views were not held in disfavor in Zurich, his theological views were. He was arrested and forced to recant his Anabaptist convictions under torture. After his release, he slipped out of the city and promptly renounced his recantation. He made his way to Moravia, where there was a high degree of toleration for dissenting views. He traveled by way of Augsburg, where he met and baptized Hans Denck, whose own career as an Anabaptist leader, while brief, was nonetheless important.

Hubmaier arrived at Nikolsburg in Moravia in July 1526. Under his leadership, Nikolsburg soon became a center for the Anabaptist movement. A large congregation, perhaps as many as twelve thousand Anabaptists, gathered there. The printer Froschauer, who had been forced to leave Zurich because of his Anabaptist views, migrated to Nikolsburg and reopened his printing firm in that city. The Protestants in Nikolsburg enjoyed the protection of Leonhard von Liechtenstein and had the sympathy, if not the support, of many of the Moravian nobility. In this refuge Hubmaier wrote a long list of works on the Eucharist and on free will, which were published by Froschauer at his new press. He also defended his teaching on baptism against Zwingli and opposed the radical views of Hans Hut, the Austrian Anabaptist, who refused to bear arms or pay war taxes.

Following the death of King Louis of Hungary and Bohemia, the Austrian authorities insisted that Hubmaier be extradited, not because of his religious activity but because of his political involvement in Waldshut. The Moravian nobility, who would have resisted extradition on charges of heresy, were not willing to risk their lives to protect someone who was charged with treason. Hubmaier was surrendered to the Austrians, who promptly whisked him off to Vienna, where he was imprisoned briefly before his transfer to the castle of Kreuzenstein in Lower Austria. While in prison in Kreuzenstein, he composed twenty-seven articles, which he sent to King Ferdinand. In these articles he made certain concessions in his views, though he held fast to the main lines of his theology. If he had hoped to ameliorate his situation by writing this defense of his views, he was sadly mistaken in his assessment of the disposition of the Austrian authorities. He was returned to Vienna, where he was tortured and burnt at the stake on March 10, 1528. Three days after his execution, his wife was drowned in the Danube by the same authorities who had condemned her husband to death by fire.

Hubmaier's theology is, as we have already noted, a curious blend of conservation and radical ideas. On the question of grace and free will, for example, Hubmaier attempted to steer a middle course between Luther and the older traditions of medieval theology. Medieval Catholic theologians pointed to the mystery that, even before men and women consciously choose to disobey the will of God, they are already in a state of alienation from their Creator, and that this state, though it is the common lot of every human being, is nevertheless profoundly unnatural. Human beings do not become sinners by sinning. Their alienation from God precedes their conscious willing and choosing, and their sinful acts are only a symptom and expression of that alienation. How this happens is a mystery, though all human beings experience it as a fact.

The majority of medieval theologians did not believe that human beings have forgotten what the good is or that they have lost all taste for it. They still have conscience, which knows what is good, and a faculty called synderesis, which prefers it. The nominalists even argued that, while sin had damaged human nature, the character of that damage was psychological rather than metaphysical.[9] Fallen human beings could still love God above everything else in the world and their neighbors as themselves. By exercising their natural powers to seek God, they could dispose themselves for the reception of grace. There are, in other words, for all but the most Augustinian of medieval theologians,[10] innate resources in men and women that survive the shock of the fall and form the indispensable basis for the renewal of their broken relationship to God.[11]

In medieval thought, baptism is regarded as the remedy for original sin. It is not necessary for an infant to have faith in order to receive the benefits that accompany baptism. The sacraments are not merely signs or symbolic actions, which act out a moment in the church's life without conferring grace, except, perhaps in the limited sense of stirring up a psychological response. The sacraments of the Catholic church confer grace *ex opere operato*, on the basis of the performance of the rite. They are effective signs that convey to the recipients what they symbolize. The ontological transformation of human beings is effected through the external rites of the church.

Luther opposed the medieval view of justification and argued that the scholastic theologians had been seduced by Aristotle into believing that sin and righteousness were qualities of the soul.[12] For Luther righteousness is not a human property, not something one possesses. It is, rather, God's total judgment over the whole person. Like righteousness, sin is also total, not in the sense that the individual sinner commits every known sin but in the sense that sin involves the total person in that person's total relationship to God. There is no part of the human personality untouched by idolatry, by the universal tendency to turn away from the Word of God and in upon oneself. Luther rejects the common late medieval view that there are natural resources that enable men and women to dispose themselves for the reception of grace. Sinners are utterly unable to reconstitute their broken relationship with God.

Zwingli agreed more or less with Luther in his view of justification but differed with him over the role of the sacraments.[13] While Luther argued that

God works on the inner person by means of external signs to which he has attached his promise, Zwingli distinguished sharply between inner and outer baptism. The Holy Spirit in his sovereign freedom cannot be bound to creaturely elements, nor can external things cleanse the inner self. The inner baptism by the Spirit takes place independently of baptism by water. God acts directly on the soul by his Spirit rather than indirectly by means of water. Water baptism belongs to the response of the church to the grace of God already given or, in the case of infants, in anticipation of it. Inner baptism is the gracious act of God that creates faith. It is given to the elect by the direct action of the Spirit. Because Zwingli laid stress on the sovereign activity of the divine Spirit rather than on the human response of faith and on the decree of election rather than on the experience of regeneration, he was willing to administer the sacrament to infants. Children of Christian parents belong to the covenant of God just as Hebrew children inherited the covenant given to their fathers and mothers. As circumcision was the outer seal of the Old Covenant, so infant baptism is the outer seal of the New.

Hubmaier also defended a covenantal understanding of baptism, though he meant by covenant something different from what Zwingli meant. The principal actor in Zwingli's covenant is the triune God, who initiates in Christ a covenant with the elect, by his mercy providing redemption in Christ and applying it to the elect on the basis of his justice. The benefits of God's reconciling act in Jesus Christ are communicated to the elect by the Holy Spirit, who acts directly on the inner person, creating and awakening faith. In response to this grace the elect take part in the sacramental life of the church, both for themselves and for their children.

The principal actor in Hubmaier's covenant is the believing individual, who responds to God's regenerating act in his or her own life by entering into covenant with God and with the church through baptism.[14] Candidates for baptism confess their faith in Jesus Christ and their intention of living a disciplined life of obedience to Christ. The church, by agreeing to administer baptism to such candidates, confesses that it recognizes in them the signs of true disciples of Jesus Christ. Whereas Zwingli emphasized divine initiative and the freedom of the Holy Spirit, Hubmaier stressed the human response to grace and the freedom of the will.

In defending the freedom of the human will over against Luther, Hubmaier returned in part to the medieval Catholic views in which he had been raised, though without embracing the medieval sacramental system. Like the nominalists, Hubmaier distinguished between the absolute and the ordained power of God.[15] God can do whatever he chooses, since God's absolute power means that he is not subject to any law outside his own will. However, by God's ordained power God has chosen to act in certain ways and not in others. While the absolute will of God is hidden from us and not a fit subject for speculation, the ordained will of God has been revealed and may be investigated. The harsh things Paul has to say in the ninth chapter of Romans about the sovereignty of God and the ability of God to deal with human beings as a potter deals with clay should be referred to the hidden or absolute will of God. Hubmaier does not deny that God could deal with men and women in such an arbitrary fashion, but he clearly regards it as a hypothetical possibility that God has chosen not to actualize. The revealed will of God makes it clear that he has invited all human beings to participate in salvation. Just as God compels no one to enter the kingdom, so he places no obstacles in the path of any person. The universal offer of salvation is seriously meant. If it is not fully realized, the fault lies with human beings rather than with God. While Hubmaier wished to affirm the Augustinian understanding of the prevenience of grace, he rejected the Augustinian understanding of predestination.

Hubmaier argued that a limited freedom of the will has survived the trauma of the fall and forms the natural anthropological resource for the return to God.[16] Hubmaier believed with Erasmus that human beings were created as tripartite beings—spirit, soul, and flesh. The will of the spirit was unscathed by the fall and still desires the good,[17] though it cannot guide the soul and body back to God without the assistance of the external preaching of the Word and inner illumination by the Holy Spirit. By making use of their limited freedom, sinners dispose their wills for the reception of grace, which cannot be given to them without their free and uncoerced consent. When sinners respond to the offer of the gospel, God must regenerate them, not because of the quality of their response but because God has bound himself by his promises to justify whoever responds to the gospel.[18] Insofar as Hubmaier thinks of a covenant between God and humankind, he thinks of a two-sided covenant in which there are mutual obligations binding on both parties and to which human response provides the key. While God has taken the initiative in establishing the structure in which men and women may be saved, God's act of regenerating any person is itself a response to the human act of fulfilling a condition of the covenant. God draws men and women to salvation or permits them to be damned, if they will not be saved. But in neither case does God act the part of the free sovereign of Augustinian theology. In the last analysis it is human choice and not divine sovereignty that is decisive. The will of God is the guarantee of the reliability of the gospel, but not of its ultimate triumph.

Since free human decision is essential as a precondition for the reception of baptism, it follows that baptism cannot be administered to infants.[19] The church does not embrace the entire community but is rather a voluntary society of the baptized, who live in conscious tension with the world.[20] Hubmaier did not make the tension between the church and the world as fierce as some of the other Anabaptist thinkers, who taught nonresistance,[21] but it is nonetheless fairly severe. God's acceptance of sinners rests on his work of grace in them rather than on his total judgment over them. That work of grace in human beings does not exclude the possibility of attaining at least a relative perfection in

Radical Reformers

this life. The baptism by water and the Spirit will be completed by the baptism of blood in the constant warfare with evil.

Hubmaier faced in two directions. His view of baptism and of the voluntary church represented a break with the past and the anticipation of new currents that gained in significance after his death. But his views of grace and free will represented a continuation into the sixteenth century of conservative theological motifs from the later Middle Ages over against the radical theological insights of Luther. The thesis that the Anabaptist stress on human ethical transformation represents a more radical view of justification than the "merely" forensic doctrine of Luther will not hold water. Luther was no less interested in human ethical renewal than were Biel or Hubmaier. His new and radical insight, which proved to be a too heady brew for both the scholastics and the Anabaptists, was that this renewal formed no part of the basis for God's acceptance of sinners. On this point the magisterial and the Radical reformations parted company, not because the Radical reformers were too radical, but because, from the perspective of Luther and Calvin, they were not radical enough.

19

HANS DENCK

(1500?–1527)

The Universal Word

IF ONE WERE TO analyze the modern religious temper, one would certainly have to list as ingredients of that disposition the feeling that religion is essentially a private matter, that inner spirituality is more important than the performance of ritual acts, and that the test of authentic piety is its ability to motivate men and women to achieve concrete ethical goals. How it happens that average persons in the pew, whatever the public posture of the religious group to which they belong, have come to hold these convictions as their own is a long story whose telling need not concern us here. What is important to note here is only the fact that during the Reformation voices were raised that expressed similar sentiments. There were men and women who devalued the corporate sacramental life of the church and who defined the essence of Christianity as obedience to the will of God. One of the most eloquent and learned representatives of this group was also the youngest to rise to prominence in the early decades of the sixteenth century. His name was Hans Denck, by training a humanist and by occupation a schoolmaster.

Denck was born at Habach near Huglfing in Upper Bavaria, probably in 1500.[1] In 1517 he matriculated at the University of Ingolstadt, where he received his baccalaureate in 1519. He specialized in languages and won recognition as a master of Greek, Hebrew, and Latin. After his graduation from Ingolstadt he went to Basel, where he studied at the university under Oecolampadius[2] and took a job as proofreader and editor in the printing firm owned by Curio. At the university he listened to Oecolampadius lecture on Isaiah. He also played a major role, while in Basel, in the editing of Theodore Gaza's multivolume Greek grammar.

Oecolampadius took an interest in Denck and when the post of principal at Saint Sebald's School in Nuremberg fell vacant successfully nominated him for that position. Denck was glad for a secure post in a city where he could begin to sink down his roots. For several years (1519–23) he had wandered from place to place throughout South Germany, and, while his position at Curio's was a good one, it was not as well suited to his abilities as the more demanding job of schoolmaster. His tenure at Saint Sebald's, however, proved all too brief. He was caught in the cross fire of the various religious factions in Nuremberg and forced to resign.

Nuremberg was the center of a distinguished group of humanists who in 1516 had welcomed Staupitz with open arms and had made Nuremberg the scene of his greatest triumph. They were reform minded, but they understood that reform in terms of the improvement of the moral and devotional life of individuals. The path to renewal for the church lies in the imitation of Christ (*Nachfolge Christi*) and total surrender to the will of God (*Gelassenheit*). Denck, who was influenced by late medieval mysticism as well as Erasmus, found the emphasis of the humanists a wholesome one and shared their distrust of the Lutheran teaching of *sola fide*.

The Lutherans, however, led by the pastor of the Church of Saint Lorenz, Andreas Osiander, continued to gain influence in the city. When certain "ungodly painters," led by Sebald Behaim, were brought before the civil authorities on the charge that they held unacceptable views of baptism and the Lord's Supper, their testimony implicated Denck as well. Denck was brought to trial and ordered to give his views of several doctrinal issues, especially baptism and the Lord's Supper. In spite of certain ambiguities in his thought, which made it difficult for the Lutherans to know exactly what he meant, they were able to decipher enough to make clear to themselves that his views were not satisfactory. On January 21, 1525, Denck was banished from the city forever.

According to Oecolampadius, Denck's first stop after his banishment from Nuremberg was the city of Mühlhausen, where he took a job as teacher. Since Mühlhausen is associated with the name of Thomas Müntzer, this may have been the Basel reformer's way of saying that Denck belonged to the circle of Müntzer's disciples, a thesis that contemporary scholarship tends to discredit. However, even if Denck did go to Mühlhausen, he did not remain there for more than a few months. By June 1525 he could be found in the home of an Anabaptist in St. Gall. Vadian and Kessler,[3] who describe his visit to St. Gall, accuse him of teaching universalism and of holding to the heretical position of Origen that even the devil will at last be saved.

Through the intervention of two noblemen, Bastians von Freyburg and Jörg Regel, Denck was offered a position as teacher in the city of Augsburg. He accepted and moved from St. Gall to Augsburg during the fall of the same year. The Protestant party in Augsburg was badly divided over the subject of the Lord's Supper with hostile Lutheran and Zwinglian factions. The situation was not helped by the fact that Urbanus Rhegius, the leading reformer in Augsburg, could not seem to make up his mind between the two factions and listed one day toward Wittenberg and the next toward Zurich. His fundamental orientation, however, was toward Luther, and his views increasingly took on a Lutheran cast.

The visit of Balthasar Hubmaier to Augsburg in 1526 proved decisive for Denck's theological development. Though Denck had had contact with the Anabaptists, especially with the Swiss Brethren, he had not joined their ranks. Hubmaier was now able to persuade him that the Anabaptist understanding of believer's baptism was the correct view and that he himself should be rebaptized as an adult. A few months later, Denck in his turn was able to persuade Hans Hut to follow his example and submit to adult baptism. Although Denck did not found a congregation of Anabaptists in Augsburg, his work did lead in time to the formation of a South German Anabaptist movement, distinct in its emphases and spirit from the Swiss Brethren.

Denck did not escape suspicion in Augsburg. An ugly rumor circulated that he had been expelled from Nuremberg because of his political views. When that rumor was quashed, another took its place. The charge of Kessler and Vadian that Denck taught universalism was revived and whispered over the back fences and in the local taverns. Urbanus Rhegius, who felt an obligation to see whether the rumor had any foundation in fact, invited Denck to a theological discussion, at first in private and later before a group of local clergy. When the discussions yielded no satisfactory result, Rhegius suggested that the issues be debated before the city council. Denck agreed, but on the day set for the debate he slipped out of the city. He had gone through this experience once before in Nuremberg and had no desire to repeat it.

He arrived in Strasbourg in the fall of 1526. Neither Capito nor Bucer was glad to see him arrive, since they had been given to understand that he had been driven out of Nuremberg because of his denial of the doctrine of the Trinity. Though the charge was groundless, Bucer challenged him to a theological disputation and attempted to refute his position. Denck's ideas were also opposed by Michael Sattler, the Anabaptist leader of the Swiss Brethren in Strasbourg. Sattler and his followers were committed to a high view of Scripture and rejected Denck's position, which subordinated Scripture to direct revelation. Their views were summarized in the Schleitheim Confession of 1527.

Forced to leave Strasbourg, Denck wandered up the Rhine Valley through Bergzabern and Landau to Worms. In Worms he joined forces with Ludwig Haetzer to make the first German translation of the Prophets, a work they had begun when they were in Strasbourg. The translation was accurate and was used by Luther and by the translators of the Zurich Bible in preparing their own versions. Denck left Worms when a public defense of Anabaptist teaching in the marketplace by Denck, Ludwig Haetzer, and Jakob Kautz backfired and provoked a reaction against Protestantism in all its forms.

The next months were spent on the road, traveling from Worms to Basel to Zurich and then to Augsburg, where he attended the so-called Martyrs' Synod in August 1527. At the synod he was able to come to a détente with Hans Hut, who agreed not to preach his controversial views concerning the end of the world and the last judgment to the congregation at Augsburg unless specifically requested to do so. From Augsburg Denck rejoined Haetzer, who was now in Nuremberg, and together they met with Wilhelm Reublin in Ulm.

Oecolampadius allowed Denck to return to Basel but not without exacting a price: he required Denck to compose a recantation of his views. The confession that Denck wrote in compliance with the wishes of Oecolampadius is a very modest document and represents, on the whole, no important change in his position. He still regards infant baptism as unscriptural, though he no longer insists that Christians must submit to rebaptism as adults.[4] The whole tenor of the document is less a recantation than a reaffirmation of his characteristic emphases. If there is a shift, it is away from Anabaptism and in the direction of Spiritualism. Nevertheless, even though the document is a summary of Denck's views rather than a denial of them, Oecolampadius treated the document as though it were all that he had hoped for. Shortly after composing this confession, Denck contracted the plague and died.

Denck's theology can be understood in part as the dialectical antithesis to Martin Luther's thesis.[5] That is not to say that there were no positive impulses in Denck's theology that existed prior to, or at least apart from, his encounter with Luther. Denck was not simply a naysayer and did not relish the role of critic. But it is true that his positive theological motifs can be best understood when seen against the background of the theology he opposed.

Both Luther and Denck agreed that God can only be known through his self-revelation in the Word. But here the agreement ends and the differences begin to multiply. For Luther the Word of God is something external before it is something internal. It is not the case that the Word of God speaks to the human heart without external mediation. The Word of God is something spoken, written, and preached—all external acts. God has made himself known in the concrete humanity of Jesus Christ. He has bound his Spirit to the apostolic testimony of Holy Scripture. God comes to men and women from without, through the elements of bread and wine or through the proclamation of the gospel. Faith is not something that by a kind of spontaneous generation sprouts up suddenly in the human heart. It is an answer to a Word spoken to it from without.

The Spiritualists, by beginning with what they believed to be the still, small voice of God spoken in secret in their hearts, made it impossible to distinguish the voice the God from the voice of their own imaginations. Even more dangerously, they unwittingly provided human beings with an excuse for disobedience to God. If revelation is an inner voice, then God is bound to the sensitivity and strength of human religious intuition. Those who have no religious experiences cannot be held accountable for their rebellion against God. For Luther it was precisely because the Word of God is not dependent on human receptivity that it can effectively unmask human pretension and sin. God's

Word has universal validity apart from human experience and even, perhaps, in spite of it.

Denck believed that Luther had inverted the correct understanding of the meaning of the Word of God. The fact that God reveals himself immediately to the human heart does not undercut human responsibility but rather establishes it. God's Word is not an esoteric or fantastic religious experience. It is the voice of the Logos, who calls men and women to obedience to God. While there are millions of people who have not read the Bible and who cannot hear the proclamation of the gospel, there is no one who has not heard the voice of God speaking within. Because the word of God speaks to all men and women, all are equally responsible to God and cannot plead that they have never heard the message of redemption or were not predestined to receive grace. Human beings do not initiate their own salvation, but they are free to accept or reject the claim of God laid immediately on them by the divine Word. If they are not saved, they cannot shunt the responsibility for their condition aside or lay the blame on God.

Denck enlarged the sphere of human responsibility by denying both the Lutheran doctrine of predestination and the Stoic doctrine of fate. Luther believed that God had chosen some men and women for salvation and others for damnation. He saw no other way to protect the gratuity of justification than by affirming the Augustinian doctrine of double predestination. The doctrine of predestination grows for both Luther and Calvin out of the surprise of the elect that they believe, even though they are not worthy, when many fine people, who seem far more deserving, do not believe. Predestination is not a speculative doctrine but is affirmed as the only possible explanation for the mystery of faith.

Though Luther accepted the doctrine of double predestination, out of a pastoral concern for the weak in faith he did not preach it. The strong in faith have no need to concern themselves with this doctrine, since believers ought, if their faith is mature, to be willing to be damned for the glory of God. And the weak in faith have no business concerning themselves with predestination, since it will only cause them needless anxiety. Cling to God's saving act in Christ, and leave the hidden will of God to the angels.

Even though Luther taught predestination, he did not teach the Stoic doctrine of fate, though he could talk at times as though he did. He was in philosophical matters an indeterminist. The doctrine of predestination does not mean that all of a human being's moral acts are foreordained or that the drama of history is a kind of charade in which events are robbed of significance and mystery. Predestination means that sinners cannot, by taking thought, reconstitute their broken relationship with God. It does not mean that they have been foreordained from all eternity to eat turtle soup on Thursday next.

Denck, however, understood Luther's doctrine of predestination and his denial of the freedom of the will as another form of the Stoic assault on human

Radical Reformers

freedom and responsibility. He was not correct in this belief, but his error is understandable. There is, he argued, no secret will of God that stands in dialectical relationship to his revealed will. The believer has no reason to fear that what God has spoken to the church will be invalidated by what he has not yet revealed. God summons Christians to the obedience exemplified in Jesus Christ. He has not made that obedience impossible either by predestination or by original sin. Human beings have the freedom to respond and the obligation to do so.

Holy Scripture is not valueless, but it is not identical with the Word of God.[6] There is a soteriological necessity for the Word of God to be independent of Holy Scripture. Scripture, therefore, is not the Word of God but is rather a witness to the Word. It is a letter from God, but it is opaque and cannot be understood until one has encountered God through the Word that speaks to the heart. Like the sacrament of the Lord's Supper, Scripture is a kind of outward witness to an inward grace. It does not mediate the grace, but it witnesses to a grace already present in the heart.

Like the late medieval mystics from the school of Tauler and Eckhart, Denck was more interested in the discarnate Christ than he was in the man, Jesus of Nazareth. To be sure, Jesus plays an important role as an example to be imitated in the human struggle to attain perfect surrender to the will of God. But it is the discarnate Lord who speaks directly to the heart and who makes redemption universally accessible. Unlike Tauler and Eckhart, however, Denck had no real interest in anthropology. He even denied the teaching of the Rhineland mystics that God unites with human beings in some inner ground or spark of the soul, a faculty that has survived the trauma of the fall and provides the indispensable anthropological resource for the return to God. When the Word speaks to a person, he speaks to the whole person and not to some isolated faculty.

Kessler and Vadian accused Denck of universalism; that is, of teaching that grace will in the end triumph over all evil, even the disobedience and seemingly implacable hostility of Satan. There is, however, no evidence in Denck's own writings that he ever taught such a doctrine, though the witness of his contemporaries cannot simply be discounted.[7] What his writings teach is a universalism of opportunity and responsibility. All sinners stand on the same plane with respect to the possibility of their salvation. The Word speaks in every heart, and every human being has the same capacity to respond. Whether or not Denck actually took the step of moving from the affirmation of the possibility of universal salvation to the confession of the fact is an issue that cannot be decided on the basis of the writings that have survived.

Denck understood Christianity, finally, as an ethical religion. He therefore opposed anything in the teaching of the reformers that seemed to him to cloud or obfuscate the moral imperatives that lie at the heart of the gospel. Original sin, predestination, a stress on preaching and sacrament seemed to him to weaken the resolution of sinners to yield themselves totally to the will of God or to give them a convenient excuse for rejecting the stringent ethical demands of the Christian kerygma. The gospel is the summons to imitate Christ, and authentic faith is obedience to that summons. Therefore, in his last confession, Denck could weaken his ties to the Anabaptist doctrine of believer's baptism without surrendering anything essential to his faith. Inner spirituality is more important than the performance of ritual acts, and the test of authentic piety is its ability to motivate men and women to achieve concrete ethical goals. By affirming that conviction, Denck became the spokesman for a new disposition in religion, a disposition that found a fresh embodiment in the later moralism and inward religion of the Enlightenment.

20

PILGRAM MARPECK
(1495?–1556)

The Church and the Old Testament

THE RELATIONSHIP BETWEEN the two Testaments is a knotty problem that has puzzled Christian thinkers ever since an ancient shipowner named Marcion suggested that there was no relationship whatever between them.[1] Unlike some of the Fathers, who claimed that the trouble with the Jews was that they did not understand the Old Testament typologically, Marcion rejected typological exegesis and insisted that the Old Testament should be understood literally. When the Old Testament is taken literally, he argued, it becomes clear that the God of the Old Testament is a God of justice and law who knows nothing of mercy. Marcion wanted nothing to do with this kind of God or with any book, for that matter, that talks about this God. He rejected the Old Testament and put what he believed to be the gospel in its place.

In back of Marcion's attitude toward the Old Testament and his sharp contrast between Jewish and Christian thought lay his struggle to resolve still another problem, the riddle of the existence of evil. Marcion found that his experience of the world was dual. He encountered just enough joy, beauty, and love in the world to make the affirmation of the goodness of God plausible. On the other hand, he stumbled over just enough pain and pointless suffering to make that affirmation seem like an exercise in pious self-deception. This duality could only be explained if one took the contrast between the Old and the New Testaments with absolute seriousness.

Human experience of the goodness and evil of the world is dual because there are two Gods rather than one God. There is the God who created this world, the God of whom the Old Testament speaks and whom the Jews worshipped. Then there is the God who is the Redeemer, the God of mercy, love, and grace, who was revealed in Jesus Christ. All evil and pain is traceable back to the Creator-God of the Old Testament, who is responsible not only for the pain of childbirth but also for such useless and annoying pests as alligators and termites. God the Redeemer was utterly unknown until he made himself known in Jesus Christ. The New Testament, then, is a message from this God of love, who is in no way identifiable with the God of the Old Testament.

Marcion's views, though they were accepted by many Christians, were rejected by the main body of the church. His theology, however, was not without effect on the church. By his insistence on the absolute discontinuity between the two Testaments, he brought the church to a clearer apprehension of the fact that the Creator and the Redeemer are one God, that Yahweh of Israel and the Father of Jesus Christ are the same. He also prompted it to think through the problem of divine mercy and justice and to affirm at last that mercy and justice are combined in one God. This is a paradox the church cannot escape through the easy solution of positing the existence of two Gods.

While the church rejected the solution of Marcion, it was not prepared to argue that the Old Testament and the New were precisely on the same level or that there was no significant difference between them.[2] The Old Testament was, as many Christian theologians liked to put it, the shadow of which the New Testament is the substance. The events of the Old Testament are not significant in themselves but only as typological foreshadowings of the saving events that take place in the New. While the Old Testament belongs by right to the church as well as to ancient Israel, there is nothing in it that is not possessed in a fuller and more complete way in the New. The New Testament stands on a higher plane than the Old, as fulfillment is higher than anticipation. This conviction about the superiority of the New Testament to the Old was reflected in the Middle Ages in the church's teaching concerning the efficacy of the sacraments. According to medieval theology, ancient Israel also possessed certain sacraments, such as, for example, the ceremony of circumcision. The sacraments of the old law, however, were regarded as less effective than the sacraments of the new. Whereas the sacraments of the church are effective *ex opere operato* ("on the basis of the performance of the rite"), the sacraments of Israel were only effective *ex opere operantis* ("on the basis of the disposition of the recipient"). The sacraments of the Old Covenant merely signify God's grace; they do not convey it as a matter of course. The sacraments of the New Covenant, on the other hand, are effective signs that convey to believers what they symbolize.

Although Marcion did not succeed in his attempt to persuade the church to abandon the Old Testament, he did not suffer total defeat. The church erected a wall of partition between the two Testaments, less formidable than the barrier erected by Marcion but nevertheless real. The Old Testament, theologians argued, is directed toward the natural end of human beings, while the New Testament is related to the higher goal of their supernatural end. The Old Covenant was marked by *timor* ("fear"), while the New Covenant is characterized by *amor* ("love"). The Pauline vision of the church as the wild olive branch grafted into the tree of Israel was generally lost in the scramble to assert the uniqueness of the church and the abrogation of the covenant with Israel.

A strong counteroffensive against the residual Marcionite tendencies in the theology of the church was launched by Zwingli and his successor, Bullinger. These theologians opposed all theories of salvation history marked by discontinuity. Israel and the church were understood by the Zurich reformers as part of one covenant people of God. The fundamental covenant, which affects the destiny of both Israel and the church, is the covenant with Abraham, which is brought to fruition but not abrogated in Jesus Christ. There is no distinction, with respect to their effectiveness, between the sacraments of the Old Testament and the sacraments of the New. While there are differences between the Old Testament and the New—the ritual celebrations and festivals of Israel, for example, are not binding on the church—still these differences are accidental rather than substantial. The meaning of God's saving act in Jesus Christ can only be rightly discerned when it is seen in the framework of the covenant with Abraham.

The Reformed insistence on the unity of salvation history and the fundamental nature of the covenant with Abraham meant that the Reformed were in a position to appreciate the doctrine of the kingship of Christ over the earth.[3] When the church begins to interpret the New Testament in the light of the Old, it is compelled to reject the kind of spirituality that turns its back on the world. Human salvation is not deliverance from the world, but redemption together with it. Creation is not the work of an alien God but the context and ultimate goal of redemption.

The Reformed solution to the problem of the relation of the two Testaments was not the only answer proposed in the sixteenth century. The Anabaptists also struggled with the problem and attempted to elaborate a constructive solution. One of the most significant alternatives to the Reformed position was the theory elaborated by Pilgram Marpeck, the leader of the South German Anabaptists.

Marpeck was not a theologian by training but a civil engineer.[4] He was born around the year 1495 in Rattenberg in the Inn Valley of Austria. His family was reasonably well-to-do, and several relatives had served in the local government of Rattenberg. He attended Latin school and in 1520 entered the Rattenberg brotherhood of miners. In 1523 he became a member of the town council and in 1525 was given the post of mining judge. The income from his public office and his private business enabled him to own two homes and to travel in Germany. His comfortable financial status also made it possible for him to adopt three children.

There is a mystery surrounding Marpeck's conversion to the Anabaptist cause. Apparently, he was very much impressed by the preaching of Leonhard Schiemer and Hans Schlaffer, two Anabaptist missionaries who were executed in Rattenberg in 1528. It also seems probable that he attended Anabaptist meetings in Kitzbühl and in the Münichau Castle during 1527. At any rate, he was dismissed from his post as mining judge on January 28, 1528, because of his unwillingness to aid the authorities in Innsbruck in their efforts to apprehend the Anabaptists in the Rattenberg area. There is every reason to believe that his reluctance to persecute the Anabaptists stemmed not simply from his generally humane and tolerant feelings toward them but from the fact that he shared their theological convictions. Shortly after his dismissal from office he fled from Rattenberg, leaving his property to be confiscated by the authorities.

He arrived in Strasbourg, where he purchased citizenship and a house. The imperial city of Strasbourg under Bucer and Capito was relatively tolerant of religious dissent, and many of the more important figures in the Radical reformation took up residence there, men such as Schwenckfeld, Sebastian Franck, Johannes Bünderlin, and Jakob Kautz. Marpeck soon established himself as one of the leaders of the Anabaptist movement in Strasbourg.

The Strasbourg city council was delighted to have an engineer with Marpeck's training and experience on the payroll of the city and gave him a post as civil engineer. Strasbourg needed lumber from the Black Forest as well as from the valley of the Ehn and the Klingental. Marpeck constructed the flumes that made it possible to float logs from the rich timberlands to the east and west of Strasbourg down the Rhine to the timberless city. His services were well performed and highly regarded by the city council. If he had not been an Anabaptist, he could have lived out his days in Strasbourg.

In 1531, however, the city council of Strasbourg, acting in part in response to the initiative of Marpeck, summoned a meeting of its members and the Committee of Twenty-one to investigate Marpeck's theological views. The pressure to clarify the lines between the magisterial and the Radical reformers came mainly from Bucer. Capito was, on the whole, inclined to take a rather more relaxed view of the Radicals than was his colleague.

On December 9, 1531, Marpeck was called before the council to defend his views against the charges leveled against him by Bucer. Marpeck summarized his position in twenty-three articles, which Bucer attempted to refute point by point.[5] Marpeck defended the Anabaptist view of adult baptism and of the independence of the church from the state. Bucer, who rejected Marpeck's theology of the church, advocated the practice of infant baptism by drawing the typically Reformed analogy between Israel and the church and between circumcision and baptism.[6] The city council upheld Bucer's theology of baptism over Marpeck's and informed Marpeck that if he did not abandon his views he would have to leave Strasbourg for good. He agreed to their decision and asked for a little time to dispose of his property. In January 1532, he turned his back on Strasbourg, forced for the second time in his life to leave his home and his position for his faith.

Comparatively little is known about his activities over the next decade. He became, together with Leupold Scharnschlager, the leader of a group of South

Radical Reformers

German Anabaptists scattered over a wide territory from Moravia in the east to Alsace in the west.[7] In 1542 he began a controversy with Schwenckfeld that stretched over several years. Marpeck could accept neither Schwenckfeld's Christology nor his excessive individualism. The debate between the two theologians, who apparently had come to know each other in Strasbourg, is one of the more important in the sixteenth century and states the position of the evangelical Anabaptists over against that of the Spiritualists.

In 1544 Marpeck settled permanently in Augsburg, where he was once again given the post of city engineer with a salary of 150 florins a year. The city of Augsburg was Protestant, though certainly not Anabaptist. This could have meant trouble for Marpeck, who made no attempt to hide the fact that he was an Anabaptist elder. The city council, however, seems to have satisfied itself with wrist-tapping warnings to Marpeck to stop his activities as an Anabaptist. There are four warnings on record, issued in 1545, 1550, 1553, and 1554. When Marpeck died in 1556, the city still had not taken any more severe action against him than these pro forma expressions of disapprobation.

Marpeck's views on a whole range of issues—for example, his view of the freedom of the will, of the necessity of adult baptism, of the nature of the church as a voluntary community living in conscious tension with the world—are not very different from the views of Balthasar Hubmaier and the other South German Anabaptists.[8] These views, however, had come under fire from two directions, from Bucer and Bullinger on the right and from Schwenckfeld on the left.

Bucer and the Reformed defended infant baptism by stressing the unity between the two Testaments and the consequent validity of the analogy between circumcision and infant baptism. Marpeck correctly perceived that it was impossible to maintain the doctrine of believer's baptism over against Bucer and Bullinger without addressing the issue of the relationship between the two Testaments. It was impossible to be wrong on that issue and still be right on the other.

Marpeck's view of the Old Testament presupposed a sharp distinction between it and the New Testament.[9] The Old Testament represents "yesterday"; the New Testament "today." The contrast between yesterday and today rested for Marpeck on his understanding of the decisiveness of the Christ-event. The Old Testament saints were not redeemed until Jesus Christ suffered and died on their behalf. When the Israelites were delivered from bondage in Egypt, though this exodus was an authentic act of God, it was nothing more than a physical redemption from physical bondage. It has, of course, typological significance as a signpost pointing ahead toward the saving act of God in Christ, but considered in itself it is an act of God of a fundamentally different order. The Old Testament saints are first redeemed in the New Testament. The descent into hell is the act by which God releases them from their spiritual bondage. In other words, the saving acts of God have consequences but not pre-effects.

Because the New Covenant and the Old Covenant are fundamentally different, just as physical and spiritual redemption are distinct, analogies between the
Old and New Testaments are both dangerous and misleading. The moral standards of the New Testament are higher than those of the Old, and any
attempt to reinstitute the lower standards of the Old Testament destroys
Christian freedom. Christians may not carry the sword simply because it was
carried in the Old Testament; nor may infants be baptized because they were
circumcised in Israel. To be sure, one finds symbolically in the Old Testament
foreshadowings of the rites and events of the New. But that does not for a
minute mean that symbol and essence are on the same level or that one should
forsake the reality that has come to light in the New Testament for the shadows
of the Old. The meaning of baptism, of the church, of Christian ethics must be
defined from the gospel. The uniqueness of the saving event in Jesus Christ
means that the New Testament provides its own framework of interpretation.

Though Marpeck did not echo the Marcionite rejection of the Old
Testament, he did make it clear that the New Testament is primary and that
the Old Testament represents a more primitive and dated level of revelation.
The new deed of God in Christ has made the old deeds through Abraham and
Moses obsolescent. The Old Testament is useful to the church precisely to the
extent that its preliminary character is recognized and respected. Any confusion of the two Testaments will result in an obscuring of the uniqueness of the
person and work of Jesus Christ or in a lessening of the stringent ethical demands of the New Covenant.

Bucer and Bullinger misunderstood the nature of the new covenant community in Christ because of their obsession with the old covenant community
of Israel. The danger from Schwenckfeld was of a different sort altogether.
Schwenckfeld, by his individualistic spiritualization of the gospel, threatened
to dissolve the idea of community and replace it with a religion of the isolated
believer in the presence of God. In the face of the Spirit-dominated Christianity
of Schwenckfeld, Marpeck wished to reaffirm the importance of the letter,
without lapsing into the biblical literalism that characterized many of the Swiss
Anabaptists. He tried to strike a balance by reinterpreting the meaning of the
magisterium of the church.

The classic statement of the problem of the magisterium or teaching office
of the church was developed by Vincent of Lérins in the first half of the fifth
century. Vincent admitted that Holy Scripture could be interpreted in several
ways. But there was a simple test for what is catholic truth. One should believe
as true what has been believed everywhere (*ubique*), always (*semper*), and by all
(*ab omnibus*). A proper interpretation of Scripture can and must meet this three-
fold test. This means that ancient truth is always to be preferred to theological
novelty.

Vincent believed that all theological truths were revealed at the very beginning of the Christian Era. There was a doctrinal deposit entrusted to the earli-

est church. Whatever one teaches in the present can, and must, be nothing more than an explanation and unfolding of the truth found in this original deposit.

Vincent believed, furthermore, that there has been from the very beginning a real doctrinal consensus in the truth. This is, of course, not the dispassionate judgment of an historical scholar who has sifted the evidence and discovered this consensus. It is the judgment of a theologian who posits on theological grounds the existence of such a consensus before he goes looking for it.

Finally, Vincent was convinced not only that such a doctrinal consensus exists in the church and has existed from the very beginning but that it is ascertainable. But who has the time and competence to go looking for this doctrinal consensus? The church needs a magisterium, a teaching office, someone with the time and the competence to seek out and identify this doctrinal consensus, which is believed to exist before it has ever been found.

Some theologians in the later Middle Ages regarded the doctors of the church as the true bearers of this teaching office.[10] Those who felt this way held that there is a single source of revelation from which the Christian church draws its teaching and that source is Holy Scripture. Every doctrine the church wishes to teach is found in Holy Scripture. Indeed, it must be found there, or the church has no business teaching it. That does not mean that these theologians appeal to Scripture alone and reject the tradition of the church as a useless appendage that, if listened to, will distort the meaning of Holy Scripture. On the contrary, the tradition of the church is highly respected as an aid for the understanding of Holy Scripture. The wisdom of the past is not rejected. But neither is it looked upon as a second source of revelation. It is an aid for the understanding of Holy Scripture, nothing more. The Christian attempts to understand the Bible with the assistance of those who have labored on it before him. This is essentially the position taken by Luther and Calvin during the Reformation.

Other theologians regarded the bishops as the possessors of the charism of truth, as the authentic interpreters of Holy Scripture. Theologians who felt this way often tended to believe that revelation is richer and fuller than Holy Scripture. Not all of the revelation committed to the apostles was written down by them. Some teachings were passed on orally. These are the unwritten traditions of the church, which are to be regarded as of equal authority with Holy Scripture. The Roman Catholic church at the Council of Trent affirmed this understanding of the relationship of Scripture and tradition.

Marpeck rejected both the Roman Catholic and the main-line Protestant understanding of the teaching office of the church. His emphasis on *sola scriptura* implied a more radical rejection of the tradition of the church than did the position of Luther and Calvin. On the other hand, he did not retreat into a bare literalism. The letter of Scripture without the simultaneous witness of the Spirit kills rather than makes alive. However, the bearer of the teaching office of the church is not the Spirit-instructed individual, as Schwenckfeld maintained, but rather the community of the regenerate and baptized believers. The interpretation of Scripture is a communal activity, in which the exegesis of individual members of the church is subject to the community as a whole. Tradition is the living voice of the voluntary community of believers as that community is instructed by the Spirit through Scripture. It is not the doctors of the church nor the bishops, but the community as a whole that is the bearer of the charism of truth. The covenant community is the authentic interpreter of Holy Scripture.

In his view of the relation of the two Testaments and by his emphasis on the corporate nature of the interpretation of Holy Scripture, Marpeck represents a maturing and refining of the Anabaptist position. Other Anabaptist leaders were more imaginative, some were more learned, but none was wiser or more temperate. He corrected the excesses of earlier Anabaptists and gave their faith balance and form.

NOTES

ABBREVIATIONS

CR   *Corpus Reformatorum.* (Halle, Berlin, Brunswick, Leipzig, and Zurich, 1834–)

LW   *Luther's Works.* 55 Volumes. (Philadelphia: Fortress Press; St. Louis: Concordia, 1955–)

WA   *D. Martin Luthers Werke: Kritische Gesamtausgabe.* (Weimar, 1883–1983)

WABr   *D. Martin Luthers Werke: Briefwechsel.* (Weimar, 1930–70)

WATR   *D. Martin Luthers Werke: Tischreden.* (Weimar, 1912–21)

I. JOHANNES GEILER VON KAYSERSBERG

1. The most useful histories of Strasbourg in English are Miriam Usher Chrisman, *Strasbourg and the Reform*, and Franklin L. Ford, *Strasbourg in Transition, 1648–1789* (New York: Norton, 1966). Note: Works listed in the bibliography for each chapter are cited in shortened form in the notes to that chapter.

2. For the biography of Geiler, see L. Dacheux, *Un réformateur catholique à la fin du XVe siècle.* There is a brief biography in Chrisman, *Strasbourg and the Reform*, pp. 68–78.

3. For a discussion of the relationship of Geiler to humanism, see E. J. Dempsey Douglass, *Justification in Late Medieval Preaching*, pp. 206–7. The following characterization of Geiler's theology is heavily dependent on the research of Douglass.

4. Douglass, *Justification in Late Medieval Preaching*, p. 203.

5. The most important seminal study of nominalist thought is Heiko A. Oberman, *The Harvest of Medieval Theology.* For a brief and more popular discussion see Heiko A. Oberman, *Forerunners of the Reformation* (New York: Holt, Rinehart and Winston, 1966), pp. 123–41.

6. Douglass, *Justification in Late Medieval Preaching*, pp. 82–91.

7. Ibid., pp. 30–7.

2. JOHANNES VON STAUPITZ

1. On this problem see Ernst Wolf, *Staupitz und Luther*, pp. 138–68. Wolf's conclusions are briefly summarized in his article "Johann von Staupitz und die theologische Anfänge Luthers," *Luther-Jahrbuch* 9 (1929): 43–86. For more recent discussions see my *Misericordia Dei* and *Luther and Staupitz*.

2. For an extensive discussion of the possible meanings of Augustinian in the later Middle Ages, see my *Luther and Staupitz*.

3. For an informative, if harshly critical, essay on this problem see Reinoud Weijenborg, "Neuentdeckte Dokumente im Zusammenhang mit Luthers Romreise," *Antonianum* 32 (1957): 147–202. Weijenborg's conclusions were subjected to searching criticism by Franz Lau, "Pere Reinoud und Luther: Bemerkungen zu Reinhold Weijenborgs Lutherstudien," *Luther-Jahrbuch* 27 (1960): 64–122.

4. WATR 2, no. 2255 (18 Aug.–26 Dec. 1531); WATR 4, no. 4091 (6–9 Nov. 1538); LW 54, 320; WATR 5, no. 5371 (Summer 1540).

5. For a systematic survey of Staupitz's theology see my *Misericordia Dei* and *Luther and Staupitz*. See also Markus Wriedt, *Gnade und Erwählung*.

6. Johannes von Staupitz, *Hiob* (1497–98) 5.32.26–33; 7.44.36–37; 7.44.41–45; 30.229.2–4; 18.153.19–21; *Libellus* (1517) 3; *Lieb Gottes* (1518), ed. Knaake, 94.

7. Staupitz, *Libellus* 22, 26, 27, 33; *Lieb Gottes* 111.

8. Staupitz, *Libellus* 36, 40, 86, 131, 152.

9. Staupitz, *Lieb Gottes* 105.

10. Staupitz, *Hiob* 1.3.8–10; *Libellus* 8, 9, 13, 14, 33.

11. Staupitz, *Libellus* 26.

12. Staupitz, *Libellus* 62; *Glauben* (1525), ed. Knaake, 126–7.

13. Staupitz, Hs: bV8, St. Peter (1512), Sermon 12, folio 58.

14. Staupitz, *Hiob* 11.95.5–11.

15. Gabriel Biel, *Sermones Dominicales de Tempore* (Hagenau, 1510), 4 A; *Sermones de Festivitatibus Christi* (Hagenau, 1510), 12 E. For a discussion of Biel on this distinction see Heiko A. Oberman, *Harvest of Medieval Theology* (Cambridge: Harvard University Press, 1963), pp. 217–35.

16. WABr 2.566–68, no. 512 (27 June 1522).

17. WABr 3.155–57, no. 659 (17 Sept. 1523).

18. The text of this letter is reprinted in T. Kolde, *Die Deutsche Augustiner-Congregation und Johann von Staupitz*, pp. 446–47.

3. GASPARO CONTARINI

1. Hubert Jedin, *A History of the Council of Trent*, vol. 1, *The Struggle for the Council*, pp. 355–6.

2. Ibid., p. 356.

3. G. R. Elton, *The New Cambridge Modern History*, vol. 2, *The Reformation, 1520–59*, pp. 175–6. (Hereafter cited as *The Reformation*.)

4. Jedin, *A History of the Council*, p. 372.

5. Ibid.

6. Elton, *The Reformation*, p. 176.

7. Jedin, *A History of the Council*, p. 374.

8. Ibid., pp. 376–7.

9. Ibid., p. 377.

10. Walter Lipgens, *Kardinal Johannes Gropper (1503–1559) und die Anfänge der katholischen Reform in Deutschland*, pp. 68–9.

11. On the medieval doctrine of justification and Luther's relationship to it see Heiko A. Oberman, "'Iustitia Christi' and 'Iustitia Dei': Luther and the Scholastic Doctrines of Justification."

12. Lipgens, *Kardinal Johannes Gropper*, pp. 100–101.

13. Hastings Eells, "The Origin of the Regensburg Book," p. 371.

14. Elton, *The Reformation*, p. 178.

15. Heinz Mackensen, "Contarini's Theological Role at Ratisbon." See Hubert Jedin, "Ein 'Turmerlebnis' des jungen Contarini."

16. Contarini's dependence on Thomas Aquinas has been traced in detail by Hanns Rückert, *Die theologische Entwicklung Gasparo Contarinis*. Heinz Mackensen has challenged Rückert's conclusions and has rightly argued that Contarini was more Augustinian in his doctrine of original sin than was Thomas. See especially Mackensen, "Contarini's Theological Role at Ratisbon," p. 46.

17. Jedin, *A History of the Council*, pp. 378–9.

18. Eells, "The Origin of the Regensburg Book," See R. Stupperich, "Der Ursprung des Regensburger Buches von 1541 und seine Rechtfertigungslehre."

19. Gasparo Contarini, "Liber Ratisbonensis."

20. Richard M. Douglas, *Jacopo Sadoleto, 1477–1547: Humanist and Reformer* (Cambridge: Harvard University Press, 1959), p. 158.

21. Friedrich Hünermann, introduction to *Gasparo Contarini: Gegenreformatorische Schriften, 1530–1542*, p. xx.

22. Gasparo Contarini, "Epistola de Iustificatione," in *Gasparo Contarini: Gegenreformatorische Schriften*, pp. 24, 33.

23. Jedin, *A History of the Council*, p. 384.

24. Ibid., p. 385.

25. Ibid.

26. Elton, *The Reformation*, p. 178.

27. Jedin, *A History of the Council*, p. 386.

4. FABER STAPULENSIS

1. This brief sketch of medieval hermeneutics is especially dependent on the following studies: Gerhard Ebeling, "Die Anfänge von Luthers Hermeneutik," *Zeitschrift für Theologie und Kirche* 48 (1951): 172–230, and "Hermeneutik," in *Die Religion in Geschichte und Gegenwart*, 3d ed. (Tübingen: J.C.B. Mohr, 1957–65), vol 3., cols. 242–62, and "Der hermeneutische Ort der Gotteslehre bei Petrus Lombardus und Thomas von Aquin," *Zeitschrift für Theologie und Kirche* 61 (1964): 283–326; Wilfred Werbeck, *Jacobus Perez von Valencia: Untersuchungen zu seinem Psalmenkommentar* (Tübingen: J.C.B. Mohr, 1959). See also: Beryl Smalley, *The Study of the Bible in the Middle Ages*, 2d ed. (New York: Philosophical Library, 1952); P. C. Spicq, *Esquisse d'une histoire de l'Exégèse Latine au Moyen Age* (Paris: J. Vrin, 1944).

2. "Now what man of intelligence will believe that the first and the second and the third day, and the evening and the morning existed without the sun and moon and stars? And the first day, if we may so call it, was even without a heaven?" Origen *De principiis* 4.3.1, transl. G. W. Butterworth (New York: Harper & Row, 1966).

3. Origen *De principiis* 4.2.4.

4. Augustine, *Epistola ad Vincentium* 8.24.

5. Augustine, *De doctrina Christiana* 3.10.14; 3.15.23.

6. Thomas Aquinas, *Summa Theologiae* 1, q.1, a.10.

7. Thomas Aquinas, VII *Quodlibetales* 6.14–16.

8. Thomas Aquinas, *Summa Theologiae* 1, q.1, a.10 ad 1.

9. See Gerhard Ebeling, "Luthers Psalterdruck vom Jahre 1513," *Zeitschrift fur Theologie und Kirche* 50 (1953): 43–99.

10. For Faber's hermeneutic see Fritz Hahn, "Faber Stapulensis und Luther," pp. 356–432, and the more reliable Heiko A. Oberman, *Forerunners of the Reformation*, pp. 281–96.

11. There is no definitive biography of Faber. Still useful is Karl Henrich Graf, "Jacobus Faber Stapulensis." In English see George V. Jourdan, *The Movement towards Catholic Reform in the Early Sixteenth Century*, and John Woolman Brush, "Lefèvre d'Etaples."

12. Faber, preface to *Quincuplex Psalterium*. For an English translation, see Oberman, *Forerunners of the Reformation*, pp. 297–301.

13. This is made clear in the preface to the *Sancti Pauli Epistolae XIV*. For an English translation, see Oberman, *Forerunners of the Reformation*, pp. 302–7.

14. On the circle of Meaux, see especially R.-J. Lovy, *Les origines de la Réforme Française*.

15. Faber articulates this ideal in the introduction to the *Commentarii Initiatorii in Quatuor Evangelia*. For the English text, see J. B. Ross and M. M. McLaughlin, eds., *The Portable Renaissance Reader* (New York: Viking Press, 1958), pp.84–86.

16. On Noel Beda see Walter F. Bense, "Noel Beda and the Humanist Reformation at Paris, 1504–1534" (Ph.D. diss., Harvard University, 1967).

17. See Oberman, *Forerunners of the Reformation*, p. 291.

18. On this point, see François Wendel, *Calvin: Origins and Development of His Religious Thought* (New York: William Collins, 1963), p. 130. See Hermann Dörries, "Lefèvre und Calvin."

19. See in this connection the careful essay by W. F. Dankbaar, "Op de Grens der Reformatie."

20. "Zelf is hij niet door die deur gegaan. Maar hij heeft de deur geopend"; Dankbaar, "Op de Grens der Reformatie," p. 345.

5. REGINALD POLE

1. The most complete and authoritative biography of Pole is Wilhelm Schenck, *Reginald Pole, Cardinal of England*.

2. For the English text of this treatise see Reginald Pole, *Pole's Defense of the Unity of the Church*.

3. In this connection see George B. Parks, "The Parma Letters and the Dangers to Cardinal Pole."

4. For the history of the period from Regensburg to Trent see Hubert Jedin, *A History of the Council of Trent*, vol. 1, *The Struggle for the Council*.

5. Reginald Pole, quoted by Joseph G. Dwyer in his introduction to *Pole's Defense*, p. xxix.

6. For Pole's theological role at Trent, see Marvin W. Anderson, "Trent and Justification (1546)." See also Jedin, *A History of the Council*.

7. See Hubert Jedin, "Kardinal Pole und Vittoria Colonna."

8. Reginald Pole, as quoted by Edward G. Boland in "An Appreciation of Cardinal Pole," p. 125.

9. For the Marian epoch, see H. F. M. Prescott, *Mary Tudor*.

6. PHILIP MELANCHTHON

1. WATR 3, no. 3619 (1 Aug. 1537); LW 54:245.

2. WATR 5, no. 5511; LW 54: 339–40. See WA 18.601.3; translation in *Luther and Erasmus: Free Will and Salvation*, trans. and ed. E. Gordon Rupp and Philip S. Watson, Library of Christian Classics 17 (Philadelphia: Westminster Press, 1969), p. 102.

3. In this connection see the illuminating essay by Wilhelm Pauck, "Luther and Melanchthon," in *Luther and Melanchthon*, ed. Vilmos Vajta, pp. 13–31.

4. CR 6:474, 880, 882.

5. Luther felt that Melanchthon was often too severe with his students during examinations. WATR 4, no. 4056.

6. WATR 1, no. 17 (1531); WATR 3, no. 3520, LW 54: 219–20; WATR 4, no. 4444.

7. WATR 1, no. 80. See WABr 5.412.19.

8. WATR 5, Nr. 6443. See WATR 4, no. 4909.

9. Franz Hildebrandt, *Melanchthon: Alien or Ally?*

10. The most recent biographies of Melanchthon in English are Clyde Manschreck, *Melanchthon, The Quiet Reformer*, and Robert Stupperich, *Melanchthon*.

11. Hildebrandt and Pauck follow an older tradition in historiography that believes that humanism represents a philosophical position very close to the teaching of Erasmus. Hildebrandt remarks concerning Melanchthon's continuing humanism after his conversion to the Lutheran reformation that Melanchthon "enables us to define how far a Lutheran can go in humanism without becoming a heretic." Hildebrandt, *Melanchthon*, p. xii. Nevertheless, as an evangelical humanist, Melanchthon walked a different path from the Reformed theologians who shared a common background in humanism. Melanchthon's commitment to Luther meant that "it was impossible for him to understand the Bible in the moralistic-legalistic way of Zwingli, Butzer, or Calvin. Evangelical humanists which they were, they attached special value to the connection between faith and morality. But Melanchthon was inspired by Humanism to cultivate especially the connection between *faith* and *intellectual culture*." Pauck, "Luther and Melanchthon," p. 17. This view of humanism has been challenged by many historians, especially Paul O. Kristeller.

12. Philip Melanchthon, *The Loci Communes of Philip Melanchthon*, pp. 68–9.

13. CR 11:280, 282.

14. CR 21:790; 12:433; 11:272.

15. CR 11:280, 282.

16. CR 1:613, 695; 3:362; 11:280, 282; 13:655; 10:690; 21:370.

17. CR 12:399, 568, 608; 5:582; 3:826, 985; 11:272; 8:49.

18. CR 11:273.

19. Wilhelm Maurer, "Melanchthon as Author of the Augsburg Confession," pp. 153–67.

20. CR 10:70, 785; 21:332, 652, 659.

21. CR 21:658.

22. CR 21:742.

23. Fraenkel has argued that Melanchthon's shift in eucharistic theology is due in part to his study of the eucharistic teaching of the fathers, a road he was prompted to follow by the stimulus of Oecolampadius, the reformer of Basel. Melanchthon's doctrine is characterized by what Fraenkel calls its "functional element, i.e., the concentration on processes rather than things." Peter Fraenkel, "Ten Questions Concerning Melanchthon, the Fathers and the Eucharist," in *Luther and Melanchthon*, ed. Vilmos Vajta, pp. 146–64.

24. Melanchthon makes it clear that he does not believe that this is a test Luther himself would have imposed. CR 1:287, 406; 6:170.

7. JOHANNES BUGENHAGEN

1. WATR 3, no. 2898, LW 54:179; WATR 4, no. 4956.

2. The most helpful interpretive essay on Bugenhagen is Ernst Wolf, "Johannes Bugenhagen, Gemeinde und Amt."

3. Older but still useful biographies of Bugenhagen are Karl A. T. Vogt, *Johannes Bugenhagen Pomeranus*, and Hermann Hering, *Doctor Pommeranus, Johannes Bugenhagen*.

4. For Bugenhagen's view of the Lord's Supper see his "Von der Evangelischen Messe, 1524," "Ein Ratschlag, wie man das Sakrament geniessen soll, 1524," and "Bekentnis von seinem Glauben und seiner Lehre, 1529."

5. The text of this church order has been edited by Hans Lietzmann: *Johannes Bugenhagens Braunschweiger Kirchenordnung*. For his work in composing and revising liturgies see Johannes H. Bergsma, *Die Reform der Messliturgie durch Johannes Bugenhagen (1485–1558)*.

8. ANDREAS OSIANDER

1. For the life of Osiander see W. Möller, *Andreas Osiander*, and Gottfried Seebass, *Das reformatorische Werk des Andreas Osiander*.

2. Osiander's attitude toward Copernicus and the controversy that surrounds his composition of the preface is treated in some detail by John Dillenberger in *Protestant Thought and Natural Science*, pp. 41–9. See Heinrich Bornkamm, "Kopernikus im Urteil der Reformatoren," in *Das Jahrhundert der Reformation*, pp. 177–85.

3. The fundamental study of Osiander's theology is E. Hirsch, *Die Theologie des Andreas Osiander und ihre geschichtlichen Voraussetzungen*. Also helpful is Hans Emil Weber, *Reformation, Orthodoxie, und Rationalismus*, vol. 1, pt. 1, pp. 258–321.

4. For Reuchlin see Lewis William Spitz's, *The Religious Renaissance of the German Humanists*, pp. 61–80 (Cambridge: Harvard University Press, 1963).

9. NIKOLAUS VON AMSDORF

1. See Robert Kolb, *Nikolaus von Amsdorf*, for an introduction to Amsdorf. Still useful for biographical detail is Theodor Pressel, *Nicolaus von Amsdorf*.

2. For this period of Amsdorf's life see Peter Brunner, *Nicholas von Amsdorf als Bishof von Naumburg*.

3. A brief but useful exposition of Amsdorf's theology is Otto Henning Nebe, *Reine Lehre*.

4. Nikolaus von Amsdorf, *Nikolaus von Amsdorff: Ausgewählte Schriften*, ed. Otto Lerche, p. 93.

5. Ibid., p. 79.
6. Ibid., p. 88.
7. Ibid., p. 84.
8. Ibid., pp. 86–7.
9. Ibid., p. 104.
10. Ibid., p. 85.
11. Ibid., p. 128.
12. Ibid., p. 129.
13. Ibid., p. 130.
14. Ibid., p. 96.

10. JOHANNES BRENZ

1. For the early theology of Brenz see the excellent book by Martin Brecht, *Die frühe Theologie des Johannes Brenz.*
2. On this question see James M. Estes, "Church Order and the Christian Magistrate according to Johannes Brenz."
3. See F. W. Kantzenbach, "Der Beitrag des Johannes Brenz zur Toleranzidee."

11. MARTIN BUCER

1. For a general biography of Bucer in English see Hastings Eells, *Martin Bucer.*
2. Martin Bucer, "Martin Butzers an ein christlichen Rath und Gemeyn der statt Weissenburg Summary seiner Predig daselbst gethon 1523," in *Martin Bucers Deutsche Schriften*, vol. 1 (1960), pp. 69–147.
3. See Wilhelm Pauck, "Luther and Butzer," in *The Heritage of the Reformation*, pp. 73–83.
4. On the relation of Bucer and Calvin see Pauck, "Calvin and Butzer," pp. 85–99.
5. See Gerrit Jan van de Poll, *Martin Bucer's Liturgical Ideas.*
6. For a brief survey of Bucer's theology, see Otto Ritschl, *Dogmengeschichte des Protestantismus*, vol. 3, pp. 122–56 (Leipzig: J. C. Hinrichs, 1908–27).
7. For the career of Gropper see Walter Lipgens, *Kardinal Johannes Gropper (1503–1559) und die Anfänge der katholischen Reform in Deutschland* (Münster in Westphalia: Aschendorff, 1951).
8. For Bucer's activity in England see Constantin Hopf, *Martin Bucer and the English Reformation.*

12. HEINRICH BULLINGER

1. The most authoritative biography of Bullinger until his inauguration at Zurich is Fritz Blanke, *Der junge Bullinger, 1504–1531.* For a brief survey of scholarship on Bullinger see Rudolf Pfister, "Bullinger-Forschung," *Archiv für Reformationsgeschichte* 51 (1960): 90–7. Old but still useful as an introduction to Bullinger is Carl Pestalozzi, *Heinrich Bullinger: Leben und ausgewählte Schriften* (1858).
2. On the meaning of the covenant in early Reformed thought, see Gottlob Schrenk, *Gottesreich und Bund im älteren Protestantismus: Vernehmlich bei Johannes Coccejus* (Gütersloh: Bertelsmann, 1923); Jens G. Møller, "The Beginnings of Puritan Covenant Theology," *Journal of Ecclesiastical History* 14 (1963): 46–67; Joseph C. McLelland,

"Covenant Theology: A Re-evaluation," *Canadian Journal of Theology* 3 (1957): 182–8; J. Rodman Williams, "The Covenant in Reformed Theology," *Austin Seminary Bulletin* 78 (1963): 24–38; and Lyle D. Bierma, "Federal Theology in the Sixteenth Century: Two Traditions?" *Westminster Theological Journal* 45 (Fall 1983): 304–21.

3. Bullinger's view of the covenant is conveniently summarized in sermon 6 of the third *Decade*, pp. 167–217. For an excellent treatment of Bullinger's understanding of covenant, see A. J. van't Hooft, *De theologie van Heinrich Bullinger in betrekking tot de Nederlandsche Reformatie.*

4. Joachim Staedke, *Die Theologie des jungen Bullinger*, p. 69.

5. On this point see Gottfried W. Locher, "The Change in the Understanding of Zwingli in Recent Research," *Church History* 34 (1965): 19. The most comprehensive study of the *Decades* and their influence is Walter Hollweg, *Heinrich Bullingers Hausbuch.*

6. On the Second Helvetic Confession see the collection of important essays edited by Joachim Staedke, *Glauben und Bekennen.*

7. An important exception to this generalization is the excellent study of Bullinger's influence in France and the French-speaking cantons of Switzerland by André Bouvier, *Henri Bullinger.*

8. For Bullinger's relation to Anabaptism see Heinold Fast, *Heinrich Bullinger und die Täufer.*

13. JOHN HOOPER

1. I am using the term "Puritan" throughout this essay to describe a spirit later embodied in the later Puritan movement and of which Hooper was representative. Puritanism as a movement begins in the reign of Elizabeth I. In that sense Hooper was never a Puritan.

2. For a brief biography of Hooper see Everett H. Emerson, *English Puritanism from John Hooper to John Milton*, pp. 47–50.

3. "For if they be kept in the Church as things indifferent, at length they will be maintained as things necessary." John Hooper, *Early Writings*, p. 534.

4. A point forcefully made by Marshall Knappen, *Tudor Puritanism*, p. 86.

5. J. Gairdner, "Bishop Hooper's Visitation of Gloucester, 1551," *English Historical Review* (1904): 98–121.

14. PETER MARTYR VERMIGLI

1. For Peter Martyr's early life see Philip McNair, *Peter Martyr in Italy.*

2. George H. Williams provides a brief introduction to Valdés in *The Radical Reformation* (Philadelphia: Westminster Press, 1962), pp. 529–36, as does Angel M. Mergal in *Spiritual and Anabaptist Writers*, ed. George H. Williams and Angel M. Mergal, Library of Christian Classics 25 (Philadelphia: Westminster Press, 1957), pp. 297–319.

3. On Ochino see Roland H. Bainton, *The Travail of Religious Liberty* (New York: Harper, 1958), pp. 149–76.

4. For a comprehensive treatment of Peter Martyr's doctrine of the Lord's Supper see Joseph C. McLelland, *The Visible Words of God.*

5. On the problem of sacrifice see Franz Hildebrandt, *I Offered Christ* (Philadelphia: Fortress Press, 1967).

6. On the Marburg colloquy see Walther Köhler, *Zwingli und Luther*, vol. 2

(Gütersloh: C. Bertelsmann, 1953). See Ernst Bizer, *Studien zur Geschichte des Abendmahl-streits im 16. Jahrhundert*, 2d ed. (Darmstadt: Wissenschaftliche Buchgesellschaft, 1962). For a brief and helpful introduction to Zwingli's eucharistic thought, see Gottfried W. Locher, "The Shape of Zwingli's Theology," *Pittsburgh Perspective* 8 (1967): 5–26.

7. For a brief statement of Luther's understanding of the Lord's Supper see Paul Althaus, *The Theology of Martin Luther* (Philadelphia: Fortress Press, 1966), pp. 375–403. See also "Scripture and the Lord's Supper," chapter 7 of my *Luther in Context* (Grand Rapids: Baker Books, 1986 [1995]) pp. 72–84.

8. Calvin's teaching on the Eucharist is helpfully discussed by Ronald S. Wallace in *Calvin's Doctrine of the Word and Sacrament* (Edinburgh: Oliver and Boyd, 1953). See Kilian McDonnell, *John Calvin, the Church, and the Eucharist* (Princeton: Princeton University Press, 1967). See also "Calvin and his Lutheran Critics," chapter 12 of my *Calvin in Context* (New York: Oxford University Press, 1995), pp. 172–186.

9. On the importance of this theme in Calvin's thought see especially Heiko A. Oberman, "Die 'Extra'-Dimension in der Theologie Calvins," in *Geist und Geschichte der Reformation: Festgabe Hanns Rückert zum 65. Geburtstag*, ed. Heinz Liebing and Klaus Scholder (Berlin: de Gruyter, 1966), pp. 323–56.

10. For the function of this doctrine as a way of preserving the Trinitarian character of the human knowledge of God and of oneself see E. David Willis, *Calvin's Catholic Christology*, Studies in Medieval and Reformation Thought 2 (Leiden: E. J. Brill, 1966).

15. THEODORE BEZA

1. An older but still useful biography of Beza in English is Henry M. Baird, *Theodore Beza*.

2. In this connection see Waldo S. Pratt, *The Music of the French Psalter of 1562*.

3. For this controversy see Robert M. Kingdon, *Geneva and the Consolidation of the French Protestant Movement, 1564–1572*, pp. 37–137.

4. See Basil Hall, "Calvin against the Calvinists," pp. 19–37.

5. Theodore Beza, *Tractationes Theologicae*, 1:171, 183.

6. Ibid., 3:248, 256.

7. Ibid., 1:170–1.

8. Ibid., 1:344, 362, 418; 3:404.

9. I owe this insight to Richard A. Muller of Calvin Theological Seminary.

16. ANDREAS BODENSTEIN VON CARLSTADT

1. The most complete biography of Carlstadt is the two-volume work by Hermann Barge, *Andreas Bodenstein von Karlstadt*. See also Gordon Rupp's treatment of Carlstadt in his *Patterns of Reformation* (Philadelphia: Fortress Press, 1969), pp. 49–153; and George H. Williams, *The Radical Reformation*, pp. 38–44, 68–75, 101–6.

2. For the theology of Staupitz see my *Misericordia Dei: The Theology of Johannes von Staupitz in Its Late Medieval Setting*, Studies in Medieval and Reformation Thought 4 (Leiden: E. J. Brill, 1968) and *Luther and Staupitz: A Essay in the Intellectual Origins of the Protestant Reformation*, Duke Monographs in Medieval and Renaissance Studies 4 (Durham, N.C.: Duke University Press, 1980).

3. These theses are reprinted in *Karlstadt und Augustin*, ed. Ernst Kähler, pp. 8*–37*.

4. Ibid., pp. 3–122.

5. Ibid., p. 67, ll. 28 ff.; 81.31 ff.; 29.1 ff.; 30.19.

6. Note especially thesis 109: "Lex evangelii scripta est vetus." On this subject see Gordon Rupp, "Word and Spirit in the First Years of the Reformation," *Archiv für Reformationsgeschichte* 49 (1958): 13–26. See Andreas Bodenstein von Carlstadt, *Karlstadts Schriften aus den Jahren 1523–25*, 2:13.10–11; 2:77.10–11. (Hereafter cited as *Schriften*.)

7. Carlstadt, *Schriften*, 2:18.29–19.8. On this question see also Hans J. Hillerbrand, "Andreas Bodenstein of Carlstadt, Prodigal Reformer."

8. See Bernd Moeller, "Tauler und Luther," in *La mystique rhénane* (Paris: Presses universitaires de France, 1963), pp. 157–68; Heiko A. Oberman, "Simul Gemitus et Raptus: Luther und die Mystik," in *The Church, Mysticism, Sanctification, and the Natural in Luther's Thought* (Philadelphia: Fortress Press, 1967), pp. 20–59.

9. Andreas Bodenstein von Carlstadt, *Was gesagt ist: Sich gelassen* (1523), A iv.

10. Erich Hertzsch is in general agreement with this point of view; see *Schriften*, 1:xvi–xvii.

11. Carlstadt, *Schriften*, 1:59.14–60.15.

12. Andreas Bodenstein von Carlstadt, *Von Abtuhung der Bilder und das keyn Bedtler unther den Christen seyn sollen*.

13. WA 10.1–64; LW 51:70–100.

14. Carlstadt, *Schriften*, 2:7–49.

15. Andreas Bodenstein von Carlstadt, *Auslegung dieser Wort Christi* (Basel, 1524), d iiij. See also his *Schriften*, 2:22.31–3.

16. Carlstadt, *Schriften*, 2:13.38 ff.

17. CASPAR SCHWENCKFELD

1. CR 8:740.

2. Caspar Schwenckfeld, *Corpus Schwenckfeldianorum*, 2:132–39. (Hereafter cited as *CS*.)

3. *CS* 2:191 ff.

4. *CS* 2:205 ff.

5. *CS* 3:153, 626; 12:535.

6. WA 19.123.

7. *CS* 2:62.

8. *CS* 14:110 ff.; 3:44, 77 ff.

9. *CS* 4:39; 14:116; 2:354.

10. *CS* 2:346; 3:376.

11. *CS* 2:621; 3:721; 5:674; 13:248; 14:379; 9:718.

12. *CS* 11:435; 10:413.

13. *CS* 5:170.

14. *CS* 13:985; 10:707; 3:509.

15. *CS* 2:574, as translated by Paul L. Maier in *Caspar Schwenckfeld on the Person and Work of Christ*, p. 22.

16. *CS* 7:507, 547.

17. *CS* 6:86 ff.

18. *CS* 7:740; 17:326–438.

19. *CS* 9:812.

20. *CS* 8:667.

21. *CS* 4:27, 37; 10:846–48; 5:782; 12:899.

22. *CS* 7:566; 7:545; 12:370; 7:505; 7:323; 6:134; 4:680; 11:424.

23. *CS* 3:902 ff.

24. *CS* 3:858.

25. *CS* 4:795.

26. *CS* 7:450.

18. BALTHASAR HUBMAIER

1. Roland H. Bainton, "The Left Wing of the Reformation," *Journal of Religion* 21 (1941): 124–34.

2. George H. Williams, *The Radical Reformation*, pp. xxiii–xxxi.

3. Albert Henry Newman, *A History of Anti-Pedobaptism* (Philadelphia: American Baptist Publication Society, 1902), and Robert A. Mackoskey, "The Life and Thought of Balthasar Hubmaier, 1485–1528," (Ph.D. diss., University of Edinburgh, 1956).

4. For the biography of Hubmaier, see Henry C. Vedder, *Balthasar Hubmaier*, and Torsten Bergsten, *Balthasar Hubmaier*. A brief biographical sketch is included in Balthasar Hubmaier, *Schriften*, pp. 9–43.

5. On the problem of the relationship of Eck to nominalism see Erwin Iserloh, *Die Eucharistie in der Darstellung des Johannes Eck*, Reformationsgeschichtliche Studien und Texte 73 / 74 (Münster in Westphalia: Aschendorff, 1950), p. 344; and Walter L. Moore, Jr., "Between Mani and Pelagius: Predestination and Justification in the Early Writings of John Eck" (Ph.D. diss., Harvard University, 1967).

6. Balthasar Hubmaier to Johannes Sapidus, October 26, 1521, in *Elsass*, vol. 1, *Stadt Strassburg, 1522–1532*, Quellen zur Geschichte der Täufer, 7 (Gütersloh: Gerd Mohn, 1959), pp. 40–2.

7. In this connection see Thor Hall, "The Possibilities of Erasmian Influence on Denck and Hubmaier in Their Views on the Freedom of the Will."

8. There is reason to believe that the relationship between nominalism and humanism is closer than was once thought. See especially on this question Heiko A. Oberman, "Some Notes on the Theology of Nominalism with Attention to Its Relation to the Renaissance," *Harvard Theological Review* 53 (1960): 47–76. For the points of agreement between Erasmus and nominalism, see John Barton Payne, *Erasmus: His Theology of the Sacraments* (Richmond, VA: John Knox Press, 1970).

9. For the most authoritative study of these questions see Heiko A. Oberman, *The Harvest of Medieval Theology* (Cambridge: Harvard University Press, 1963), pp. 120–84.

10. Johannes von Staupitz is an excellent representative of this Augustinian sentiment in theology. See my *Misericordia Dei: The Theology of Johannes von Staupitz in Its Late Medieval Setting*, Studies in Medieval and Reformation Thought 4 (Leiden: E. J. Brill, 1968), pp. 57–74; *Luther and Staupitz: An Essay in the Intellectual Origins of the Protestant Reformation*, Duke Monographs in Medieval and Renaissance Studies 4 (Durham, N.C.: Duke University Press, 1980).

11. Steven E. Ozment has written an illuminating study of the theological significance of synderesis in late medieval doctrines of justification. See his *Homo Spiritualis: A Comparative Study of the Anthropology of Johannes Tauler, Jean Gerson, and Martin Luther (1509–16) in the Context of Their Theological Thought*, Studies in Medieval and Reformation Thought 6 (Leiden: E. J. Brill, 1969).

12. For a brief introduction to Luther's understanding of justification see Gerhard Ebeling, *Luther: An Introduction to His Thought* (Philadelphia: Fortress Press, 1970), pp.

110–74; Heinrich Bornkamm, "Iustitia Dei in der Scholastik und bei Luther," *Archiv für Reformationsgeschichte* 39 (1942): 1–46 and "Zur Frage der Iustitia Dei beim jungen Luther," 52 (1961): 16–29 and 53 (1962): 1–60; Heiko A. Oberman, "'Iustitia Christi' and 'Iustitia Dei'": Luther and the Scholastic Doctrines of Justification," *Harvard Theological Review* 59 (1966): 1–26. On Luther's rejection of the habit of grace see Reinhard Schwarz, *Fides, Spes, und Caritas beim jungen Luther* (Berlin: De Gruyter, 1962).

13. For an introduction to Zwingli's theology that reflects recent advances in critical scholarship see Gottfried W. Locher, *Die Theologie Huldrych Zwinglis im Lichte seiner Christologie*, vol. 1 (Zurich: 1952); Jaques Courvoisier, *Zwingli: A Reformed Theologian* (Richmond, VA: John Knox Press, 1963). Locher's point of view on Zwingli is briefly summarized in Gottfried W. Locher, "The Shape of Zwingli's Theology: A Comparison with Luther and Calvin," *Pittsburgh Perspective* 8 (June 1967): 5–26.

14. The most helpful discussion of Hubmaier's doctrine of baptism is found in Rollin Stely Armour, *Anabaptist Baptism*, pp. 19–57.

15. Hubmaier, *Schriften*, pp. 416–7.

16. Ibid., pp. 382–97.

17. Ibid., p. 386.

18. Ibid., p. 418.

19. Ibid., pp. 313–5.

20. Ibid., pp. 315–6.

21. Ibid., pp. 434–57.

19. HANS DENCK

1. For a brief biography of Denck see Jan J. Kiwiet, "The Life of Hans Denck (ca. 1500–1527)."

2. On Oecolampadius see Gordon Rupp, *Patterns of Reformation* (Philadelphia: Fortress Press, 1969), pp. 3–53.

3. On Vadian and Kessler see Rupp, *Patterns of Reformation*, pp. 357–78.

4. Hans Denck, *Schriften*, vol. 2 (1956), p. 109.

5. For a survey of Denck's theology see Jan J. Kiwiet, "The Theology of Hans Denck."

6. Denck, *Schriften*, vol. 2 (1956), p. 106. See Claude R. Foster, Jr., "Hans Denck and Johannes Buenderlin."

7. See William Klassen, "Was Hans Denck a Universalist?"

20. PILGRAM MARPECK

1. For a brief statement of the position of Marcion, see F. L. Cross, *The Early Christian Fathers* (London: G. Duckworth, 1960), pp. 40–1. See Adolf Harnack, *Marcion: Das Evangelium von einem fremden Gott* (Leipzig: J. C. Hinrichs, 1924).

2. In this connection see Heiko A. Oberman, "The Protestant Tradition," in *The Convergence of Traditions*, ed. Elmer O'Brien (New York: Herder and Herder, 1967), pp. 67–135.

3. Arnold A. van Ruler, *Die Christliche Kirche und das Alte Testament* (Munich: C. Kaiser, 1955), p. 75.

4. For the biography of Marpeck, see Jan J. Kiwiet, *Pilgram Marpeck*; John C. Wenger, "The Life and Work of Pilgram Marpeck"; Harold S. Bender, "Pilgram Marpeck."

5. See Manfred Krebs and Hans Georg Rott, eds., *Elsass*, vol. 1, *Stadt Strassbourg, 1522–1532, Quellen zur Geschichte der Täufer*, 7.

6. For Bucer's doctrine of the church, see Jaques Courvoisier, *La notion d'église chez Bucer* (Paris: 1933).

7. For letters from this period, see Torsten Bergsten, "Two Letters by Pilgram Marpeck."

8. See Alvin J. Beachy, "The Grace of God in Christ as Understood by Five Major Anabaptist Writers."

9. For Marpeck's theology, see John C. Wenger, "The Theology of Pilgram Marpeck"; William Klassen, *Covenant and Community*; Rollin Stely Armour, *Anabaptist Baptism*, pp. 113–34.

10. Heiko A. Oberman, "Quo Vadis Petre? The History of Tradition from Irenaeus to Humani Generis," *Harvard Divinity Bulletin* 26 (1962): 1–25.

BIBLIOGRAPHY

1. JOHANNES GEILER VON KAYSERSBERG

Primary Sources

Geiler von Kaysersberg, Johannes. *Die ältesten Schriften Geilers von Kaysersberg*. Edited by L. Dacheux. Freiburg im Breisgau, 1882. Reprinted Amsterdam: Editions Rodopi 1965.

———. *Geilers von Kaisersberg ausgewählte Schriften nebst einer Abhandlung über Geilers Leben und echte Schriften*. Edited by Philipp de Lorenzi. 4 vols. Trier, 1881–83.

Secondary Sources

Abray, Lorna J. *The People's Reformation: Magistrates, Clergy, and Commons in Strasbourg: 1500–1598*. Ithaca: Cornell University Press, 1985.

Chrisman, Miriam Usher. *Strasbourg and the Reform*. New Haven: Yale University Press, 1967.

Dacheux, L. *Un réformateur Catholique à la fin du XVe siècle, Jean Geiler de Kaysersberg: Etude sur sa vie et son temps*. Paris, 1876.

Douglass, E. J. Dempsey. *Justification in Late Medieval Preaching: A Study of John Geiler of Kaysersberg*. Studies in Medieval and Reformation Thought 1. Leiden: E. J. Brill, 1966.

Eisemann, Susanne. *Sed corde dicemus: das volkstumliche Element in den deutschen Predigten des Geiler von Kaysersberg*. New York: Peter Lang, 1996.

Israel, Uwe. *Johannes Geiler von Kaysersberg (1445–1510): der Strassburger Münsterprediger als Rechtsreformer*. Berlin: Duncker & Humbolt, 1997.

Oberman, Heiko A. *The Harvest of Medieval Theology*. Cambridge: Harvard University Press, 1963.

2. JOHANNES VON STAUPITZ

Primary Sources

Unprinted Works—Johannes von Staupitz

Sermones, Codex Hs: bV8, Saint Peter; Codex Hs: bII11, Saint Peter; Codex Hs: 23 E 16, Nonnberg. All three codices are found in the Library of the Benedictine Abbey, Salzburg, Austria.

Constitutiones Fratrum Heremitarum sancti Augustini ad Apostolicorum Privilegiorum Formam pro Reformatione Alemanie. Nuremberg, 1504.

Decisio Questionis de Audiencia Misse in Parrochiali Ecclesia Dominicis et Festivis Diebus. Tübingen, 1500.

Johannis Staupitii: Opera Quae Reperiri Poterunt Omnia: Deutsche Schriften. Edited by J. F. K. Knaake. Vol. 1. Potsdam, 1867.

Libellus de Executione Eterne Predestinationis. Nuremberg, 1517. Parts of this treatise appear in English translation in Heiko A. Oberman, *Forerunners of the Reformation* (New York: Holt, Rinehart and Winston, 1966), pp. 175–203.

Sämtliche Schriften: Abhandlungen, Predigten, Zeugnisse, Lateinische Schriften. 2 vols. Edited by Lothar Graf zu Dohna and Richard Wetzel. Spätmittelalter und Reformation, Texte und Untersuchungen, vols. 13–14. Berlin: W. de Gruyter, 1987.

Staupitz, Tübinger Predigten. Edited by Georg Buchwald and Ernst Wolf. Quellen und Forschungen zur Reformationsgeschichte 8. Leipzig: M. Heinzius, 1927.

Secondary Sources

Jeremias, Alfred. *Johannes von Staupitz, Luthers Vater and Schuler.* Leipzig: Eberhard Arnold Verlag, 1926.

Keller, Ludwig. *Johann von Staupitz und die Anfänge der Reformation.* Leipzig, 1888.

Kolde, T. *Die deutsche Augustiner-Congregation und Johann von Staupitz.* Gotha, 1879.

Steinmetz, David C. *Luther and Staupitz: An Essay in the Intellectual Origins of the Protestant Reformation.* Monographs in Medieval and Renaissance Studies 4. Durham, N.C.: Duke University Press, 1980.

———. *Misericordia Dei: The Theology of Johannes von Staupitz in Its Late Medieval Setting.* Studies in Medieval and Reformation Thought 4. Leiden: E. J. Brill, 1968.

Wolf, Ernst. *Staupitz und Luther: Ein Beitrag zur Theologie des Johannes von Staupitz und deren Bedeutung für Luthers theologischen Werdegang.* Quellen und Forschungen zur Reformationsgeschichte 9. Leipzig: M. Heinzius, 1927.

Wriedt, Markus. *Gnade und Erwählung: Eine Untersuchung zu Johann von Staupitz und Martin Luther.* Veröffentlichungen des Instituts für Europäische Geschichte Mainz, Abteilung Religionsgeschichte 141. Mainz: P. von Zabern, 1991.

3. GASPARO CONTARINI

Primary Sources

Contarini, Gasparo. *Casparo Contarini Cardinalis Opera.* Farnborough, England: Gregg International, 1968.

———. *Gasparo Contarini: Gegenreformatorische Schriften, 1530–1542.* Corpus Catholicorum 7. Münster in Westphalia, 1923.

———. "Liber Ratisbonensis, Art. 5, De Justificatione Hominis." In *Corpus Reformatorum*, edited by Karl Gottlieb Bretschneider and Heinrich Ernst Bindseil, vol. 4, 198–201. Halle, 1834–60.

————. "Protestantes ad Caesarem de Libro Ratisbon." In *Corpus Reformatorum*, edited by Karl Gottlieb Bretschneider and Heinrich Ernst Bindseil, vol. 4, pp. 476–91. Halle, 1834–60.

Secondary Sources

Brieger, Theodore. "Die Rechtfertigungslehre des Cardinal Contarini, kritisch dargestellt und verglichen mit der des Regensburger Buches." *Theologische Studien und Kritiken* 45 (1872): 87–150.

Eells, Hastings. "The Origin of the Regensburg Book." *Princeton Theological Review* 26 (1928): 355–72.

Elton, G. R., ed. *The New Cambridge Modern History*, Vol. 2. *The Reformation, 1520–1559*. Cambridge, England: Cambridge University Press, 1958.

Gleason, Elizabeth G. *Gasparo Contarini: Venice, Rome, and Reform*. Berkeley: University of California Press, 1993.

Hünermann, Friedrich. "Die Rechtfertigungslehre des Kardinals Gasparo Contarini." *Theologische Quartalschrift* 120 (1921): 1–22.

Jedin, Hubert. "Ein 'Turmerlebnis' des jungen Contarini." In *Kirche des Glaubens— Kirche der Geschichte*, vol. 1, pp. 167–80. Freiburg im Breisgau: Herder, 1966.

————. *A History of the Council of Trent*. Vol. 1. *The Struggle for the Council*. Translated by Dom Ernest Graf. St. Louis: B. Herder, 1957.

Lipgens, Walter. *Kardinal Johannes Gropper (1503–1559) und die Anfänge der katholischen Reform in Deutschland*. Münster in Westphalia: Aschendorff, 1951.

Mackensen, Heinz. "Contarini's Theological Role at Ratisbon in 1541." *Archiv für Reformationsgeschichte* 51 (1960): 36–57.

Matheson, Peter. *Cardinal Contarini at Regensburg*. Oxford: Clarendon Press, 1993.

Oberman, Heiko A. "'Iustitia Christi' and 'Iustitia Dei': Luther and the Scholastic Doctrines of Justification." *Harvard Theological Review* 59 (1966): 1–26.

Rückert, Hanns. *Die Theologische Entwicklung Gasparo Contarinis*. Bonn: A. Marcus und E. Weber, 1926.

Stupperich, Robert. "Der Ursprung des Regensburger Buches und seine Rechtfertigungslehre." *Archiv für Reformationsgeschichte* 36 (1939): 88–116.

4. FABER STAPULENSIS

Primary Sources

Faber Stapulensis, Jacobus. *Commentarii Initiatorii in Quatuor Evangelia*. Paris, 1522.

————. *Quincuplex Psalterium*. Paris, 1509.

————. *Sancti Pauli Epistolae XIV*. Paris, 1512.

Secondary Sources

Bedouelle, Guy. *Lefèvre d'Etaples et l'intelligence des écritures*. Travaux d'Humanisme et Renaissance 152. Geneva: Droz, 1976.

————. *Le Quincuplex Psalterium de Lefèvre d'Etaples: Un Guide de Lecture*. Travaux d'Humanisme et Renaissance 171. Geneva: Droz, 1979.

Brush, John Woolman. "Lefèvre d'Etaples: Three Phases of His Life and Work." In *Reformation Studies: Essays in Honor of Roland H. Bainton*, edited by Franklin H. Littell, pp. 117–28. Richmond, VA: John Knox Press, 1962.

Dagens, J. "Humanisme et Evangélisme chez Lefèvre d'Etaples." In *Courants religieux et humanisme*. Paris: Presses universitaires de France, 1959.

Dankbaar, W. F. "Op de Grens der Reformatie: De Rechtvaardigings-leer van Jacques Lefèvre d'Etaples," *Nederlands Theologisch Tijdschrift* 8 (1954): 327–45.

Dörries, Hermann. "Lefèvre und Calvin," *Zeitschrift für Kirchengeschichte* 44 (1925): 544–81.

Gelder, H. A. Enno van. *The Two Reformations in the Sixteenth Century*. The Hague: M. Nijhoff, 1964.

Graf, Karl Heinrich. "Jacobus Faber Stapulensis: Ein Beitrag zur Geschichte der Reformation in Frankreich." *Zeitschrift für Historische Theologie* 22 (1852): 3–86, 165–237.

Hahn, Fritz. "Faber Stapulensis und Luther." *Zeitschrift für Kirchengeschichte* 57 (1938): 356–432.

Hughes, Philip Edgecombe. *Lefèvre: Pioneer of Theological Renewal in France*. Grand Rapids: Eerdmans, 1984.

Jourdan, George V. *The Movement towards Catholic Reform in the Early Sixteenth Century*. London, 1914.

Lovy, R.-J. *Les origines de la Réforme Française: Meaux, 1518–1546*. Paris: Diffuseur: Librarie protestante, 1959.

Lubac, Henri de. "Les humanistes chrétiens due XV–XVI siècle et l'herméneutique traditionelle." In *Herméneutique et tradition*, pp. 173–7. Rome: Instituto de studi filosofici 1963.

Oberman, Heiko A. *Forerunners of the Reformation*. New York: Holt, Rinehart and Winston, 1966.

5. REGINALD POLE

Primary Sources

Brewer, J. S., et al. *Letters and Papers of the Reign of Henry VIII*. 22 vols. London, 1862–1932.

Pole, Reginald. *De Concilio*. Rome, 1562.

———. *Epistolae*. Edited by A. M. Quirini. 5 vols. Brescia, 1744–57.

———. *Pole's Defense of the Unity of the Church*. Translated by Joseph G. Dwyer. Westminster, Md.: Newman Press, 1965.

———. *A Treatie of Justification*. Ilkley, England: Scholar Press, 1976.

———. *Reformatio Angliae*. Rome, 1562.

Secondary Sources

Anderson, Marvin W. "Trent and Justification (1546): A Protestant Reflection." *Scottish Journal of Theology* 21 (1968): 385–406.

Boland, Edward G. "An Appreciation of Cardinal Pole." *Unitas* 14 (1962): 120–6.

Fenlon, Dermot. *Heresy and Obedience in Tridentine Italy: Cardinal Pole and the Counter Reformation*. Cambridge, England: Cambridge University Press, 1972.

Gasquet, F. A. *Cardinal Pole and His Early Friends*. London: G. Bell and Sons, Ltd., 1927.

Haile, Martin. *The Life of Reginald Pole*. New York: Longmans, Green, 1910.

Jedin, Hubert. *A History of the Council of Trent*. 2 vols. St. Louis: B. Herder, 1957–61.

———. "Kardinal Pole und Vittoria Colonna." In *Kirche des Glaubens—Kirche der Geschichte*, Vol. 1, pp. 181–94. Freiburg: Herder, 1966.

Parks, George B. "The Parma Letters and the Dangers to Cardinal Pole." *Catholic Historical Review* 46 (1960): 299–317.

Prescott, H. F. M. *Mary Tudor*. New York: Macmillan, 1953.

Schenck, Wilhelm. *Reginald Pole, Cardinal of England*. New York: Longmans, Green, 1950.

Zimmermann, A. *Kardinal Pole: Sein Leben and seine Schriften*. New York, 1893.

6. PHILIP MELANCHTHON

Primary Sources

Melanchthon, Philip. *Commentary on Romans*. Translated by Fred Kramer. St. Louis: Concordia, 1992.

———. *The Loci Communes of Philip Melanchthon*. Translated by Charles Leander Hill. Boston: Meador, 1944.

———. *Melanchthon and Bucer*. Edited by Wilhelm Pauck. Library of Christian Classics 19. Philadelphia: Westminster Press, 1969.

———. *Melanchthon on Christian Doctrine*. Edited by Clyde L. Manschreck. Library of Protestant Thought. New York: Oxford University Press, 1965.

———. *Melanchthon: Selected Writings*. Translated by Charles Leander Hill. Minneapolis: Augsburg, 1962.

———. *Melanchthons Werke* (Studienausgabe). Edited by Robert Stupperich et al. 6 vols. Gütersloh: C. Bartelsman, 1951–83.

Secondary Sources

Bizer, Ernst. *Theologie der Verheissung: Studien zur Theologie des jungen Melanchthon (1519–1524)*. Neukirchen, Germany: Neukirchener Verlag des Erziehungsvereins, 1964.

Bornkamm, Heinrich. *Das Jahrhundert der Reformation*. Göttingen: Vandenhoeck & Ruprecht, 1961.

Dillenberger, John. *Protestant Thought and Natural Science*. New York: Doubleday, 1960.

Elert, Werner. *The Structure of Lutheranism*. St. Louis: Concordia, 1962.

Fraenkel, Pierre. *Testimonia Patrum: The Function of the Patristic Argument in the Theology of Philip Melanchthon*. Geneva: E. Droz, 1961.

———, et al. *Zwanzig Jahre Melanchthonstudium*. Geneva: Droz, 1967.

Hildebrandt, Franz. *Melanchthon: Alien or Ally?* Cambridge, England: Cambridge University Press, 1946.

Kusukawa, Sachiko. *The Transformation of Natural Philosophy: The Case of Philip Melanchthon*. Cambridge, England: Cambridge University Press, 1995.

Manschreck, Clyde L. *Melanchthon, The Quiet Reformer*. New York: Abingdon Press, 1968.

Maurer, Wilhelm. *Der junge Melanchthon*. Vol. 1. Gottingen: Vandenhoeck & Ruprecht, 1967.

———. "Melanchthon as Author of the Augsburg Confession." *Lutheran World* 7 (1960): 153–67.

———. *Melanchthon-Studien*. Gütersloh: Gütersloher Verlagshaus, G. Mohn, 1964.

McGiffert, A. C. *Protestant Thought before Kant*. New York: Harper, 1961.

Oyer, John S. *Lutheran Reformers against Anabaptists*. The Hague: M. Nijhoff, 1964.

Richard, James W. *Philip Melanchthon, The Protestant Preceptor of Germany*. New York: Putnam's, 1898.

Stupperich, Robert. "The Development of Melanchthon's Theological-Philosophical World View." *Lutheran World* 7 (1960): 168–80.

———. *Melanchthon*. Translated by Robert H. Fischer. Philadelphia: Westminster Press, 1965.

———. *Der unbekannte Melanchthon*. Stuttgart: W. Kohlhammer, 1961.

Vajta, Vilmos, ed. *Luther and Melanchthon*. Philadelphia: Muhlenberg Press, 1961.

Wengert, Timothy J. *Human Freedom, Christian Righteousness: Philip Melanchthon's Exegetical Dispute with Erasmus of Rotterdam*. New York: Oxford University Press, 1998.

———. *Law and Gospel: Philip Melanchthon's Debate with John Agricola of Eisleben*. Grand Rapids: Baker Books, 1997.

———. *Philip Melanchthon's Annotationes in Johannem in Relation to Its Predecessors and Contemporaries*. Geneva: Librairie Droz, 1987.

7. JOHANNES BUGENHAGEN

Primary Sources

Bugenhagen, Johannes. *Johannes Bugenhagens Braunschweiger Kirchenordnung*. Edited by Hans Lietzmann. Kleine Texte für Vorlesungen und Übungen 88. Bonn: A. Marcus und E. Weber, 1912.

———. *J. Bugenhagens Briefwechsel*. Edited by Otto Vogt. Photographic reprint of the editions Stettin (1888–99) and Gotha (1910). Hildesheim: Olms, 1966.

———. "Von der Evangelischen Messe, 1524," "Ein Ratschlag, wie man das Sakrament geniessen soll, 1524," and "Bekentnis von seinem Glauben und seiner Lehre, 1529." In *Reformatorische Verkündigung und Lebensordnung*, edited by Robert Stupperich, pp. 105–20. Klassiker des Protestantismus 3. Bremen: Schünemann, 1963.

Secondary Sources

Bergsma, Johannes H. *Die Reform der Messliturgie durch Johannes Bugenhagen (1485–1558)*. Hildesheim: Bernward Verlag, 1966.

Bieber, Anneliese. *Johannes Bugenhagen zwischen Reform und Reformation*. Göttingen: Vandenhoeck and Ruprecht, 1993.

Hering, Hermann. *Doktor Pomeranus, Johannes Bugenhagen: Ein Lebensbild aus der Zeit der Reformation*. Schriften des Vereins für Reformationsgeschichte 22. Halle, 1888.

Leder, Hans G. *Johannes Bugenhagen: Gestalt und Wirkung*. Berlin: Evangelische Verlagsanstalt, 1984.

Vogt, Karl A. T. *Johannes Bugenhagen Pomeranus: Leben und ausgewählte Schriften*. Elberfeld, 1867.

Wolf, Ernst. "Johannes Bugenhagen, Gemeinde und Amt." In *Peregrinatio*, pp. 257–78. Munich: C. Kaiser, 1965.

————. "Johannes Bugenhagen und die 'Ordnung der Gemeinde.'" In *Zwischenstationen: Festschrift für Karl Kupisch*, edited by Helmut Gollwitzer et al., pp. 281–98. Munich: C. Kaiser, 1963.

8. ANDREAS OSIANDER

Primary Sources

Osiander, Andreas. *De Unico Mediatore Iesu Christo et Iustificatione Fidei: Confessio Andreae Osiandri*. Königsberg, 1551.
————. *Ein Disputation von der Rechtfertigung des Glaubens*. Königsberg, 1551.
————. *Gesamtausgabe*. Edited by G. Müller. Gütersloh: Gütersloher Verlagshaus Gerd Mohn, 1975.

Secondary Sources

Bornkamm, Heinrich. *Das Jahrhundert der Reformation*. Göttingen: Vandenhoeck & Ruprecht, 1961.
Dillenberger, John. *Protestant Thought and Natural Science*. New York: Doubleday, 1960.
Heberle, A. "Andreas Osiander's Lehre in ihrer frühesten Gestalt." *Theologische Studien und Kritiken* 17 (1844): 371–414.
Hirsch, E. *Die Theologie des Andreas Osiander und ihre geschichtlichen Voraussetzungen*. Göttingen: Vandenhoeck & Ruprecht, 1919.
Möller, W. *Andreas Osiander: Leben und ausgewählte Schriften*. Elberfeld: R. L. Friderichs, 1870.
Seebass, Gottfried. *Das Reformatorische Werk des Andreas Osiander*. Einzelarbeiten aus der Kirchengeschichte Bayerns 44. Nuremberg: Verein für Bayerische Kirchengeschicte, 1967.
Stupperich, Martin. *Osiander in Preussen 1549–1552*. Arbeiten zur Kirchengeschichten 44. Berlin: W. de Gruyter, 1967.
Weber, Hans Emil. *Reformation, Orthodoxie, und Rationalismus*. Vol.1, pt. 1. Gütersloh: C. Bertelsmann, 1937.

9. NIKOLAUS VON AMSDORF

Primary Sources

Amsdorf, Nikolaus von. *Nikolaus von Amsdorff: Ausgewählte Schriften*. Edited by Otto Lerche. Gütersloh: C. Bertelsmann, 1938.

Secondary Sources

Brunner, Peter. *Nikolaus von Amsdorf als Bischof von Naumburg*. Schriften des Vereins für Reformationsgeschichte 179. Gütersloh: G. Mohn, 1961.
Kolb, Robert. *Nikolaus von Amsdorf (1483–1565). Popular Polemics in the Preservation of Luther's Legacy*. Bibliotheca Humanistica et Reformatorica 24. Nieuwkoop: De Graaf, 1978.
Lerche, Otto. *Amsdorff und Melanchthon*. Berlin: 1937.

Nebe, Otto Henning. *Reine Lehre: Zur Theologie des Niklas von Amsdorff.* Göttingen: Vandenhoeck & Ruprecht, 1935.

Pressel, Theodor. *Nicolaus von Amsdorf.* Elberfeld, 1862.

10. JOHANNES BRENZ

Primary Sources

Brenz, Johannes. *Katechismus.* Leipzig, 1852.

———. *Predigten des Johannes Brenz.* Edited by E. Bizer. Stuttgart: Quell-Verlag, 1955.

———, *Schriftauslegungen.* Tübingen: J. C. B. Mohr, 1986– .

———. *Werke.* Tübingen: J. C. B. Mohr, 1970– .

———. *Würtembergishes Kirchenbuch.* Stuttgart, 1782.

Köhler, Walther. *Bibliographia Brentiana.* Berlin: C. A. Schwetschke, 1904.

Pressel, Theodor. *Anecdota Brentiana.* Tübingen, 1868.

Secondary Sources

Brandy, Hans-Christian. *Die späte Christologie des Johannes Brenz.* Beiträge zur historischen Theologie 80. Tübingen: J. C. B. Mohr, 1991.

Brecht, Martin. *Die frühe Theologie des Johannes Brenz.* Beiträge zur historischen Theologie 36. Tübingen: J. C. B. Mohr, 1966.

Estes, James M. *Christian Magistrate and the State Church: The Reforming Career of Johannes Brenz.* Toronto: Toronto University Press, 1982.

———. "Church Order and the Christian Magistrate according to Johannes Brenz." *Archiv für Reformationsgeschichte* 59 (1968): 5–24.

Hartmann, Julius, and Karl Jäger. *Johann Brenz.* 2 vols. Hamburg: Friedrich Perthes, 1840–42.

Hermelink, H. *Johannes Brenz als lutherischer und schwäbisher Theologe.* Stuttgart: Im Quell-Verlag der Evang. Gesellschaft, 1949.

Kantzenbach, F. W. "Der Anteil des Johannes Brenz an der Konfessionspolitik und Dogmengeschichte des Protestantismus." In *Reformatio und Confessio: Festschrift für D. Wilhelm Maurer,* pp. 113–29. Berlin: Lutherisches Verlagshaus, 1965.

———. "Der Beitrag des Johannes Brenz zur Toleranzidee." *Theologische Zeitschrift* 21 (1965): 38–64.

11. MARTIN BUCER

Primary Sources

Bucer, Martin. *De Regno Christi.* Edited by François Wendel. Opera Latina 15. Paris: Presses Universitaires de France, 1955.

———. *Enarratio in Evangelium Iohannis.* Edited by Irena Backus. Series 2, Martini Buceri Opera Omnia 2. Leiden: E. J. Brill, 1988.

———. *Instruction in Christian Love.* Translated by Paul T. Fuhrmann. Richmond, VA: John Knox Press, 1952.

———. *Martin Bucers Deutsche Schriften.* Edited by Robert Stupperich. Vols. 1, 2, 3, 7. Gütersloh: Gütersloher Verlagshaus G. Mohn, 1960– .

————. *Melanchthon and Bucer*. Edited by Wilhelm Pauck. Library of Christian Classics 19. Philadelphia: Westminster Press, 1969.

Wright, David F., editor and translator. *Common Places of Martin Bucer*. Courtenay Library of Reformation Classics 4. Abingdon: Sutton Courtenay Press, 1972.

Secondary Sources

Anrich, Gustav. *Martin Bucer*. Strasbourg: K. J. Trübner, 1914.

Bornkamm, Heinrich. *Das Jahrhundert der Reformation*. Göttingen: Vandenhoeck & Ruprecht, 1961.

Burnette, Amy Nelson. *The Yoke of Christ: Martin Bucer and Christian Discipline*. Sixteenth Century Essays and Studies 26. Kirksville, MO: Truman State University, 1994.

Chrisman, Miriam Usher. *Strasbourg and the Reform*. New Haven: Yale University Press, 1967.

Courvoisier, Jaques. *La notion d'église chez Bucer*. Paris: F. Alcan, 1933.

Eells, Hastings. *Martin Bucer*. New Haven: Yale University Press, 1931.

Greschat, Martin. *Martin Bucer: ein Reformator und seine Zeit*. Munich: Beck, 1990.

Hopf, Constantin. *Martin Bucer and the English Reformation*. New York: Macmillan, 1947.

Littell, Franklin H. "New Light on Butzer's Significance." In *Reformation Studies*, edited by Franklin H. Littell, pp. 145–67. Richmond, VA: John Knox Press, 1962.

Pauck, Wilhelm. *The Heritage of the Reformation*. Glencoe, Ill.: Free Press, 1961.

————. *Das Reich Gottes auf Erden*. Berlin: W. deGruyter, 1928.

Poll, Gerrit Jan van de. *Martin Bucer's Liturgical Ideas*. Theologische Bibliotheek 27. Assen, Netherlands: Royal van Gorcum, 1954.

Pollet, J. V. *Martin Bucer: Etudes sur la correspondance*. vol. 1. Paris: Presses Universitaires de France, 1958.

Stephens, Peter. *The Holy Spirit in the Theology of Martin Bucer*. London: Cambridge University Press, 1970.

12. HEINRICH BULLINGER

Primary Sources

Bullinger, Heinrich. *The Decades*. Edited for the Parker Society. 5 vols. Cambridge, 1849–52.

————. *Werke*. Edited by Fritz Büsser. Zürich: Theologischer Verlag, 1972– .

Secondary Sources

Baker, Wayne J. *Heinrich Bullinger and the Covenant: The Other Reformed Tradition*. Athens, Ohio: Ohio University Press, 1980.

Blanke, Fritz. *Der junge Bullinger, 1504–1531*. Zurich: Zwingli-Verlag, 1942.

Bouvier, André. *Henri Bullinger, Le successeur de Zwingli*. Paris: E. Droz, 1940.

Fast, Heinold. *Heinrich Bullinger und die Täufer*. Weierhof: Pfalz, 1959.

Hollweg, Walter. *Heinrich Bullingers Hausbuch*. Neukirchen: Kreis Moers, Verlag der Buchhandlung des Erziehungsvereins, 1956.

Hooft, A. J. van't. *De theologie van Heinrich Bullinger in betrekking tot de Nederlandsche Reformatie*. Amsterdam, 1888.

McCoy, Charles S., and J. Wayne Becker. *Fountainhead of Federalism: Heinrich Bullinger and the Covenantal Tradition*. Louisville: John Knox Press, 1991.

Staedke, Joachim. *Die Theologie des jungen Bullinger*. Zurich: Zwingli-Verlag, 1962.

———, ed. *Glauben und Bekennen: Vierhundert Jahre Confessio Helvetica Posterior*. Zurich: Zwingli-Verlag, 1966.

Walser, Peter. *Die Pradestination bei Bullinger*. Zurich: Zwingli-Verlag, 1957.

13. JOHN HOOPER

Primary Sources

Hooper, John. "A Declaration of Christ and His Office." In *English Reformers*, edited by T. H. L. Parker, pp. 193–218. Library of Christian Classics 26. Philadelphia: Westminster Press, 1966.

———. *Early Writings*. Parker Society Edition. Cambridge, 1848.

———. *Later Writings*. Parker Society Edition. Cambridge, 1852.

Secondary Sources

Constant, G. *The Reformation in England*. Vol. 2, *Introduction of the Reformation into England: Edward VI (1547–1553)*. London: Sheed and Ward, 1942.

Dugmore, C. W. *The Mass and the English Reformers*. London: Macmillan, 1958.

Emerson, Everett H. *English Puritanism from John Hooper to John Milton*. Durham, N.C.: Duke University Press, 1968.

Hughes, Philip. *The Reformation in England*. 3 vols. New York: Macmillan, 1963.

Hughes, Philip E. *Theology of the English Reformers*. London: Hodder and Stoughton, 1965.

Hunt, F. W. *The Life and Times of John Hooper (c. 1500–1555): Bishop of Gloucester*. Lewiston, N.Y.: Edwin Mellen Press, 1992.

Knappen, Marshall. *Tudor Puritanism*. Chicago: University of Chicago Press, 1939.

Rupp, E. Gordon. *Studies in the Making of the English Protestant Tradition*. Cambridge, England: Cambridge University Press, 1949.

14. PETER MARTYR VERMIGLI

Primary Sources

Kingdon, Robert M. *The Political Thought of Peter Martyr Vermigli: Selected Texts and Commentary*. Geneva: Droz, 1980.

The Peter Martyr Library. Edited by John Patrick Donnelly and Joseph C. McLelland. Sixteenth Century Essays and Studies. Kirksville. MO: Thomas Jefferson University Press, 1994– .

Vermigli, Peter Martyr. *Defensio Doctrinae Veteris et Apostolicae de Sacrosancto Eucharistiae Sacramento*. Basel, 1581.

Secondary Sources

Anderson, Marvin W. *Peter Martyr Vermigli, a Reformer in Exile (1542–1562)*. Bibliotheca Humaniastica et Reformatorica 10. Nieuwkoop: De Graaf, 1975.

Donnelly, John Patrick. *Calvinism and Scholasticism in Vermigli's Doctrine of Man and Grace*. Studies in Medieval and Reformation Thought 18. Leiden: E. J. Brill, 1976.

James, Frank A. *Peter Martyr Vermigli and Predestination: The Augustinian Inheritance of an Italian Reformer*. New York: Oxford University Press, 1998.

McLelland, Joseph C. *The Visible Words of God*. Edinburgh: Oliver and Boyd, 1957.

McNair, Philip. *Peter Martyr in Italy*. New York: Oxford University Press, 1967.

Schlosser, Friedrich Christoph. *Leben des Theodor de Beza und des Peter Martyr Vermigli*. Heidelberg, 1809.

Schmidt, C. *Peter Martyr Vermigli: Leben und ausgewählte Schriften*. Elberfeld, 1858.

Strype, John. *Annals of the Reformation and Establishment of Religion*. Vol. 1, pt. 1. Oxford, 1824.

———. *Memorials of Archbishop Cranmer*. 3 vols. Oxford, 1848–54.

15. THEODORE BEZA

Primary Sources

Beza, Theodore. *Correspondance*. Edited by F. Aubert et al. 4 vols. Geneva: Droz, 1960– .

———. *Cours sur les Epîtres aux Romains et aux Hébreux, 1564–66*. Edited by Pierre Fraenkel and Luc Perrotet. Travaux d'humanisme et Renaissance 226. Geneva: Droz, 1988.

———. *De Iure Magistratuum*. Edited by Klaus Sturm. Neukirchen: Neukirchener Verlag, 1965.

———. *Tractationes Theologicae*. 3 vols. Geneva, 1582.

Secondary Sources

Backus, Irena. *The Reformed Roots of the English New Testament: The Influence of Theodore Beza on the English New Testament*. Pittsburgh: Pickwick Press, 1980.

Baird, Henry M. *Theodore Beza, The Counselor of the French Reformation, 1519–1605*. New York: Putnam's, 1899.

Bray, John S. *Theodore Beza's Doctrine of Predestination*. Nieuwkoop: De Graaf, 1975.

Geisendorf, Paul. F. *Theodore de Bèze*. Geneva: Jullien, 1967.

Hall, Basil. "Calvin against the Calvinists." In *John Calvin*, edited by F. L. Battles et al., pp. 19–37. Courtenay Studies in Reformation Theology 1. Appleford, England: Sutton Courtenay Press, 1966.

Kickel, Walter. *Vernunft und Offenbarung bei Theodor Beza*. Neukirchen: Neukirchener Verlag, 1967.

Kingdon, Robert M. *Geneva and the Coming of the Wars of Religion in France, 1555–1563*. Travaux d'humanisme et Renaissance 22. New York: G. Lounz, 1956.

———. *Geneva and the Consolidation of the French Protestant Movement, 1564–1572*. Madison: University of Wisconsin Press, 1967.

Maruyama, Tadataka. *The Ecclesiology of Theodore Beza: The Reform of the True Church*. Geneva: Droz, 1978.

Monter, E. William. *Calvin's Geneva*. New York: Wiley, 1967.

Pratt, Waldo S. *The Music of the French Psalter of 1562*. New York: Columbia University Press, 1939.

Raitt, Jill. *The Colloquy of Montbéliard, 1586: Politics and Religion in the Sixteenth Century*. New York: Oxford University Press, 1992.

―――. *The Eucharistic Theology of Theodore Beza: Development of the Reformed Doctrine.* AAR Studies in Religion 4. Chambersburg, Pa.: American Academy of Religion, 1972.

16. ANDREAS BODENSTEIN VON CARLSTADT

Primary Sources

Carlstadt, Andreas Bodenstein von. *The Essential Carlstadt: Fifteen Tracts.* Translated and edited by E. J. Furcha. Waterloo, Ontario: Herald Press, 1995.

―――. *Karlstadts Schriften aus den Jahren 1523–25.* Edited by Erich Hertzsch. 2 vols. Halle: M. Niemeyer, 1956.

―――. *Karlstadt und Augustin.* Edited by Ernst Kähler. Halle, 1952.

―――. *A Reformation Debate: Karlstadt, Emser, and Eck on Sacred Images.* Translated and edited by Bryan Mangrum and Giuseppe Scavizzi. Toronto: Centre for Reformation and Renaissance Studies, 1998.

―――. *Von Abtuhung der Bilder und das keyn Bedtler unther den Christen seyn sollen.* Edited by Hans Lietzmann. Kleine Texte für Vorlesungen und Übungen 74. Bonn: A. Marcus und E. Weber, 1911.

Sider, Ronald J., ed. *Karlstadt's Battle with Luther: Documents in a Liberal-Radical Debate.* Philadelphia: Fortress Press, 1978.

Secondary Sources

Barge, Hermann. *Andreas Bodenstein von Karlstadt.* 2 vols. Leipzig: Friedrich Brandstetter, 1905.

Hillerbrand, Hans J. "Andreas Bodenstein of Carlstadt, Prodigal Reformer." *Church History* 35 (1966): 379–98.

Oyer, John S. *Lutheran Reformers against Anabaptists.* The Hague: M. Nijhoff, 1964.

Pater, Calvin. *Karlstadt as the Father of the Baptist Movements: The Emergence of Lay Protestantism.* Toronto: Uiversity of Toronto Press, 1984.

Preus, James S. *Carlstadt's Ordinaciones and Luther's Liberty: A Study of the Wittenberg Movement, 1521–22.* Harvard Theological Studies 26. Cambridge: Harvard University Press, 1974.

Rupp, E. Gordon. "Andrew Karlstadt and Reformation Puritanism." *Journal of Theological Studies* 10 (1959): 308–26.

―――. *Patterns of Reformation.* Philadelphia: Fortress Press, 1969.

―――. "Word and Spirit in the First Years of the Reformation." *Archiv für Reformationsgeschichte* 49 (1958): 13–26.

Sider, Ronald J. *Andreas Bodenstein von Karlstadt: The Development of His Thought, 1517–1525.* Studies in Medieval and Reformation Thought 11. Leiden: E. J. Brill, 1974.

Williams, George H. *The Radical Reformation.* Philadelphia: Westminster Press, 1962.

17. CASPAR SCHWENCKFELD

Primary Sources

Schwenckfeld, Caspar. "An Answer to Luther's Malediction." In *Spiritual and Anabaptist Writers,* edited by George H. Williams and Angel M. Mergal, pp. 163–81. Library of Christian Classics 25. Philadelphia: Westminster Press, 1957.

————. *Commentary on the Augsburg Confession.* Translated by Fred A. Grater. Pennsburg, Pa.: Schwenkfelder Library, 1982.

————. *Corpus Schwenckfeldianorum.* Edited by C. D. Hartranft, E. S. Johnson, and S. G. Schultz. Vols. 1–15.[1] Leipzig: Breitkopf and Härtel, 1907–39. Vols. 15²–19. Pennsburg, Pa.: Board of Publication of the Schwenkfelder Church, 1959–61.

Secondary Sources

Ecke, Karl. Fortsetzung der Reformation: *Kaspar von Schwenckfelds: Schau einer apostolischen Reformation.* Gladbeck, Germany: Schriftenmissions-Verlag, 1978.

Furcha, Edward J. *Schwenckfeld's Concept of the New Man.* Pennsburg, Pa.: Board of Publication of the Schwenkfelder Church, 1970.

Jones, Rufus M. *Spiritual Reformers in the Sixteenth and Seventeenth Centuries.* London: Macmillan, 1914.

Loetscher, Frederick William. *Schwenckfeld's Participation in the Eucharistic Controversy of the Sixteenth Century.* Philadelphia: MacCalla, 1906.

Maier, Paul L. *Caspar Schwenckfeld on the Person and Work of Christ.* Assen, Netherlands: Royal Van Gorcum, 1959.

————. "Caspar Schwenckfeld: A Quadricentennial Evaluation." *Archiv für Reformationsgeschichte* 54 (1963):89–97.

McLauchlin, R. Emmet. *Caspar Schwenckfeld, Reluctant Reformer: His Life to 1540.* New Haven: Yale University Press, 1986.

Schultz, Selina Gerhard. *Caspar Schwenckfeld von Ossig.* Pennsburg, Pa.: Board of Publication of the Schwenkfelder Church, 1946.

Séguenny, André. *The Christology of Caspar Schwenckfeld: Spirit And Flesh in the Process of Life Transformation.* Translated by Peter C. Erb and Simone Nienwoldt. Texts and Studies in Religion 35. Lewiston, N.Y.: Edwin Mellen Press, 1987.

Seyppel, Joachim H. *Schwenckfeld, Knight of Faith.* Pennsburg, Pa.: Board of Publication of the Schwenkfelder Church, 1961.

Wach, Joachim. *Types of Religious Experience, Christian and Non-Christian.* Chicago: University of Chicago Press, 1951.

Williams, George H. *The Radical Reformation.* Philadelphia: Westminster Press, 1962.

18. BALTHASAR HUBMAIER

Primary Sources

Hubmaier, Balthasar. *Balthasar Hubmaier, Theologian of Anabaptism.* Translated and edited by Wayne Pipkin and John H. Yoder. Scottdale, Pa.: Herald Press, 1989.

————. "On Free Will." In *Spiritual and Anabaptist Writers,* edited by George H. Williams and Angel M. Mergal, pp. 112–35. Library of Christian Classics 25. Philadelphia: Westminster Press, 1957.

————. *Schriften.* Edited by Gunnar Westin and Torsten Bergsten. Quellen zur Geschichte der Täufer 9. Gütersloh: Gerd Mohn, 1962.

Secondary Sources

Armour, Rollin Stely. *Anabaptist Baptism: A Representative Study.* Studies in Anabaptist and Mennonite History 11. Scottdale, Pa.: Herald Press, 1966.

Beachy, Alvin J. "The Grace of God in Christ as Understood by Five Major Anabaptist Writers." *Mennonite Quarterly Review* 37 (1963): 5–33, 52.

Bergsten, Torsten. *Balthasar Hubmaier: Seine Stellung zu Reformation und Täufertum.* Acta Universitatis Upsaliensis, Studia Historico-Ecclesiastica Upsaliensia 3. Kassel, 1961.

Hall, Thor. "The Possibilities of Erasmian Influence on Denck and Hubmaier in Their Views on the Freedom of the Will." *Mennonite Quarterly Review* 35 (1961): 149–70.

Rempel, John D. *The Lord's Supper in Anabaptism: A Study in the Christology of Balthasar Hubmaier, Pilgram Marpeck, and Dirk Philips.* Studies in Anabaptist and Mennonite History. Waterloo, Ontario: Herald Press, 1993.

Steinmetz, David C. "The Baptism of John and the Baptism of Jesus in Huldrych Zwingli, Balthasar Hubmaier and Late Medieval Theology." In *Continuity and Discontinuity in Church History.* Festschrift for George H. Williams, edited by F. F. Church and T. George, pp. 169–81. Leiden: E. J. Brill, 1979.

————. "Luther und Hubmaier im Streit um die Freiheit des menschlichen Willens." *Evangelische Theologie* 43 (November / December 1983): 512–26.

Vedder, Henry C. *Balthasar Hubmaier, The Leader of the Anabaptists.* New York: Putnam's, 1905.

Williams, George H. *The Radical Reformation.* Philadelphia: Westminster Press, 1962.

Windhorst, Christof. *Täufrisches Taufverständnis: Balthsar Hubmaiers Lehre zwischen traditioneller und reformatorischer Theologie.* Studies in Medieval and Reformation Thought 16. Leiden: E. J. Brill, 1976.

Yoder, John. *Täufertum und Reformation in der Schweiz.* Schriftenreihe des Mennonitischen Geschichtesvereins 6. Karlsruhe: H. Schneider, 1962.

19. HANS DENCK

Primary Sources

Denck, Hans. *Schriften.* Quellen zur Geschichte der Täufer 6. Gütersloh: Bertelsmann, 1955–56.

————. *Selected Writings of Hans Denck.* Translated by Edward J. Furcha with Ford Lewis Battles. Pittsburgh Original Texts and Translations, series 1. Pittsburgh: Pickwick Press, 1975.

————. *Selected Writings of Hans Denck 1500–1527.* Edited by E. J. Furcha. Texts and Studies in Religion 44. Lewiston, N.Y.: Edwin Mellen Press, 1989.

————. "Whether God Is the Cause of Evil." In *Spiritual and Anabaptist Writers,* edited by George H. Williams and Angel M. Mergal, pp. 88–111. Library of Christian Classics 25. Philadelphia: Westminster Press, 1957.

Secondary Sources

Baring, Georg. "Hans Denck und Thomas Müntzer in Nürnberg, 1524." *Archiv für Reformationsgeschichte* 50 (1959):145–81.

Bauman, Clarence. *The Spiritual Legacy of Hans Denck: Interpretation and Translation of Key Texts.* Studies in Medieval and Reformation Thought 47. Leiden: E. J. Brill, 1991.

Beachy, Alvin J. "The Grace of God in Christ as Understood by Five Major Anabaptist Writers." *Mennonite Quarterly Review* 37 (1963): 5–33, 52.

Coutts, Alfred. *Hans Denck, 1495–1527: Humanist and Heretic*. Edinburgh: Macnive & Wallace, 1927.

Foster, Claude R., Jr. "Hans Denck and Johannes Buenderlin: A Comparative Study." *Mennonite Quarterly Review* 39 (1965):115–24.

Hall, Thor. "Possibilities of Erasmian Influence on Denck and Hubmaier in Their Views on the Freedom of the Will." *Mennonite Quarterly Review* 35 (1961):149–70.

Jones, Rufus M. *Spiritual Reformers in the Sixteenth and Seventeenth Centuries*. London: Macmillan, 1914.

Keller, Ludwig. *Ein Apostel der Wiedertäufer*. Leipzig, 1882.

———. *Johann von Staupitz und die Anfänge der Reformation*. Leipzig, 1888.

Kiwiet, Jan J. "The Life of Hans Denck (ca. 1500–1527)." *Mennonite Quarterly Review* 31 (1957): 227–59.

———. "The Theology of Hans Denck." *Mennonite Quarterly Review* 32 (1958): 3–27.

Klassen, William. "Was Hans Denck a Universalist?" *Mennonite Quarterly Review* 39 (1965): 152–54.

Lohse, Bernhard. "Hans Denck und der 'linke Flügel' der Reformation." In *Humanitas-Christianitas: Walther von Loewenich zum 65. Geburtstag*, edited by K. Beyschlag et al., pp. 74–83. Witten: Luther-Verlag, 1968.

Packull, Werner O. *Mysticism and the Early South German-Austrian Anabaptist Movement 1525–1531*. Scottdale, Pa.: Herald Press, 1977.

Rupp, E. Gordon. "Word and Spirit in the First Years of the Reformation." *Archiv für Reformationsgeschichte* 49 (1958): 13–26.

Williams, George H. *The Radical Reformation*. Philadelphia: Westminster Press, 1962.

———. "Sanctification in the Testimony of Several So-Called 'Schwärmer.'" In *The Church, Mysticism, Sanctification, and the Natural in Luther's Thought*, edited by Ivar Asheim, pp.194–211. Philadelphia: Fortress Press, 1967.

Yoder, John H. "The Hermeneutics of the Anabaptists." *Mennonite Quarterly Review* 41 (1967): 291–308.

20. PILGRAM MARPECK

Primary Sources

Bergsten, Torsten. "Two Letters by Pilgram Marpeck." *Mennonite Quarterly Review* 32 (1958): 192–210.

Marpeck, Pilgram. "Glaubensbekenntnis." In *Quellen zur Geschichte der Täufer*, Vol. 7. *Elsass*, pt. 1, *Stadt Strasbourg, 1522–32*, edited by Manfred Krebs and Hans Georg Rott, pp. 416–527. Gütersloh: Gerd Mohn, 1959.

———. "Verantwurtung." In *Quellen und Forschungen zur Geschichte der oberdeutschen Taufgesinnten im 16. Jahrhundert*, edited by Johannes Loserth. Vienna and Leipzig: Carl Fromme, 1929.

———. *The Writings of Pilgram Marpeck*. Translated and edited by William Klassen and Walter Klaassen. Kitchener, Ontario: Herald Press, 1978.

Secondary Sources

Armour, Rollin Stely. *Anabaptist Baptism: A Representative Study*. Studies in Anabaptist and Mennonite History 11. Scottdale, Pa.: Herald Press, 1966.

Beachy, Alvin J. "The Grace of God in Christ as Understood by Five Major Anabaptist Writers." *Mennonite Quarterly Review* 37 (1963): 5–33, 52.

Bender, Harold S. "Pilgram Marpeck, Anabaptist Theologian and Civil Engineer." *Mennonite Quarterly Review* 38 (1964): 231–65.

Boyd, Stephen Blake. *Pilgram Marpeck: His Life and Social Theology.* Duke Monographs in Medieval and Renaissance Studies 12. Durham, N.C.: Duke University Press, 1992.

Kiwiet, Jan J. *Pilgram Marbeck: Ein Führer der Täuferbewegung im süddeutschen Raum.* Kassel, 1957.

Klassen, William. *Covenant and Community: The Life, Writings and Hermeneutic of Pilgram Marpeck.* Grand Rapids: Eerdmans, 1968.

Wenger, John C. "The Life and Work of Pilgram Marpeck." *Mennonite Quarterly Review* 12 (1938): 137–65.

———. "The Theology of Pilgram Marpeck." *Mennonite Quarterly Review* 12 (1938): 205–56.

INDEX